ROUTLEDGE LIBRARY EDITIONS: THE ECONOMICS AND BUSINESS OF TECHNOLOGY

Volume 2

TRADE UNIONS AND TECHNOLOGICAL CHANGE

TRADE UNIONS AND TECHNOLOGICAL CHANGE

A Research Report Submitted to the 1966 Congress of Landorganisationen i Sverige

Edited by
S. D. ANDERMAN

LONDON AND NEW YORK

First published in 1967 by George Allen & Unwin

This edition first published in 2018
by Routledge
2 Park Square, Milton Park, Abingdon, Oxon OX14 4RN

and by Routledge
711 Third Avenue, New York, NY 10017

Routledge is an imprint of the Taylor & Francis Group, an informa business

© 1967 George Allen & Unwin Ltd

All rights reserved. No part of this book may be reprinted or reproduced or utilised in any form or by any electronic, mechanical, or other means, now known or hereafter invented, including photocopying and recording, or in any information storage or retrieval system, without permission in writing from the publishers.

Trademark notice: Product or corporate names may be trademarks or registered trademarks, and are used only for identification and explanation without intent to infringe.

British Library Cataloguing in Publication Data
A catalogue record for this book is available from the British Library

ISBN: 978-1-138-50336-6 (Set)
ISBN: 978-1-351-06690-7 (Set) (ebk)
ISBN: 978-1-138-56126-7 (Volume 2) (hbk)
ISBN: 978-0-203-71089-0 (Volume 2) (ebk)

Publisher's Note
The publisher has gone to great lengths to ensure the quality of this reprint but points out that some imperfections in the original copies may be apparent.

Disclaimer
The publisher has made every effort to trace copyright holders and would welcome correspondence from those they have been unable to trace.

Trade Unions and Technological Change

A RESEARCH REPORT
SUBMITTED TO THE 1966 CONGRESS OF
LANDORGANISATIONEN I SVERIGE

(*The Swedish Confederation of Trade Unions*)

EDITED AND TRANSLATED BY

S. D. ANDERMAN

Staff Tutor in Industrial Relations
University of Oxford
Delegacy for Extra-Mural Studies

London
GEORGE ALLEN & UNWIN LTD
RUSKIN HOUSE · MUSEUM STREET

FIRST PUBLISHED IN 1967

This book is copyright under the Berne Convention. Apart from any fair dealing for the purposes of private study, research, criticism or review, as permitted under the Copyright Act, 1956, no portion may be reproduced by any process without written permission. Enquiries should be addressed to the publisher.

© *George Allen & Unwin Ltd*, 1967

PRINTED IN GREAT BRITAIN
in 11 *on* 12 *point Times Roman type*
BY SIMSON SHAND LTD
LONDON, HERTFORD AND HARLOW

FOREWORD

This research report by the Swedish Confederation of Trade Unions, or LO as it is popularly known, constitutes one of the first major attempts by a trade union, employer or government group in a country experiencing sustained full employment and widespread scarcity of labour to examine systematically the manpower problems associated with rapidly changing technology. This effort is indeed timely. For until now public discussion and intensive research in this area have been largely confined to the United States. And, while the American exchange has had the virtue of awakening other countries to the need to understand and prepare measures to cope with the consequences of accelerating technological change, the relative scarcity of systematic study in other countries has meant that research has too frequently been focused on the problems of technology and structural unemployment in the context of a relatively high—i.e. about 4 per cent—level of aggregate unemployment.

Yet, as the present study indicates, structural unemployment and redundancy are only two of a host of difficulties accompanying technological progress. Internal job transfers as well as continuous changes in job content, skill requirements, systems of payment and methods of job evaluation entail sginficant costs to the worker in terms of loss of income, decreased job satisfaction and a less favourable occupational adjustment. Moreover, even under sustained full employment, where the aggregate unemployment level rarely exceeds $1\frac{1}{2}$ per cent, certain groups of workers, notably those of advanced years, are called upon to pay a disproportionate share of the price of generating a continuous increase in general living standards through a rapid pace of technological change. To countries such as those in Western Europe which have long experienced employment levels in the order of 98–99 per cent, these findings are particularly relevant and meaningful. They may also suggest new emphases if not new avenues of exploration to researchers and policy-makers in the United States.

This study is the product of a group of LO economists—Dr Rudolf Meidner, its chairman, Sven F. Bengtson, Gösta Dahlström, K. G. Karlsson, Eric Pettersson, Bo Jonsson, all members of LO's research division, and Evert Holmberg of the Swedish Metal Workers Union. The group has drawn extensively on the advice and services of a number of experts including Dr Erik Bolinder, LO's specialist in industrial medicine, Olle Gunnarsson, head of LO's works council division, Professor Bengt J. Andersson, Royal College of Technology in Stockholm, and Professor Edmund Dahlström of the University of Gothenburg.

The programme of active research on the project extended over a period of three years, starting in December 1962, and included numerous meetings with management and trade union officials, visits to plants, and study visits to England, West Germany and the United States.

In addition to the present report, this research activity has given rise to two other publications (in Swedish) on the adjustment problems created by technological change: *The Individual and the Industrial Environment*, by Dr Erik Bolinder, a special investigation of the medical aspects of technology; and *Technological Change and Work Adjustment*, edited by Professor Edmund Dahlström, a study by a group of sociologists of the problems of worker adjustment to change in industry. Both have been used too as the basis for much of the reasoning and many of the conclusions in the present study.

The LO group has moreover conducted a sample survey among about 0·5 per cent of the LO membership, which now numbers over 1·5 million workers. In the present report the survey is cited as the LO Membership Survey. As well, the group produced an extensive case study of the shutdown of the 'Vargen' textile plant in Norrköping.

Finally, a series of lengthy monographs on the manpower consequences of technological change in different industries and certain large firms has been prepared by the group in collaboration with the national unions, employers' associations and individual firms. The industries covered are metal working and engineering, textiles, building and construction, and forestry. The enterprise studies include Swedish Railways and LKAB, the state-owned corporation in the iron ore mining industry.

It has now become an established tradition for the Swedish labour movement to commission a research paper on an important social or economic problem to be presented and discussed at LO congresses. The precedent was first set when the Committee of

Foreword

Fifteen submitted its study on *The Trade Union Movement and Modern Society* to the 1941 LO congress. This report centred on the responsibilities of the trade union movement to the community, its relation to the State and the powers of the LO to pursue a centralized trade union wages policy. Its successor, *Trade Unions and Full Employment*, was presented to the 1951 LO congress, and contained a blueprint for government stabilization policy and trade union wages policy under full employment. This report contained one of the first published suggestions that the government incorporate an 'active labour market policy' as a complement to fiscal and monetary policies. A modified version was published in English in 1953. In 1961, two studies were submitted to the LO congress. One, *Trade Unions and Industrial Democracy*, remained untranslated. The other, *Economic Expansion and Structural Change*, was edited and translated by T. L. Johnston, then lecturer in political economy, University of Edinburgh, and published by George Allen and Unwin.

The editing of the text of the present report has been marginal. The views of its authors have been preserved throughout its length. Inevitably, however, it has not been possible to give a verbal translation of the Swedish text. Every effort has been made to convey the exact shades of meaning and emphasis of the original, but it has often been necessary to introduce changes of phraseology in order to translate the differences of Swedish grammar and linguistic style into readable English.

Rewley House, *Steven D. Anderman*
Wellington Square, Oxford *January* 1967

CONTENTS

FOREWORD   *page* 7

1. INTRODUCTION   19
   From *The Trade Union Movement and Modern Society* to *Economic Expansion and Structural Change*   19
   Focusing on the Adjustment Problems of the Individual   22
   Technology is only *one* Factor in the Process of Change   24

2. VALUES AND PREMISES   26
   Increased Industrial Efficiency   26
   Man and Work   27
   Full Employment   29
   The Adjustment of the Individual to the Work Environment   30
   A Higher Standard of Living   32
   Labour-Management Consultation and Technological Change   34
   To Estimate Productive Efficiency   34
   Conflict and Harmony of Objectives   36

3. TECHNOLOGICAL CHANGE   39
   Some Definitions and Premises   39
   The Process of Technological Change   42
   Technological Change in Different Sectors of Industry   49
   The Pace of Technological Advance   55

4. MANAGERIAL ORGANIZATION, ADMINISTRATIVE SYSTEMS AND TECHNOLOGICAL CHANGE   60
   Management's 'Organizational Ideology'   62
   The Growth of Personnel Administration   64
   Managerial Organization and Systems of Wages Payment   65
   The Structure of Power and Influence Within the Business Organization   67
   Changes in Job Content   69

5. TECHNOLOGICAL CHANGE,
   EMPLOYMENT AND UNEMPLOYMENT 74
   The Classical Economists' View 75
   The Compensation Theory versus the Theory of
   Underconsumption 77
   The 'Structuralists' versus the 'Aggregate Demand'
   School 80
   Technological Change Constitutes No Threat to Full
   Employment 85
   Employment Trends for the Swedish Economy as a
   Whole 86

6. CHANGES IN THE STRUCTURE OF
   EMPLOYMENT 89
   Employment Trends in Major Swedish Sectors 89
   Trends in Employment and Productivity in
   Manufacturing Industries 93
   Technological Change and the Structure of
   Unemployment 102
   Regional Shifts in the Distribution of the
   Population 104

7. THE IMPACT OF CHANGING
   TECHNOLOGY ON THE OCCUPATIONAL
   STRUCTURE 108
   Changes in the Occupational Structure 108
   Qualitative Changes in the Occupational Structure 111
   Some Conclusions and a Perspective for the Future 116

8. LABOUR MOBILITY 120
   Statistical Data on Labour Mobility 122
   Redeployment Difficulties and Loss of Income in
   Relation to Plant Shutdowns 130
   Internal Transfers 136

9. WORKER ADJUSTMENT AND
   TECHNOLOGICAL CHANGE 138
   Need Adjustment 138
   Physical Adjustment 141
   Psychological Adjustment 144
   Job Satisfaction 147

Job Involvement	150
Individual Capacity and the Preconditions for Adjustment	153

10. HOURS OF WORK ... 158
    Changes in Hours of Work and Current Conditions ... 159
    Leisure—Hours of Work ... 161
    Occupational Adjustment and Hours of Work ... 166

11. SYSTEMS OF WAGE PAYMENT ... 171
    Work Study and Work Measurement ... 172
    Piecework and Timework Systems ... 176
    Job Evaluation and Merit Rating ... 179
    Wage Systems and Technological Change ... 182
    Systems of Payment and Worker Adjustment ... 188

12. INCOME SECURITY AND TECHNOLOGICAL CHANGE ... 194
    Income Guarantees and Internal Transfers ... 194
    Income and Age ... 199
    Examples from Other Countries ... 200
    Income Security and Redundancy ... 202

13. THE DISTRIBUTION OF INCOME AND WEALTH ... 209
    Constancy of the Wage and Salary Share and Growing Inequities in Distribution of Income and Wealth ... 210
    The Dilemma Between Increased Capital Formation and a More Even Distribution of Income and Wealth ... 211
    Increased Company Savings (A Higher Self-Financing Capacity) ... 212
    Measures to Stimulate Personal Savings ... 214
    Measures to Increase Collective Savings ... 215
    Capital Formation through Collective Bargaining ... 217

14. TECHNOLOGICAL CHANGE AND
    LABOUR-MANAGEMENT CO-OPERATION
    IN THE PLANT 222
    LO-SAF Agreements 223
    The Individual Worker and the Process of
    Technological Change 225
    Labour-Management Co-operation in Managing
    Change at the Workplace 227
    Different Displacement Situations 229
    Technical Change and Labour-Management
    Relations in the Plant 231
    The Rights of Employees to Participate in
    Management Decision-Making 232
    The Orientation of Information and Consultation 235

15. CONCLUSIONS AND RECOMMENDATIONS 238
    The Issues 238
    Expanded Labour Market and Labour Force
    Research 239
    The Follow-through on Measures Taken 240
    Forecasting Measures 241
    The Employment Exchanges 242
    Displacement Within the Firm 244
    Special Measures for Difficult-to-Place Workers 245
    Retraining and the Occupational Structure 247
    Wages Policy and Systems of Payment 249
    Income and Job Security 250
    Occupational Adjustment 253
    Hours of Work, Part-time Work, Shift-work 256
    A More Even Distribution of Income 257
    The 'Management' of Change 257

FIGURES

1. Production, Employment and Productivity in
   Several Industries, 1950–65 *page* 99
2. Employment in the Mining Industry as a Whole
   and in LKAB Mines, 1959–65 100
3. Examples of Different Piecework Systems 177
4. Different Methods of Differentiating Pay 182
5. The Distribution of LO Members in Different
   Income Classes and Age Groups 199

TABLES

1. Changes in Labour Productivity, 1923–80 *page* 59
2. Production, Input of Capital and Labour, Capital and Labour Productivity and Capital Intensity, 1950–65 87
3. Changes in Employment and Productivity, 1950–80 90
4. Production, Employment and Productivity Within Manufacturing, 1950–65 94
5. Changes in Production, Employment and Productivity for the Periods 1951–4, 1955–8, 1959–62 and 1963–5. Annual Averages as Percentages 98
6. Productivity Increases and Unemployment Levels for Certain Industries 102
7. Unemployment in Selected Industrial Unemployment Insurance Societies, 1956–64, as a Percentage of Total Insured 103
8. Unemployment Among Forestry Workers in April and May in Relation to Annual Averages, 1956–63 103
9. Unemployment Among Insured Workers in Different Regions, 1961–4, as a Percentage of Total Insured 104
10. The Swedish Population Distributed by Major Sectors of the Economy, 1900, 1930 and 1960 in % 105
11. Demographic Changes During Decades, 1910–60, in % 106
12. Changes in Administrative Staff as a Proportion of Total Employment in Swedish Manufacturing, 1946–63 111
13. Job Separations as a % of Employed Workers, 1947–64 123
14. Entries Into and Withdrawals From the Swedish Textile Workers Union, as a Percentage of Total Membership 127

15. Labour Mobility of Different Kinds Among Manual Workers, 1945–50 and 1960–5. (Separations during one year as a % of total employed workers)   128
16. The Number of Employees Covered by Advance Notice of Curtailed Production, 1960–5   131
17. Distribution of the Total Workforce One Year After a Plant Shutdown.   131
18. The Proportions of Individuals Working Different Average Working Weeks   160
19. The Proportions of LO Membership in Different Working Weeks   160
20. The Proportions of LO Membership in Different Systems of Shift Work   165
21. The Proportion of LO Members Paid According to Different Systems of Wage Payment   178
22. The Piecework Percentage in Different Industries, 1956, 1960 and 1964   184
23. The Piecework Percentage in the Commercial Sector   186
24. Change in Level of Earnings for LO Membership as a Consequence of Internal Transfer   198
25. The Number of LO Members who have Experienced a Reduction in Earnings After Changing Jobs as a Proportion of All Those Who Changed Jobs, by Age Groups   204
26. Savings in the Business Sector as a Percentage of Investment, 1955–70   213

CHAPTER 1

Introduction

The strength of the Swedish trade union movement and its ability to play an important rôle not only as an interest group but also as an initiating force in the process of overall social change in Sweden are currently widely recognized. This has understandably led to some speculation about the reasons why the trade union movement has attained such a position in Swedish society, a position which is almost unique by international standards. The answer is neither simple nor clear-cut. The usual explanations put forward are Sweden's long, uninterrupted period of peace, its homogeneous population, the favourable rise in its living standards and the traditional intimate co-operation between the political and trade union branches of the labour movement which in turn has provided one of the foundations for its lengthy possession of political power, as well as enabling the successful implementation of a welfare policy programme of full employment and social equality.

Yet, to us it seems plain that a major source of the growth of the power and influence of the trade union movement has been its will and ability to adapt its organization and activities to social changes. An interest group that restricts itself to the promotion of its narrow self-interests runs the risk that its traditions may 'fossilize' and cause it to lose its influence over the course of events. However, to the extent that an organization is able to accept change and integrate its group interests with wider interests in adjusting to developments, its aims will be regarded as progressive and it will be afforded the opportunity to participate actively in the formulation of future public policies.

FROM *The Trade Union Movement and Modern Society*
TO *Economic Expansion and Structural Change*

At a fairly early stage in its development, the Swedish trade union movement chose the latter route. One expression of this choice has been the numerous studies presented and discussed in LO quinquennial congresses over the past decades. In the first of these studies, *The Trade Union Movement and Modern Society* (1941), the LO charted its position in the welfare society.[1] This report significantly modified the trade union movement's earlier position that the labour market must be completely independent of government regulation. By increasing LO's power to co-ordinate wage policy and changing its statutes accordingly, it was thought that the process of collective bargaining could be preserved from governmental regulation. The report also contained perhaps the first clear recognition of the fact that technical rationalization was a pre-condition of continued economic and social progress.

Ten years later, the centre of gravity had shifted to the problems of wage policy in a full employment society. Broadly speaking it can be said that whereas *The Trade Union Movement and Modern Society* struggled with the problem of drawing the line between the area of free and untrammelled collective bargaining, i.e. the area where the trade union and employer organizations could act freely, and the appropriate area for state regulation, the report *Trade Unions and Full Employment* dealt with the issue of the division of responsibility between government and trade unions for the maintenance of overall economic balance in a full employment economy threatened by inflation.[2] It was now proposed that the State was essentially responsible for maintaining an overall economic balance, and that this was a pre-condition of an acceptable wage development through wage negotiations between trade unions and employer organizations. Along with the proposed programme of stabilization measures, in which a new feature was an active labour market policy, an attempt was made to find new institutional forms for a viable wage policy within the framework of the overall economic policy constraints. It soon emerged that the form thought to be most suitable for wage policy, i.e. centralized wage bargaining, did not require any formal changes in the statutes of the central trade union confederation. LO's moral authority and increased technical resources were estimated to be sufficient to allow wages

[1] *Fackföreningsrörelsen och näringslivet.* Betänkande avgivet av LO's Femtonmannakommitté, Stockholm 1941. (Trade Unions and Modern Society.)
[2] *Trade Unions and Full Employment*, Malmö 1953.

Introduction

policy to be centrally co-ordinated, and this view has been confirmed by the practical experience since the mid-1950s.

With the passing of another decade, one dominated by the problems of stabilization and income distribution policy, an attempt was made to come to grips with the problem of the structural transformation of industry as a necessary condition for economic growth and a rising standard of living. *Economic Expansion and Structural Change* (1962) adhered closely to the declarations in favour of technical rationalization that had been made two decades earlier by a representative group of trade union leaders, in *The Trade Union Movement and Modern Society*.[1] What at the start of the 1940s appeared to be an acceptance of an apparently inevitable development, ripened twenty years later into a programme for a more active policy for structural change. With reference to the stiffening of international competition as well as Sweden's obligation to provide aid to the developing countries, the trade union movement examined various structural problems and proposed a programme of measures for more active industrial and labour market policies.

There was yet another basic theme in the 1961 report. In the 1951 LO congress, the wages policy of solidarity had been reaffirmed as the guide line for trade union wages policy. Yet this policy had been thwarted by the highly uneven wage development and incidence of wage drift throughout Swedish industries during the 1950s. It became increasingly clear that an active industrial policy in conjunction with an intensified labour market policy was not only a pre-condition of more rapid economic growth; it was also essential to the realization of trade union aspirations for greater wage equality among different worker groups. To a far greater extent than earlier LO reports, *Economic Expansion and Structural Change* was directed to the Government and thus became as much a contribution to the national economic debate as to the internal trade union debate.

At the 1961 LO Congress, another trade union report of interest in this context was also discussed, notably *Trade Unions and Industrial Democracy*.[2] There is a natural link between this study and *Economic Expansion and Structural Change*. A more active

---

[1] *Economic Expansion and Structural Change*, London 1963.
[2] *Fackföreningsrörelsen och företagsdemokratin*, Stockholm 1961. (Trade Unions and Industrial Democracy.)

industrial policy which will result in a more rapid structural transformation requiring greater capital mobility and labour mobility will create greater problems of worker adjustment. In the event, problems of the workplace will loom larger and the question of how to expand and channel the influence of workers in the management of their firm in order best to further their own interests as well as those of the firm and society will become more urgent. Moreover, the security of the individual in a changing economy must be safeguarded, and aspects of this problem were given great attention in *Trade Unions and Industrial Democracy*. There it was suggested that the problems that arise in a highly mobile labour market could not be solved by employers alone but must be dealt with by close co-operation and consultation between employers and employee organizations.

The reasoning in *Trade Unions and Industrial Democracy* provided the foundation for later negotiations between LO and the Swedish Employers' Confederation, SAF, which in turn led to changes in the Basic Agreement, a comprehensive revision of the agreement on works councils and the agreements on redundancy payments and supplementary unemployment benefits.

In this way, it has been possible to provide a greater measure of employment security for the individual and improved income security for those persons made redundant by economic and technological change. New opportunities too have been opened for closer labour-management co-operation at the place of work.

FOCUSING ON THE ADJUSTMENT PROBLEMS OF THE INDIVIDUAL

The positive approach of the Swedish trade unions to rationalization is thus well-documented and requires no further elaboration. The underpinning for this attitude has been the full employment policy which has been pursued conscientiously and successfully in Sweden for decades. In countries undergoing rapid technical change at a lower level of employment, fears have occasionally arisen that the increased utilization of advanced technological processes would constitute a threat to employment and create adverse social conditions. In Sweden, where a favourable employment situation has been experienced for almost the whole of the post-war period and manpower shortages have

Introduction

widely prevailed, such apprehensions have been less frequently felt. The most commonly feared consequence of rationalization, 'structural' unemployment, has not evidenced itself to any appreciable extent in Sweden. Moreover, relatively little attention has been directed to other adverse effects of new techniques and even less to the opportunities to apply timely measures to neutralize or prevent such effects.

The LO report on industrial policy in 1961 threw some light on the relationship between the rate of introduction and diffusion of technical improvements, structural rationalization, and the required scale of public measures designed to facilitate the attendant manpower adjustment.

In the current report, we have allotted ourselves the task of treating these adjustment problems in greater detail, and isolating and identifying some of the consequences of technological change for the individual worker. At the start of the 1940s there was a need to determine the part that the trade union movement should play in a welfare society whose outlines were distinguishable in spite of the threat of war. Ten years later a viable form for a wages policy in a full employment economy was the problem that thrust itself to the foreground. After yet another decade, a trade union programme was presented for the co-ordination of all attempts to improve the overall efficiency of industry and the expansion of worker influence in the enterprise. During these two decades, three different aspects of the problems of contending with change were tackled: the institutional, wages policy, and the structural. The individual worker had not been neglected in these studies, but he was not given undue attention as long as the key task was to determine the place of the trade union movement in a new society and to formulate trade union demands for welfare policies. It is now necessary and timely to direct greater attention to the conditions of the individual in a changing society. We shall thus complement and develop our earlier discussion in *Trade Unions and Industrial Democracy*. Our task is to determine how attempts to increase overall industrial efficiency can be made compatible with successful manpower adaptation in working life; how change in the modern industrialized society can be pursued without creating excessive insecurity for individual workers. We shall also put forward proposals for a programme of measures to cope with problems of manpower redeployment.

TECHNOLOGY IS ONLY *ONE* FACTOR IN THE PROCESS OF CHANGE

Many different forces underly the changes that have occurred in our society in recent decades. Great difficulties attend any attempt to single out one factor, such as technology, and discuss its rôle in isolation from its wider setting. This problem arises fairly early at the theoretical level when an attempt is made suitably to define these forces and describe their characteristic and conconceivable inter-relationships. And when the effort is made to apply these theoretical concepts to the practical world, the difficulties perceptibly increase. Only in exceptional cases is it possible to distinguish in a given course of events the purely 'technological' factor from other types of factors. The same is true when attempts are made to derive different types of consequences from an initiating cause. In practice, therefore, it is almost pointless to attempt to isolate the consequences flowing from a given 'technological change' from the results of other simultaneously reinforcing or counteracting forces. The same is true of the measures that can be applied to mitigate the possible adverse effects of technological change. These have rarely been so formed that they can be applied to the specific consequences of a new technique; rather they have tended to be more general in form and application.

These difficulties, while considerable, are not so great as to make a discussion of the consequences of technological change for manpower an entirely meaningless or impossible exercise. We feel, however, that it is not suitable to limit the perspective to the direct consequences of purely technological changes and restrict this discussion solely to the obvious cases of such consequences. We have chosen, rather, to treat a number of problems which we think significant for the labour force as a whole and particular groups of workers regardless of whether or not such problems are created solely or predominantly by 'the new technology'.

Underlying this decision is our interest as a group not merely in 'technology' as such but rather in its diverse and far-flung consequences. It has not been our intention to describe with particularity the components of productive technology and technological research, nor to discuss how these can be further developed, but rather to examine the problems of neutralizing or

Introduction 25

preventing the adverse effects of changes in general as well as realizing more fully their potentialities.

In the second chapter we present our values and premises. Chapter 3 contains a survey of several major features of changing technology in general and in particular sectors of industry. In Chapter 4 we examine the question of administrative innovations in managerial organization including not only those changes flowing from changing technology but also those occurring independently of technology.

In Chapter 5, the relationship between technological change, employment and unemployment is discussed with special reference to conditions in the USA; Swedish material is also presented. In the two succeeding chapters, which focus especially on conditions in Sweden, the relationship between productivity and employment in different industries and shifts in the occupational structure are described. This leads to a discussion of labour mobility—both inter-firm and intra-firm—as an adjustment phenomenon in Chapter 8. Then, in Chapter 9, the adjustment of the individual worker to a changed work environment is discussed. Technology also affects the number of hours of work as well as their disposition, shifts in the mix of systems of payment, and job and income security. These issues are taken up respectively in Chapters 10–12. Chapter 13 treats the income and wealth distribution aspects of technical progress and economic growth and discusses alternative solutions to the conflict between the demand for increased capital formation and the desire for a more even distribution of income and wealth. Chapter 14 focuses on the management of changes in the enterprise and the need for increased consultation between employers and trade unions as well as worker participation. The book concludes with specific recommendations for a programme of measures to facilitate manpower adjustment to technological change addressed to the Swedish Government, to employers and to the trade union movement.

CHAPTER 2

Values and Premises

INCREASED INDUSTRIAL EFFICIENCY

One of the most important functions of the trade union movement is to promote a higher material standard of living for its members. We have long been acutely aware of the fact that a necessary condition to the success of such efforts is a progressive increase in overall industrial efficiency. Such a development itself depends largely on two factors: a continuous stream of technological innovations, and frequent and regular improvements in management organization and administrative systems. The trade union movement is not only aware of the need for such changes but, as we have demonstrated by word and deed, we intend to co-operate actively in the process of directing and forming such developments.

The maximum utilization of the available human resources in society is an integral feature of an efficient economy. 'Full employment' is a condition to a rationally functioning economy. The concept of full employment, however, must be understood to have more than a quantitative dimension; it also has important qualitative implications. In every firm and at every job, full use must be made of the skill and potentialities of individual members of the workforce.

The effort required to secure a continuous increase in industrial efficiency will inevitably make great demands of society and the firm, but the burden to be borne by the individual worker will be particularly onerous. He will be required to perform his work tasks satisfactorily and meet the changing needs of the work organization. The exact requirements will vary from job to job but in general they will consist of fulfilling certain product quantity and quality norms, displaying a certain degree of cost consciousness, being willing to develop and improve vocational ability, accepting the existing working regulations and rules of discipline, and being rarely absent.

We agree that a continuous rationalization of industry is both necessary and desirable to attain certain objectives. Although in this book we have not primarily concerned ourselves with the ways in which this process could be facilitated and promoted, the assumption of the need for an efficiently functioning economy is basic to our entire presentation.

MAN AND WORK

It is obvious that technological progress continually introduces radical change into the work environment. Yet it is also true that changing technology is instrumental in transforming the existence of the individual outside working life, notably at leisure, as a consumer of goods and services and as a member of a family. Viewed in this perspective, technological change can engender expectations of a return primarily in improvements outside working life; i.e. in opportunities through increased leisure to satisfy social and cultural as well as material needs. But even this perspective is too narrow. Ultimately the objective must be one of increasing the opportunities for men to adjust more successfully to society and their existence. An individual's personality is indivisible. Consequently, experiences at work and within the work organization cannot help but affect the personality as a whole, either as a developing or as an inhibiting influence. In other words, work does not have merely an economic significance for the individual; it also plays a large part in forming his attitude to life and society, and of course experiences outside the work environment influence employee attitudes and behaviour at work.

In this context, we wish to dissociate ourselves from the view of human motivation that regards economic reward as the only effective incentive to greater work efforts by individuals, i.e. the view that the only motivating force for human activity and reaction in working life is material gain. We believe that a more accurate view of man is that he has an innate need of activity, a need that can equally well be expressed in creative work as in play and recreation. True, the extent to which the individual will accept and seek to achieve certain goals is dependent on the advantages and benefits he expects to reap from his efforts. But the rewards need not be solely economic in nature. We further believe that imaginative and creative organizational talent and the will to accept responsibility are characteristics that are widely distributed among the population and do not repose within an élite of natural leaders.

The business enterprise exists largely to attain certain economic goals. The decisions of the firm must therefore be directed by considerations of economic efficiency. At the same time, however, all company decisions have widespread consequences for the firm's own employees and for the public at large. We feel that these wider consequences of company actions must be taken into consideration to a greater extent in company decision-taking. The responsibility of the firm does not consist solely of paying a reasonable wage for work performed. It extends to endeavouring to ensure that the job satisfies certain fundamental needs of the individual worker, notably the need for security, social contact and exchange and the opportunity to exercise personal talents and realize personal potentialities. We are well aware of the fact that current production techniques and organizational arrangements offer few opportunities for the majority of wage earners to utilize their abilities or satisfy through work their personal, social or cultural needs to any appreciable extent. This, it would appear, has helped to create a highly 'functional' attitude to work, on the part of many employees, an attitude marked by its view of work primarily as a source of income, which can provide for greater freedom and satisfaction of needs outside the working situation.

Modern society and industrial life are organically inter-related. In order to function efficiently and rationally, the system makes great disciplinary demands on the individual worker. He is required to subject himself to certain norms and rules in his dealings with other people and be able to co-operate with other individuals in the pursuit of certain collective goals. Not all people in society can accept these norms or can adapt to the demands of working life, a truth that explains many social problems and individual tragedies. We find ourselves confronted here by the perhaps inevitable conflict between the demands of the work organization and the individual worker's need of identity and independence. At the same time, however, it should be kept in mind that technological and organizational changes are not governed by fixed and immutable 'natural laws'; their course can be influenced.

In any given situation there will be a range of acceptable but different technical and organizational solutions to apply to existing problems. In the end, the decision to select one will be dictated by the norms and values prevailing in the society. In so far as the view is accepted that work can be instrumental in satisfying the needs of the individual and facilitating occupational and social adjustment, it can influence the course of change in job content and working conditions. We assert at this point that it is desirable in itself, and compatible with the demands of increased industrial efficiency, to change production techniques and the work organization in a manner calculated to improve the occupational adjustment of many groups of workers as well as to allow many individuals currently outside the labour market to find meaningful employment.

FULL EMPLOYMENT

Full employment is an objective of the highest order for the trade union movement. This is so not merely because of the economic security and the opportunities for consumption associated with a high level of employment. Were these the only requirements, they could be satisfied by other means. Thus, society could conceivably guarantee all individuals a certain income and economic standard irrespective of whether or not they actually work. Given the norms and values prevailing in our society, however, the rôle of full employment transcends the realm of the purely economic. To be involuntarily unemployed in our society is to suffer a loss of status and to experience isolation from ones' social group as well as a feeling of worthlessness. These can never be entirely compensated for by state subsidies. The government must endeavour to secure meaningful employment for all who desire to work and are capable of working.

Every rationalization measure in industry is designed to lead and leads initially to a reduced need for labour. Clearly, this initial effect can be offset or even reversed as increased productivity gives rise to lower costs, increased sales (product) turnover, and the creation of new consumer needs. However, the labour-saving effects of technological change always hover in the background.

Indeed, in certain countries that have experienced prolonged high employment together with a rapidly changing technology, this facet of technological change has at times received the preponderant share of attention. The experience has given rise to several extremely pessimistic theories on the employment effects of technological change. It would be the better part of wisdom therefore for the trade union movement to attempt to determine in advance the likely effects of technological change on employment in Sweden, not only as regards the overall level of employment but also the employment situation in the different industries, regions and occupations. We shall discuss these issues in Chapters 5–7.

THE ADJUSTMENT OF THE INDIVIDUAL
TO THE WORK ENVIRONMENT

The concept of 'adjustment to the work environment' is multidimensional. In the following discussion we shall identify and examine four of its major aspects:

(*a*) Different job operations and work environments pose different physical requirements for the worker. At the same time, there are wide variations in physical ability and health among workers. We start with the premise that employers make every effort to minimize risks to the employee's physical health in the design of job operations and the lay-out and construction of the physical working environment. This includes the application of ergonomic principles to job design as well as a physical examination of personnel in order to determine the 'right man for the right job'. This aspect will be termed *physical adjustment.*

(*b*) The concept of adjustment also encompasses the psychological health of the individual. One difficulty here, however, is that the criteria for psychological health are less commonly accepted than those for physical health. At various times, traits such as sensitivity, self-confidence, self-realization, maturity, ability to perceive reality, ability to work with other people, independence, and emotional balance have all been regarded in the literature as expressions of psychological health. As well, studies have been made of how different job conditions affect the average psychological health profile of employees. In the following discussion, we shall refer to this aspect of adjustment as *psychological adjustment*.

(*c*) Another starting point for an analysis of adjustment is the individual employee's consciously expressed attitudes, both negative and positive, to the job and his working environment, i.e. his conscious satisfaction with and enjoyment of his work. This aspect of adjustment will be a major element in the following analysis and will be termed *job satisfaction*.

(*d*) Closely related to psychological health and personal adjustment, is a fourth dimension of adjustment, *job involvement*. A high degree of involvement means that the individual derives direct satisfaction from performing the job efficiently and identifies strongly with the work organization. The opposite extreme would be *alienation* from the job and the work organization. The alienated worker views the job as a necessary evil, providing little satisfaction apart from the income; it is dull, meaningless and disagreeable. He cannot identify with the work organization and lacks interest in the firm's activity in general; he feels himself to be an outsider, a stranger.

We are aware that many regard the entire issue of involvement or alienation in working life to be insignificant or of questionable import. As was mentioned previously, our central aim is a more complete adjustment of the individual to life and society. This aim is important in itself but its achievement will have beneficial side effects. For the extent to which an individual adjusts to society and has his needs satisfied will tend to colour his participation and performance in working life. Though the practical obstacles to such a harmonious solution are considerable, we nevertheless feel that every effort should be made to design overall working conditions and job content in the coming technological and structural transformation in such a way as to increase the opportunities for personal involvement in work.

These four analytically discrete aspects of adjustment, i.e. *the physical, the psychological, job satisfaction and job involvement*, are obviously not only overlapping but also closely interdependent in reality. However, they do not always co-vary. Thus, the increased bio-technological activity in firms could lead to a clear improvement in physical adjustment while the simultaneous increase in regulation and control of individual job operations would probably result in greater restrictions on employees and a concomitant decrease in job involvement. We shall take up the question of the adjustment of the individual to his work environment in greater detail in Chapter 9. And in Chapters 10 and 11, we shall deal respectively with the issues of hours of work and different systems of wage payment, issues which bear upon the occupational adjustment of the individual worker.

A HIGHER STANDARD OF LIVING

Though technico-economic changes in industry open up new opportunities to achieve a higher level of income and standard of life, they simultaneously create grave problems in the trade unions' sphere of interest. For the individual trade union member, there are the prospects of redundancy, change in job content, new job and training requirements, alterations in systems of wage payments, and in some cases a move to a new locality or retraining to a new occupation. If interests can be successfully safeguarded at every point, it will be possible to combine a higher level of income and a better work environment with economic guarantees against job insecurity. Yet it should be kept in mind that more favourable income trends for workers do not depend solely on improvements in productivity or profitability; these can also be achieved by a more even distribution of income and wealth. The purely economic objectives of the trade union movement are therefore twofold; *greater industrial efficiency* with its accompanying opportunity for increases in the general wage level and a *more even distribution of income and wealth.*

The issue of income distribution has several facets. LO's wages policy of solidarity consists partly of the attempt to raise the low wage earnings in its sector up to the levels recently obtained or long enjoyed by other income groups. However, traditional and deeply-ingrained social attitudes regarding practical manual work as inferior to commercial, technical and administrative work have created strong resistance to such income-levelling efforts.

There are, moreover, great disparities in the degree of security of income and employment enjoyed by different employee groups. Plainly, technological change will entail an improvement

Values and Premises

in income levels and working conditions for many, if not most, members of the labour force. Many, too, will be cushioned from such change by relatively long-term guarantees against the contingency of lower wages or redundancy. For the great majority of wage earners, however, technological change will always represent a latent threat of temporary or even long-term loss of income. We feel that such differences in economic and social security are unjustifiable; a greater measure of equality of income and employment security is necessary and warranted. We shall return to this problem in Chapter 12.

Another aspect of income distribution is the relationship between profits, interest and dividends on the one hand and wages on the other. This aspect is particularly relevant to a discussion of technological change. For a high rate of investment appears to be largely a function of favourable profit expectations. But the latter are often associated with an increased concentration of wealth. In Sweden—as well as in most other highly industrialized countries—the proportion of total investment expenditure accounted for by the public sector has greatly increased. The wage earners' direct share of ownership, however, is not particularly large. One issue of great importance to the trade union movement is how their share develops. But from the workers' standpoint it seems clear that a direct share in the profitable return of production capital is not enough; they must also enjoy some measure of influence and control over managerial decisions affecting their interests.

Greater wealth is a result not only of greater income but also of a higher propensity to save. It is not in the interests of the trade union movement to introduce compulsory saving or even recommend to the rank and file how they should dispose of their income. Our objective of increasing the wealth of wage earners is thus subject to certain constraints. Within those constraints, however, it is possible to combine consumer choice with some measure of influence in production decisions and a satisfactory return on our savings. These questions have previously been dealt with at length in trade union discussions, notably in *Economic Expansion and Structural Change*, and hence require no detailed treatment in this report. Some views on this question, however, are presented in Chapter 13.

LABOUR-MANAGEMENT CONSULTATION AND TECHNOLOGICAL CHANGE

Because managerial decisions to introduce technological or organizational innovations can so profoundly affect the economic and social welfare of the workforce, we feel that employees and their trade union organizations are entitled to be informed by management of all foreseeable changes sufficiently early and concretely to allow them independently to evaluate the consequences based on their own values and appreciation of the situation—and prescribe a programme of action.

Yet information alone is not sufficient. Employee organizations must also have the time and opportunity to influence managerial decisions on the mode of implementing innovations as well as their intended outcome. Wages and conditions of employment are closely regulated in the collective bargaining agreement. At least on these issues, therefore, employees through their trade union organizations are assured of participation in the process of managerial decision-taking. Moreover, in the Basic Agreement between LO and SAF and other central agreements, notably the LO-SAF agreement on works councils, guidelines have been laid down for formal consultation between management and employees at the plant level on such issues as the technique, organization and planning of production and individual and collective job security. But it is also crucial to the overall adjustment of the individual employee to have some direct say in decisions altering job operations or working conditions on the shop floor. However, this and many other potential forms of co-operation and consultation at the workplace have remained unexplored.

It seems likely that technological change will occur at a more rapid rate in the future. We think it desirable and appropriate therefore that trade unions increase their degree of influence on managerial policies, organizational decisions, conditions of employment and working relations in the widest sense. The traditional trade union effort to increase 'industrial democracy' must be reinvigorated. We shall take up this question in greater detail in Chapter 14.

TO ESTIMATE PRODUCTIVE EFFICIENCY

Measures of productive efficiency as well as those of individual

Values and Premises

adjustment are often unsatisfactory. Their effectiveness tends to be weakened by the chain-reaction of events set in motion by any given project. Take for example the case of a large investment project such as the establishment of a new industry. This entails investments in housing, shops, public services such as schools, community centres, etc., and these changes as well as secondary investments in the service sector and other dependent industrial sectors lead in turn to continuous shifts in population. In such a highly diversified and prolonged development it is difficult to isolate the effect of the original measures.

The interdependence of different firms, industries, consumers, producers and other groups—indeed the very complexity of industry—ensures that the effects of any given structural or technological change will rarely if ever be confined to a single workplace, firm or even industry. Occurrences in a newly established or expanding sector will be reflected in changes in other sectors. Frequently, great gains in productive efficiency in one firm coincide with moderate gains or even losses in other firms. Labour turnover and manpower adjustment patterns will also vary greatly from firm to firm.

Many efforts and sacrifices in economic life are never entered as items on the profit and loss account. For a start, within large sectors of industry price determination is shielded from competitive market forces. It is exceptionally difficult therefore, to evaluate these business operations in terms of efficiency and compare them with other business activities more directly affected by market forces. Moreover, it is extremely difficult to estimate the extent of the psychological or physical deterioration of the workforce during the course of production. Similarly, how can one measure the loss occasioned when customary forms of association and social contact are disrupted by the continuous transformation of the industrial structure? Another interesting but currently incalculable disadvantage is the loss of potential productivity caused by the fact that repetitive work utilizes such a small fraction of the total creative capacities of many individuals in the labour force. In view of all these imponderables a discussion of the possible relationships or conflicts between productive efficiency and satisfaction of individual needs through work is necessarily rather speculative. A different approach to the problem would be for employers to become more interested in it and assume reponsibility for a wider range of consequences flowing from their measures. Currently, the manpower problems that result from many industrial investment decisions and cut-backs in production, are left to be dealt with largely by the labour market administrative authorities, social welfare institutions and the trade unions. The firm does only part of the job. A greater measure of forward planning, increased consultation and co-ordination and in certain cases greater consideration for the interest of the individual worker are therefore strongly warranted. These views are basic to the proposals presented in this report.

CONFLICT AND HARMONY OF OBJECTIVES

To illustrate the way in which a conflict of values can arise let us examine the case of certain concrete measures, say, measures designed to promote vocational labour mobility. When a subsidized retraining programme is enlarged to admit persons who are already employed there will probably be certain consequences for individual firms and the economy as a whole as well as for different categories of employee. It seems clear that a well-planned retraining programme will lead to an increase in earnings and greater job opportunities for the retrained worker. The change of job and workplace that can follow from a retraining course inevitably entails some risk of friction and difficulty, but in the great majority of cases the expanded retraining measures will result in an overall improvement in occupational adjustment. In addition to utilizing more fully individual talent and interests, a training programme can help to break down traditional restrictive practices that are no longer warranted given the changed industrial conditions. In other words, social benefits can flow from subsidized retraining in addition to direct gains in productivity. These gains, however, are counter-balanced by certain costs incurred by individual firms and as well as the economy as a whole. It is still not clear what economic benefits can be set against the costs of the training programme. In so far as already employed persons are retrained and eventually move to a different job or to another firm, direct benefits will be derived by certain firms while others will incur costs. A more complete analysis would probably disclose that the net benefits in general clearly outweighed the costs. Similarly, from the standpoint of the economy as a whole, a comprehensive retraining programme would probably result in many benefits, notably a swifter structural transformation, a more rapid pace of expansion in highly productive industrial sectors and a higher rate of shutdowns in stagnating sectors. The complete account, however, includes costs as well as benefits and consequently sets the stage for different sets of values to come into conflict.

Extensive investment programmes involving a complete overhaul of productive processes and perhaps the introduction of new products are generally accompanied by more modern workplaces and more amenable physical facilities. It does not always follow, however, that workers will find conditions on the new job more acceptable in all respects than the old, discontinued job. The new job can be less interesting and make new and unaccustomed demands. The transition from physically demanding manual operations to inspection work can be regarded as a step forward by some but a retrograde step by others. Any given reorganization contains a range of choices which allow jobs to be allocated with some consideration given to worker qualifications and interests. Yet despite this, many individuals caught up in the process will not be able to find their feet. The benefits for the firm associated with technological changes, and indeed the main inducement for their introduction, must be weighed against the 'costs' in terms of adjustment difficulties that almost inevitably accompany such change. There is thus, we think, a likelihood that there will be a conflict of values in technical reorganizations. This is not to gainsay that technical reorganizations in many cases can be beneficial in many respects.

Plainly, in the case of a plant shutdown or a cut-back in production there will be both gains and losses for the firm. As we mentioned earlier, it is often difficult to obtain a complete picture of how these gains and losses are distributed. In general we can presume that such events at least in the long term involve an increase in overall economic efficiency. This economic advantage is offset, however, by the transfer and adjustment difficulties encountered by the displaced and redundant personnel. The difficulties of the individual are compounded where the firm has stagnated for a long period and its workforce has obtained an unduly large proportion of elderly and difficult-to-place workers. This situation is further exacerbated when the firm employs a considerable proportion of the labour supply in a given local labour market. For it may then prove impossible to find new positions for the redundant employees without extensive geographical movement on their part. In such situations, the two major factors that must be balanced are the adjustment problems of the individual workers and probable gains in overall efficiency. Special measures are clearly called for where structural change affects difficult-to-place workers concentrated in inefficient and relatively less productive enterprises.

Bio-technological measures and worker protection can be viewed as investments in the workplace environment, designed both to improve employee adjustment and increase productive efficiency. The extra costs entailed by such measures can be offset by the benefits in terms of a better physical and psychological adjustment on the part of the individual. Such measures generally result in increased productive efficiency and thus 'harmonize' the conflict between the objectives of efficiency and adjustment.

The foregoing description of the consequences of technological change in actual situations should serve to illustrate the kind of problems of balancing that can arise. Almost every situation will contain some element of conflict of objectives. Thus, our emphasis on the need for a satisfactory overall adjustment by individual employees raises important balancing problems within the sphere of public policy for industry. It is readily apparent from the description of the complexity of the concept of adjustment that all factors embraced by this concept cannot possibly be taken into consideration in advance. If we add to this the manifold difficulties of measuring productive efficiency and the ambiguities involved in calculating other consequences of technological change, it seems clear that the process of balancing cannot be completed *a priori*. Nor, for that matter, can it be conducted in general terms. Ultimately, it must be done against the background of the special circumstances of the particular case.

CHAPTER 3

Technological Change

SOME DEFINITIONS AND PREMISES

In the past decade, there has been a proliferation of published works on the subject of technological change and its consequences for society, industry and the individual. This exchange of ideas, however, has not produced a commonly accepted definition of the concept of 'technological change'. Indeed, in general, it is questionable whether the public discussion has even resulted in a widely accepted terminology for many aspects of the subject.

In the following chapters we shall have occasion to refer to such expressions as 'technology', 'technique', 'technological' and 'technical change' and, in conjunction with these last two terms, 'mechanization' and 'automation'. 'Technology', we suggest, is the application of scientific knowledge in technical systems and technical methods of production of different products. The term 'technique' is used to designate the way in which raw materials, machines, equipment and plant, production processes, units of production and products are utilized and combined. We draw a further distinction between 'technique' and 'organization'. The latter term refers mainly to different methods of work division and job allocation, i.e. the system of work arrangement.

We use such terms as 'technical development', 'technical progress' and 'technical advance' synonymously with 'technological change' without intending any connotation of greater desirability, complexity or refinement.

The terms 'mechanization' and 'automation' frequently recur in studies of technological change. By 'mechanization' we mean the replacement, complementation or expansion of human work inputs, which are essentially human *muscle* functions by machines.

In contrast, automation is the total or partial supplantation of certain human *mental* functions, such as measuring-selection, inspection, decision-taking and control, by machines and other apparatus.

The mechanization of human work operations is no new phenomenon. The industrial revolution starting in Britain in the eighteenth century and spreading to Sweden in the latter half of the nineteenth century marked a break-through for many significant technological innovations.

For a long while, subsequent innovations were largely characterized by their advancement of mechanization, i.e. the introduction of machines to replace physically demanding work operations in the transport and processing of raw materials and semi-finished products. In recent decades, however, this development has begun to change not only in degree but also in kind. Machines have now been devised that are capable of performing a great many information-handling functions such as quantity and quality control, direction and decision-taking in individual work operations and partial production processes. And we are moving steadily to the point where entire production processes may be automated.

The new technology, which is characterized by complicated machinery with a high degree of self-direction and self-regulation, has frequently been referred to in the technical literature as 'automation'. Unfortunately, the same concept has also been used in the public debate to describe other features of technological and structural change in industry. In the event, the term has lost a good deal of its original rather precise meaning and, because of the nature of the public debate, has acquired certain emotive connotations. We shall therefore endeavour to limit the use of the term in this report. Whenever it appears, it should be taken only in its originally rather limited sense, i.e. as the highest level on the mechanization scale.

The techniques currently applied by industry vary considerably in nature and degree of complexity, not only from industry to industry and firm to firm but also from operation to operation within the same plant. For many reasons, it would be desirable to be able to identify, classify and measure the extent of diffusion, and the position on the mechanization scale of existing techniques. Many attempts have been made to construct comprehensive systems of classification or mechanization profiles.[1] For the purposes of this study we shall rely on a rather arbitrary division of techniques into three 'levels' or 'stages of mechanization'. The *lowest level* is that of individual or craft production in which manual skill is an important factor. Even at this level certain muscle functions can be transferred to machines, but the latter are largely in the nature of hand tools. The individual worker as a rule enjoys much influence and discretion over the work process and output.

The *middle level* on the mechanization scale is characterized by complicated machines and machine combinations performing human muscle functions and thereby facilitating operator decision-taking. Machine systems sometimes run by remote control and designed to perform a fixed sequence of operations as well as measure certain qualities of the product are related to this technological level. The distinguishing feature is that the operator is essentially a machine 'tender', i.e. he remains responsible for starting, feeding, watching and controlling the equipment and handling the finished product.

The *highest level of mechanization* consists of the extensive use of advanced production and information techniques. Highly mechanized processes are characterized by the mechanization not only of direct labour activity such as assembly, but also material handling control activity, testing and inspection activity and even 'computerized' data processing. Automated techniques can be associated with simple apparatus as well as with extremely complicated machinery and equipment incorporating 'program control' in which the control system directs an intricate sequence of actions, and 'feed-back control' involving extensive self regulation and correction. Automated apparatus can correct itself *after* an operation such as the processing of a product part or *before* an operation as in the case of missile steering. At this level of technology, machines have assumed many decision-taking functions and the job remaining for the human being is largely one of inspecting or supervising an automatically-controlled operating system.

These three analytically discrete 'stages' or 'levels' of 'mechanization' are not readily distinguishable from one another in

[1] For example, Bright, J. R., *Automation and Management*, Harvard University, Boston 1958.

reality. For they are a rather crude attempt to introduce separate categories to what is essentially a continuum of technology. Thus there can be significant technological changes in a firm or industry without being classified as a shift from one mechanization 'level' to another in our scheme. For example, the introduction of the power saw significantly modified the technology of certain forms of craft production without altering its essential character as 'individual production'.

Furthermore, there are many cases where the levels of mechanization overlap in practice. Thus, even if conveyor systems and assembly lines can be viewed as a middle 'level' or 'stage of mechanization', and every work operation has been radically altered as a result of the introduction of the assembly line production method, work 'on the line' is performed largely with hand tools and has the character of a lower level of mechanization. Finally, technological change not only consists of the replacement of the mechanical equipment in a given production operation. It also involves the use of new materials in a production process, alterations in the form and size of a production unit or even a product. Consequently, terms such as mechanization and automation offer an unduly narrow and limited framework for a description of the great variety of changes that can occur. While aware of these complications, we feel that it can be nevertheless useful to take simplified models of different technological levels as a starting point for the discussion. This will allow us to throw some light on certain conditions underlying the problems of manpower adjustment.

THE PROCESS OF TECHNOLOGICAL CHANGE

Again, it would probably be more correct to talk of many processes of technological development, for the overall development can hardly be viewed as having only one fixed course or direction. However, since we will attempt to characterize the basic elements of technological advance and their inter-relationships over its course, we have selected a method of analysis which is applicable regardless of the degree of uniformity or diversity of the development. Our approach is based on the familiar concept of a chain of innovations.

Chain of Innovations
1. *Research*
   (Fund of knowledge)

2. *Invention*
   Design, Combination
   (Fund of projects)

3. *Development Work*
   Construction
   Prototype Models
   (Prototypes)

4. *Production*
   Processes
   (Products)

5. *Marketing*

Technical innovations, discoveries and changes are related to one another from the point of discovery or invention to the stage where the finished product is conveyed to the consumer. Research findings in one sector can clearly have important implications for every stage in the innovation sequence in an utterly different sector. Similarly, the launching and marketing of a new product can have implications for other production processes.

Technological innovations can be regarded as the outcome of ideas that are applicable to various stages of the sequence, for example, ideas created by scientific, or pure research. Such innovations can also be influenced by social scientific, i.e. psychological, sociological, economic or organizational ideas. At all stages, the pace of change as well as its orientation is affected by the quantity of resources—human as well as material—that have been invested.

In a short term, we can perhaps obtain some idea of the direction given research and subsequent innovations by scrutinizing the quantity of resources allocated to the different sectors. Over the longer term, however, it would be extremely difficult if not impossible to distinguish between the results of spontaneous and planned contributions. In our time, new technology has resulted from the systematic application of the stock of knowledge that has been gathered through refined basic research. It is interesting to note, however, that almost all scientific discovery that has been instrumental in furthering technological advance has occurred with little notion of its future technological implications. Copernicus, Tyco Brahe, Keppler, Galileo and Newton could hardly have imagined that their ideas would provide a scientific foundation for all types of engineering technology two or three hundred years afterwards. Faraday, Maxwell and others who already during the 1800s had formulated the laws of electromagnetism have left no record of ever conceiving of future electrical motors, generators, telephones, radios and televisions. Einstein's conclusions in his theory of relativity provided an important source for the research that led to the atom bomb during the Second World War. Only subsequently were atomic reactors designed for the peaceful production of energy. Today, in countless independent research institutions throughout the world, intensive research is being carried out on the phenomenon of magnetic hydrodynamics which is expected to lead to the discovery of the peaceful uses of thermonuclear energy. At the moment, one can only speculate about the length of time it will take for such research to produce results; it could be five years or fifty years or more. Not surprisingly, no private firm at present is willing to invest in such a development as a commercial venture, though one day, if the research gives the expected results, they will transform the entire system of energy and power supply.

Even if the outlook in most other cases is less uncertain, this extreme case illustrates the difficulties involved in evaluating research and development work according to the conventional profitability criteria of business economics.

The increasingly higher costs of research have led ineluctably to an increased government participation in such activity. In general, this participation has been guided by political and economic considerations. Military policy, for example, has justified the allocation of extensive resources to technical research and development work which has led to results with important implications outside the military sector. Radar, atomic energy, computers and transistors have all been research findings that have 'spilled over' into the civilian sector. Air traffic is another example of how a development originally classified as 'military research' has had a direct influence on the quality of civilian life. In the 1930s, air traffic was completely dependent on the vagaries of the weather; aeroplanes had made little progress in conception from the prototype of the Wright brothers in 1903. During the 1940s, with the financial support of defence budgets, radar and other electronic navigation devices were developed. For the first time it was possible to invest in the extensive factory installations necessary to mass-produce aeroplanes with a large cargo capacity and to complete the materials research that was necessary to manufacture reliable jet engines. Before 1940 an Atlantic air crossing was a hazardous venture. During the Second World War such flights became essential and after the war a regular civilian transoceanic air traffic system developed. Since 1945, the shifts from generation to generation among the larger civilian aeroplanes have become so frequent that these machines now become technologically obsolete long before being physically run down. This in turn has resulted in an abundant supply of reasonably priced, perfectly operational aeroplanes to carry charter groups alongside scheduled flights.

The relationship between the overall volume of investment in technological research and the development of new techniques is by no means simple. Though Sweden's volume of investment is relatively high by international standards, the results achieved through domestic research and development work are not sufficient to support an expanding industrial complex. Imported techniques, in the form of knowledge, technical equipment and finished products constitute an important element in Sweden's technological advance. Yet, largely because it is developing a domestic research programme of some note, it is able to participate in the international exchange and thereby increase its opportunities to learn swiftly of results obtained in countries with greater resources than our own. In these ways domestic investment in advanced research orientated to well-defined objectives has been a strong propelling force in the process of technological change.

Changing technology has also resulted in the reliable mass production of relatively complicated products which in turn enable more advanced production techniques to be employed. This feed-back in the technological development has all the characteristics of an 'accelerator effect'. Current production technology has made it possible, for example, to manufacture new micro-electronic circuits which will soon result in new types of computers which are less costly and require less space. This development in turn will increase the suitability of such machines for data processing in administrative and technical planning and in automatically-controlled production processes. Moreover, the development of new products and production methods in one industry can have important implications for the pace of technological change in rather remote sectors of business activity. The following example may serve to give some idea of the complicated inter-relationship between different industrial sectors.

In Sweden, 80 per cent of the value of advertising is transmitted via newspapers, magazines, direct advertising and shop advertising. As a consequence, the overwhelming proportion of the products of the paper and pulp industry have become media for advertising activity, Not surprisingly then, this industry has become increasingly sensitive to the interplay between the advertising world and the printing industry, and increasingly dependent on changes in the technology of the printing industry.[1]

With the advent of self-service shops, product packaging has become a key medium of the advertising message. This has led to a need for an accurate and realistic reproduction of the commodity on the package, i.e. multi-colour printing. This process in turn requires paper with a high degree of whiteness (brightness), smoothness (surface fineness) and the ability to take ink satisfactorily. Offset printing shortens the process of preparation and allows a faster printing speed. An increasingly larger proportion of paper pulp is manufactured as bleached pulp because of its suitability for printing. The process of bleaching pulp results in a loss of substance and therefore requires a greater initial supply of raw materials. Brown corrugated cardboard has not as yet been replaced by that with white

[1] The following is based on Steenberg, B., *Några synpunkter på reklamväsendets roll för pappersindustri och grafisk industri*, Svenska Handelsbankens Index 1964:10.

surface layers, or plastic faced cardboard, but such a development can be expected.

Chemically treated pulp obtained from domestic softwood fibres is a good deal stronger than hardwood pulp but does not produce paper of comparable evenness, preserved opacity or overall printability. Eucalyptus and poplar pulp from temperate climates have become more widely used. To improve the printability of paper from softwood pulp, it has been treated with kaolin (porcelainized) and a binding agent. A machine has been invented that is capable of kaolinizing paper at the same rate of speed as it is produced by the paper-making machine. The chemical industry has recently sought to develop an effective binding agent. The necessary preliminary research in that area had not been carried out in Sweden and only in recent years have we begun to participate in this technological development. While firms in the wood-processing industry have engaged in extensive research, graphic processes have been long neglected. This in turn has restricted the contact and exchange between the printing industry and the paper and pulp industry.

Future printing technology will require other qualities of printing paper than simply the ability to take a liquid ink image satisfactorily. Electrostatic printing methods, for example, transfer a picture by charging a paper surface which attracts an oppositely-charged colour pigment and then sintering (vitrifying) the pigment to the paper surface. In another form, this technology has been used for multi-colour printing on the riffled surface of corrugated cardboard. In electrostatic printing processes the paper need no longer be absorbent, or especially strong-surfaced or evenly surfaced. Rationalization and product development in the paper and pulp industry require comparable efforts in the printing industry (and vice versa) in order to obtain competitive final products. Yet this relationship is further complicated by another factor. A shift of advertising to other types of media than printed matter could have effects on the wood-processing industry not unlike the substitution of plastics for wood products. The modern petrochemical industry currently provides plastics as a substitute for traditional materials, such as wood and metals, for many manufacturing processes. This has brought about a restructuring of various industries as well as leading to the introduction of new products on the market.

Greater research efforts are sorely needed to provide further insight into and earlier warning of the consequences of technological changes. Government authorities must have some idea of the probable effects of a given technological development before it has reached the final link in the innovation chain. The relevant public administrative agency should be placed in a position to influence the development so that its economic results are both optimal and compatible with the satisfaction of the need of individual workers for income and employment security.

These two considerations, i.e. overall economic growth and the security of the individual, confront us with our essential balancing problem. It is important to recognize at the outset, however, that the balancing problem occurs in an economic system which already has its certain built-in balancing mechanisms. Thus, our economic system is based on a fair proportion of production units which strive to maximize profits. Such a criterion however entails that factors that are important from the vantage point of the overall economy are rarely taken into account in the balancing process.

There are, for example, obvious health risks involved in the use of various technical products. Also, production processes often destroy part of natural environment—industrial waste can contaminate biological systems throughout wide areas, exhaust fumes and waste gas can lead to unsanitary living conditions and noise can create great discomfort. The new technology has on the other hand presented man with new and often surprising opportunities requiring new political values in areas such as training and education, employment and the right to utilize technical products. In this way, technological change presents an important challenge to the ability of society to adjust to new conditions.

The automobile and 'automobilism' offers to everyone a palpable example of how a mechanized and partly automated production process can rapidly provide a relatively complicated product to the consumer at a reasonable price and by doing this transform transportation habits and confront society with a complicated adjustment problem.

Changes in technology have been at least equally significant for us as employees as they have been for us as consumers of technological commodities. Changes in production techniques have brought in their wake changes in work organization, job content, skill requirements and systems of payment. The ability of employees to adapt to and participate in these changes is an essential factor underlying the process of technological change.

TECHNOLOGICAL CHANGE IN DIFFERENT SECTORS OF INDUSTRY

Energy production, agriculture and forestry, raw material extraction and refining, metal working and wood processing, manufacturing, materials transport, communications, information-handling and the measurement, control and regulation of production processes have all undergone considerable technological transformation. In the energy sector, we can observe an acceleration in the growth of energy production; i.e. the production of electrical energy, more recently nuclear energy and especially energy based on oil. Oil refineries are being progressively automated. And as electric power plant production has become increasingly characterized by concentration into larger units, joint production by different units and long distance transmissions of high tension, direct current 380 MV electricity, it has proved increasingly feasible to introduce automation.

Technological change in the agricultural sector has proved to be a mixed blessing. Better plant and animal stock, new farming methods and fertilizers and access to chemical methods of pest control have resulted in greatly improved productivity. Accompanying this gain however have been greater hazards to human health and natural environmental balance. Tractors, combine harvesters and mechanical equipment for livestock care and fodder storage have transformed farming methods at a rapid rate. At the same time there has been an appreciable decrease in the number of farming units.

Improved forestry preservation has led to a more rapid growth of forests, which in turn has made the mechanization of wood processing more profitable. Mechanization in the forestry sector during the 1950s has been accomplished largely through the widespread use of the power saw.[1] Hand bark peeling has been

[1] See further Sandahl, L., *Skogsbrukets strukturomvandling och tekniska utveckling samt dess konsekvenser för arbetskraften.* An industry study by the research division of the Swedish Timber Workers Union, Stockholm 1966.

D

almost entirely replaced by mechanical bark peeling, either at processing sites or in mills. However, while trimming and lopping could readily be mechanized, this has occurred only to a small extent in processing sites and the introduction of felling and bundling machines and multi-process machines designed to fell, trim and saw, is still at the experimental stage. The decisive factor in the pace of mechanization is the feasibility of using machines in intermediate cutting and thinning operations which now affect two-thirds of the overall output of wood pulp as well as involving two-thirds of the production units. The predominant form of materials transport within the forestry sector is the tractor. Trucks have increasingly replaced log floating though the latter is beginning to be mechanized at the sorting and grading stations.

In the past fifteen years, building and construction activity —particularly transport and materials handling on the construction sites—has been extensively mechanized by cranes, lifts, concrete mixers and sliding forms.[1] Prefabrication of building components, or entire rooms, has not however become widely accepted and the continuing shortness of the 'production run' has prevented a swifter mechanization of the manufacture of prefabricated building components. The structure of the building sector is marked by a large number of small production units lacking sufficient resources to invest heavily in the capital equipment that is essential for mechanization. It seems plain that the concentration of building activity into larger units would ensure a more widespread installation of mechanized construction operations and through an increase in demand lead to a swifter industrialization of existing methods of prefabricating building blocks. Highway construction and road work methods have been significantly changed by the increased capacity of mobile machinery such as excavators, steam shovels and transport vehicles. On the whole, almost all such work is now performed with the aid of machinery.

The manufacture of cement articles is gradually becoming highly mechanized and automated. In recent years, brick manufacturing has become more highly mechanized due to the intro-

[1] See further Lindahl, S., *Byggarbetskraften och den tekniska utvecklingen*. An industry study by the research division of the Building Trade Workers. Stockholm 1966.

Technological Change 51

duction of automated tunnel kilns, improved drying methods and clay extracting and materials transport equipment. Mechanization, however, is still not widely diffused among production units. The production of window glass and glass containers is highly mechanized while the manufacture of lighting glass, domestic glassware and art glassware is characterized by much handicraft work.

Firms in the printing industry, particularly printers, have attained a high degree of mechanization through the introduction of automatically controlled cylinder and rotary presses. Technological change has impinged too on printing methods, largely through the introduction of offset printing. Moreover, computer composition of text, illustrations and their final page make-up are now technically practicable.

Changing technology in the mining industry has transformed mining and material transport methods.[1] The growth of drift mining, automatic stage-feeding drills, the increased capacity of mobile machinery, the remote control of train transport and automatically-controlled shaft frame work have all created considerable changes in production conditions. Ore is refined today far more than before by sorting, dressing and pelletizing. The course of mechanization in the metal-working industries has varied greatly from industry to industry and production unit to production unit.[2] In the preparation of billet iron for example the opportunity to use systems of remote control in the slabbing mill has led to the installation of new techniques. It now appears that automation of the entire process is technically feasible. In several cases, foundries have already been almost completely automated. Program-controlled machines have been introduced in the engineering industry in the past ten years. The number of numerically controlled machine tools is still small but growing rapidly and can be expected one day to revolutionize short-run metal-working production. The technology of metal processing has been altered by capacity turning, milling, drilling, boring, cutting, reaming, tapping and stamping machines operating at a faster speed as well as improvements in steel quality.

[1] See further *Teknisk utveckling och arbetskraften i gruvindustrin*. A company study by LKAB, Stockholm 1966.

[2] See further Almgren, H., *De tekniska förändringarnas karaktär och konsekvenser inom metall- och verkstadsindustrin*. An industry study by the Swedish Metal Workers Union, Stockholm 1966.

New processing methods such as electro-erosion and high-pressure forming are gradually spreading throughout the Swedish metal-working industry. Also, the introduction of 'transfer-machines', or machine work stations which serve to link up long sequences of metal-working operations without operator intervention, has drastically altered production methods. Assembly lines and conveyor belts have long been used in assembly work, particularly in the motor car industry and in the general metal working and electrical engineering processes. The mechanization and automation of materials transport, such as hoists and overhead trolleys, have significantly enlarged production capacity and productivity, particularly in shipyards.

Spinning and weaving as well as the production of women's stockings in the textile industry have been rapidly automated in a number of production units.[1] Moreover, in certain plants, preparation and other processing work has been highly mechanized and program-controlled. Production is now under way of plastic laminated textile products. And non-woven fabrics are now manufactured by spreading synthetic fibres on a matting and binding them together by adhesive cement.

Since the beginning of the 1950s, there has been a thoroughgoing rationalization in various branches of the textile industry. New raw materials and synthetic fibres have greatly affected the structure of the textile and ready-made clothing industries. It has not proved possible to mechanize the ready-made clothing industry to the same extent as textiles, for less than one-third of the total hours of work performed in the clothing industry involves the use of machines. Yet a shift to non-woven materials can be anticipated. Ready-made clothing manufacture will progressively replace sewing with a form of vulcanization of garment seams by heatronic welding, or high-frequency heating.

The different sectors of the wood and wood products industry, i.e. sawmilling, construction, carpentry and furniture fabrication, have been subject to varying degrees of mechanization. The particularly rapid advance of furniture fabrication can partly be explained by the nature of the product and partly by the application of high-frequency current to the rapid drying of sizing and lacquer.

[1] See further *Teknisk utveckling och arbetskraften i textilindustrin.* An industry study by LO's Research division, Stockholm 1966.

In the paper and pulp industry, changing technology has manifested itself in product refinement, manila paper production and pulp bleaching. Materials transport operations too have become highly mechanized. Pulp, boiling, bleaching, washing and drying have been transformed into continuous processes. All this has led to the need for larger production units. Automatic control of processes has been introduced in the paper and pulp industry as well as in the chemical industry. Methods of control and measurement have noticeably improved through the use of isotopes. Certain processes in the iron and steel industry have thus far eluded automatic control largely because of the difficulties of measuring temperatures and registering temperature changes in steel smelters.

In the food industry, particularly where production has the character of continuous flow processes such as in the fats and oils industry, breweries, dairies, and flour mills, but also in slaughter house and meat packing plants, chocolate factories and bakeries, continuing technological change has transformed certain production operations into highly mechanized processes. The technological structure within the sector is uneven largely because rationalization has proceeded at a slower pace in bakeries and meat packing than in other branches such as flour milling, fats and oils manufacture, and dairying. Similarly, the degree of mechanization in the transport and communications sector has varied from branch to branch. Air traffic leads the field with the automation of ticket booking, traffic supervision and flying operations. A structural transformation of shipping and the maritime trade has been brought about by an expansion of the tanker fleet and the increased size and cargo capacity of individual tankers. The manufacture of automated marine machinery is now under way. Owing to the mechanization of stevedoring and longshore work through the introduction of cranes, lifts, trucks and 'containerization', lay-over times in the ports have been considerably reduced. Ore and oil ports have been highly mechanized. A notable trend in the development of transport techniques has been the growing integration of hitherto separate stages: shipping, warehousing and storage, train and trucking. One consequence of this is an increased need for the concentration of transport volume in regionally centralized ports.

The railways have long been hosts to technological change.[1] Electrification, the shift from the steam engine to the electric locomotive, occurred decades ago along with the introduction of remote control systems for track switches (points) and signals.

The increased capacity and speed of trains and the accompanying need for safety measures have led to basic changes in train management technology. Thus, during the 1950s and 1960s automation has been introduced to track switches and signals on stretches of main lines. Another factor contributing to the structural transformation of the railroad network has been the growth of the highway system and the expansion of the trucking industry. In the road transport industry, technological change has evidenced itself in the growing number of vehicles, the capacity of individual vehicles and the greater specialization of operatives. The introduction of mechanization to hoisting, loading and unloading operations has resulted in great productivity gains. Mechanization has spread to the freight terminals and storage facilities but automation has not made any appreciable headway.

The rapid growth of pre-packed foods and other goods and improved storage equipment such as deep-freezing chambers, cold-storage units and refrigerated display cases have altered work operations in the distribution sector. The shift to self-service shops, supermarkets, and department stores has brought about a thorough going transformation of the structure of retailing.

The mechanization of administrative and office work has been a long-standing development. In the past few decades, the introduction of mechanical and electrical typewriters and adding machines, book-keeping machines, filing machines and punched card machines has resulted in the mechanization of many repetitive office tasks. In general this has been accompanied by a trend towards increased specialization of office work. The introduction of the computer in the 1950s, however, marked a watershed of technological advance in the clerical sector. For, by the 1930s, the computer expansion had fundamentally, i.e. qualitatively as well as quantitatively, altered the nature of many repetitive office operations. The applicability of the computer has not been con-

[1] See further *Den tekniska utvecklingens konsekvenser för arbetskraften vid States Järnvägär*. A company study by Swedish Railways, Stockholm 1966.

fined to this sector; in recent years they have proved their mettle in production planning, construction and scientific management. The shipbuilding industry has recently experimented with computers to translate designs expressed mathematically by issuing instructions on punched tape to numerically controlled blow torches to cut plates, etc., thus altogether eliminating the drawing stage. The actual spread of the computer, however, has been restricted mainly to the larger production units in banking and insurance, public administration, commerce and industry. The smaller firms have tended to hire computer time from special service agencies.

In the medical sector, automation has begun to spread to the laboratories and new techniques, e.g. electronic and radio techniques—have transformed medical diagnosis. Computers have also created new opportunities for integrated information handling. In other areas, as well, e.g. transport and treatment, medical services have been mechanized and automated.

Technological change in the communications sector has consisted largely of the automation of the telephone system and the growth of the television network. The former has been a process of long duration, but the 1950s and 1960s were decades of exceptionally rapid growth. The latter is a rather new development of a commodity that is orientated primarily to leisure consumption. However, the application of television to other uses is on the increase. This is particularly true in the educational sector where television is becoming an important teaching medium and in the manufacturing sector where television is increasingly being used to monitor industrial production systems.

THE PACE OF TECHNOLOGICAL ADVANCE

There seems to be little doubt that the pace of technological change varies from one technological sector to the next and from one time period to another in the same sector. However, it is beyond the scope of our competence to assess with particularity whether, for example, the computer or nuclear energy has been quantitatively and qualitatively more revolutionary than, say, electrical energy or the telephone.

It is quite possible that technological progress in a given period may appear to be rather small from the scientific point of view, because few fundamentally new ideas have been introduced, and yet display an 'accelerator effect'. For with any given stock of knowledge there are additional opportunities to produce technical 'products'. The time lag between discovery and invention and application tends to vary inversely with the quantity of resources allocated to research and development. Several attempts have been made to illustrate this idea. Two American studies[1] examining respectively twelve and twenty significant innovations found that during the period from the turn of the century to the present the time interval between technical discovery and the start of commercial application has decreased from three decades to one decade and the time lag from the introduction stage to extensive commercial application has been reduced from a decade to an average of two years, though this varied from one to fifteen years depending on the product. On the other hand, there are examples of prolongation of the time lag in the commercial exploitation of new materials, processes and products.

A crucial factor appears to be the criteria that are used to distribute resources among different projects. Profitability calculations of manufacturing and service operations by producers are based on a variety of values, objectives and target rates of return which are seldom recorded and therefore not susceptible to general evaluation. The overall economic consequences of change are rarely appreciated at the time of the discovery of an engineering invention and its commercial introduction. The earliest point appears to be the stage when the innovation has spread widely throughout the market. The explanation for this seems reasonably clear. The development process is lengthy and consequently delays our ability to evaluate it. When the effects of change gradually become evident, it is often too late to alter the process whereby such a step is warranted.

Electronic data processing is the symbol of the technology of our generation. The computer was introduced in Sweden in the middle of the 1950s.[2] Only by the beginning of the 1960s, however, had it completed its period of commercial introduction.

---

[1] *Technology and the American Economy*. Report of the National Commission on Technology, Automation and Economic Progress, Washington 1966.

[2] 'Datamaskiner i Sverige', *Industria* 1965:3; and *Fackutbildning i automatisk databehandling*, SOU 1965:56, Stockholm 1965.

Technological Change

Today, there are about 300 computers used throughout the country with 5,000–6,000 persons employed as operators, programmers, system analysts and maintenance staff. In large firms in industry, trade, banking and insurance and public administration, the computer is generally accessible. Its use, however, is still confined mainly to repetitive administrative and clerical tasks and has spread only to a small extent to process control and techniques of management, such as network planning. The next generation of computers is now gaining ground and should become fairly widely diffused within a short period. The economic longevity of the older generation of computers is estimated to be about 4–5 years. It is extremely difficult to forecast with certainty how the use of computers will spread. There is some indication that the rate of increase has slightly declined. Nevertheless it is thought that by 1967 about 8,000 persons will be directly employed in the 'computer sector'. Given that the qualitative capacity of the new generation of computers is considerably greater than that of the previous generation, a reduction in the rate of increase of the number of machines in use need not be accompanied by a similar change in trend of the volume of computer work. Process control and program-controlled machine tools are promising areas of computer use. While today there are only about 20 firms in the entire country that possess numerically controlled machine tools,[1] this number is expected to quadruple in several years' time. The distribution of numerically controlled machine tools is heavily weighted toward the large and medium-large engineering firms with both unit and mass production operations. Presently, less than 100 numerically controlled machine tools are in use and these perform mainly metal cutting operations. However, it is anticipated that this number will double itself several times in coming years. Viewed as a proportion, the current Swedish level corresponds to that reached in the USA three years ago.

While computers and numerically controlled machine tools are significant technological innovations their importance is somewhat dwarfed by the overall quantity of innovations involved in technological advance.

Technological change occurs at particular points, and each

[1] *Utvecklingen beträffande numerisk styrning i Sverige.* A report by The Swedish Association for Metal Transforming and Engineering Industries, Stockholm 1966.

occurrence can entail considerable gains in productivity. Some links in the production chain inevitably tend to lag behind and create 'bottlenecks', which in turn become particular targets for new innovations. The 'war against bottlenecks' in the production system may be viewed as a significant motive force in the overall economic development. The pace of change is related to the quantity of resources allocated to research and development work. While research and development have begun to claim an increasing share of total resources, they have started from a low base and today the proportion is only a few per cent. The distribution of investment resources between new innovations and already introduced machines and materials is continuously shifting and complicates and obscures the task of quantifying the relationship between technological change and investment.

Nor have we unearthed any direct method of measuring the effects of technological change? There are admittedly occasional examples of individual cases which display reasonably isolated and measurable productivity or employment effects. It would not be worth while, however, to reproduce such calculations in this report. Not only would the process be too time-consuming and cumbersome, but we still could not be certain that our results were representative of the overall effects. An acceptable indirect method is offered by the calculation of changes in productivity for the economy as a whole. Productivity, i.e. output per man hour, gives a measure of the net result of all changes including not only technological changes but also organizational and structural changes and increased labour effort.

It is evident from Table 1 that productivity increases prior to the 1960s were small, not only during the 1930s and the early 1940s when the economy was disorganized by high unemployment and war, but also in all other periods apart from the two periods of recovery after the First and Second World Wars. During the 1960s, however, there has been a progressive rise in the rate of annual increase and this trend is expected to continue in the foreseeable future under the assumption of no unfavourable developments in international affairs. The significance of this rate of change of productivity can readily be demonstrated by comparing the time intervals required to quadruple the national product at different rates of productivity gain. Thus at a 3 per cent annual increase in productivity, it would take

TABLE 1

Changes in Labour Productivity, 1923–80

Period	Annual increases in productivity in %
1923–29	3·5–4
1929–39	*approx* 2
1938–46	*approx* 1
1946–50	4
1950–60	3·5
1960–65	4·3
1965–70*	4·5
1970–80*	4·8

Source:
* Forecasts of the Long-Term Planning Survey. The Swedish Economy, 1966–70.

twenty-four years to quadruple the national product, at 4 per cent annual increase in productivity it would take eighteen years and at a 5 per cent annual increase it would take only fourteen years. One can conclude from this that even if there is a continuous rise in the rate of increase of productivity, we shall not be confronted by a revolutionary change in technological progress.

It appears reasonably safe too, to assume that the great majority of new products, materials, methods, processes and apparatus that will be widely diffused throughout industry in the next five to ten years are already in the introductory stage or are at least known to the researchers.

CHAPTER 4

Managerial Organization, Administrative Systems and Technological Change

Accompanying the steady stream of technological innovations at the workplace is a continuous flow of *administrative innovations* in the business organization. Changes in the internal administrative system can involve shifts in the distribution of power and influence in the firm, alterations in the pattern of the flow of information, the dismantling of traditional work communities and the formation of new work groups, or the fragmentation or enlargement of the content of particular job operations. Often, the effects of such changes on the individual and his working situation are as important as the introduction of new machinery, production processes or materials.

Technological change has not only resulted in a transformation of production methods; it has also placed at management's disposal a variety of new administrative aids and instruments. The most conspicuous innovation in the new 'information-handling and decision-taking technology' is the computer. But the new advanced mathematical and statistical methods for the collection of data and the analysis of administrative and technical production problems have been equally significant.

New developments in the science of work study and a systematic utilization of the findings in different areas of research have increased the possibilities of describing, measuring and analysing different industrial and administrative job operations. Thus, innovations in technical methods of time and motion study and planning aids such as Methods—Time—Measurement (MTM) and Universal Maintenance Standards (UMS) have been enlisted in rationalization work. As a consequence, there have been

Managerial Organization 61

radical changes not only in working methods but also in the type of overall work organization, changes which are of some significance for systems of wage payments as well as the pattern of internal transfer and promotion.

The new methods give management previously undreamt of opportunities to rationalize the systems of information and decision-taking in the firm as well as manufacturing processes. With the assistance of these new techniques, new possibilities of identifying sources of information and specifying, selecting and applying desired data have presented themselves.

This is a developmental sequence that has long been familiar to those 'on the shop floor'. It will naturally have profound and widespread implications for the entire organizational structure of the firm. The difference in this case, however, is that the repercussions will probably be greatest at various levels of management.

Within the foreseeable future, highly advanced and mechanized information techniques will probably be adopted by the larger commercial firms, public administrative agencies, military establishments and all operations requiring large quantities of relatively uniform data to be rapidly processed. These techniques however, are not expected to spread swiftly to the small- and medium-sized firms. New techniques in work study, in contrast, have already become widely diffused and are beginning to penetrate even to the smaller workplaces.

Technological change creates a need for continuous adaptation of the firms' administrative system and organization. Work assignments must be revised, contact and communication between different staff must be redirected and areas of decision-taking must be reformulated as attempts are made to fashion new organizational and administrative solutions to the new technical problems that arise.

Broadly, there appears to be some relationship between organizational forms and changing technology. Thus, tools, materials and products on a building site are basically different from those in an engineering workshop. Similarly, there are noticeable differences between the content of work assignments, the functions of supervisors, information systems, etc., in these two cases. The machinery and work operations in engineering firms differ greatly from the apparatus and processes employed in oil refineries or paper and pulp mills. These differences inevitably give rise to differences in work organization and work environment. Were we to compare two firms in the same industry using largely similar techniques, say, two motor car factories, we would certainly discover significant similarities in their organizational structures, though of course if we were to pursue the comparison and study these firms in greater detail we would undoubtedly unearth important differences. For example, machine manning practices will often vary from one firm to the next. In one firm, a skilled worker will be used for a particular job while in another firm the same job is broken down into separate steps each performed by different semi-skilled or unskilled workers. As well, in certain firms, production scheduling is centrally arranged while in others it is left largely to supervisors and foremen. And, finally, even systems of wage payment, wages structures, rules of discipline, information systems and patterns of social interactions will display much variation.

While it may be possible therefore to detect some relationship between different organizational alternatives and administrative systems and technological change, the association appears to be rather weak and unclear. Plainly, there are no fixed, unique or immutable relationships governing these two factors. At every technological 'level' and in every technological situation, it is generally possible to select from among groups of different organizational alternatives and administrative systems to promote the particular objectives of the firm. The choice itself will depend largely on the decision-taker, his aims and his views of the relative effectiveness of the available alternatives. Management has both the prerogative and the responsibility to determine the organization of the activities of the enterprise. Their views on the appropriateness of particular organizational alternatives, i.e. their 'organizational ideology', are therefore sufficiently important in this context to warrant closer examination.

MANAGEMENT'S 'ORGANIZATIONAL IDEOLOGY'

There are a host of differing views about how a firm should be managed and organized in order to function effectively. These views can ultimately be reduced to certain fundamental assumptions about the forces that motivate and drive individuals to greater work effort.[1] At a more proximate level, however, there has long been a pronounced tendency to emphasize certain organizational principles thought to be important in the practical activity of the firm. With some intentional simplification, these too can be reduced to four central elements or articles of faith:

(a) *A belief in the efficacy of the hierarchical organization of power*, decisional and informational structures based on the principle of a chain of command or 'line' of authority with each employee subordinate to and taking orders from only one superior, with areas of responsibility and decision carefully delimited and not overlapping, and with specialists in the form of 'staff' personnel performing essentially or exclusively advisory functions.

(b) *A belief in authoritarian leadership* characterized by a difference in status between subordinate and superior and the superior's wide discretionary authority over and correspondingly wide responsibility for the actions of his subordinates.

(c) *A belief in the effectiveness of the simplification of work operations* and direct control over jobs, a basic article of faith underlying traditional rationalization and work study activities.

(d) *A belief in the need for incentive wage systems and coercion* based on an underlying motivational assumption that economic reward is the only effective incentive to increased work effort.

The more extreme manifestations of these principles have probably largely disappeared from our workplaces under the pressure of internal and external events such as new technology, persistent shortages of manpower in local labour markets and a general trend towards the 'democratization' of society. New research findings in social science and the criticism directed by the researchers against traditional organizational principles have also had some effect. Today, few employers maintain that there are any 'patent' solutions—or only one 'best way'—to form a business organization.

New types of organizational forms are beginning to secure a

---

[1] For a more detailed description, see for example Chapter 4 in Dahlström, E. (Ed.), *Teknisk förändring och arbetsanpassning. Ett sociologiskt bidrag till forsknings- och planeringsdebatten*, Stockholm 1966. (Technological Change and Work Adjustment.)

footing, particularly in firms that use highly advanced production techniques and employ large groups of experts in technical and other specialist fields. Moreover, the emergence of large research organizations for military and civilian uses poses the need for entirely new forms for which classical organizational principles offer little or no guidance. Despite these developments, however, preconceptions about the need for a hierarchical form of organization, the effectiveness of the division and specialization of work assignments and direct control over job operations continue to hold sway and indeed constitute a basic element in modern managerial organizations.

THE GROWTH OF PERSONNEL ADMINISTRATION

One aspect of the administrative activity of the firm specifically devoted to the employee and his or her adjustment to the working environment is personnel administration. Narrowly defined, it encompasses five main functions, notably to recruit and hire, retain, develop and train, control and 'sever' staff.

There has been considerable variation in the emphasis in the field of personnel work over the course of time as well as in its application in different occupations and firms. Broadly speaking, however, personnel administration in the post-war period has grown from an earlier state when a few staff in the firm rather unsystematically performed several personnel functions, into a recognized and independent managerial speciality.

This development, however, cannot be directly attributed to technological change. Rather the causative factors appear to be the shift to a full employment economy, the tighter situation on the labour market, the spate of new social legislation and the 'deepening' of formal education on the part of the labour force. Moreover, trade union activity and shifts in employers organizational ideology have been contributing causes.

Despite the considerable growth in recognition of the personnel administration profession today only the largest firms assign a number of full-time specialists to a separate personnel department. In the smaller firms, personnel functions are widely distributed among different staff in different departments. Even the smaller and medium-sized firms, however, can gain access to new findings and expertise in the field by resorting to the services of outside consultants and specialists provided by independent firms and employers' associations.

Though personnel administration has developed continuously and independently of technological innovations, its rôle appears to be closely associated with such changes in certain respects. Indeed, the effects of the latter on the pattern of personnel administration work can extend over the long term. Thus, temporary measures taken to solve acute personnel problems arising from technological innovations can evolve into hard and fast managerial practices. Moreover, since technological change generally gives rise to a wide variety of problems often requiring many different types of measures for their solution, such change can directly result in an expansion of personnel administrative services.

The growth of personnel administration as a managerial speciality has undoubtedly contributed to some extent to the creation of certain norms governing the introduction of new technological processes and the concomitant redeployment of the workforce. That certain norms have evolved cannot be gainsaid. There may be some variation in detail from case to case and firm to firm but there is a similarity in the overall pattern of treatment in most cases. The pattern that frequently recurs includes such major threads as improved information to employees, the creation of new groups for joint consultation and the initiation of internal training programmes. What remains somewhat unclear, however, is the exact importance of the part played by the personnel specialists in the planning and implementation of technological changes.

MANAGERIAL ORGANIZATION AND SYSTEMS OF WAGES PAYMENT

Swedish firms must take into account the fact that wage policy is largely pre-determined at the 'industry-wide' level, i.e. negotiations between the employer association and national union for the particular industry, and at the 'central level', i.e. negotiations between the Swedish Employers Confederation and the Confederation of Swedish Trade Unions. There is of course some scope for manoeuvre and negotiation at the enterprise level, notably in the case of new or revised piece rates, but an essential characteristic of the Swedish system is that the firm is advised to offset increases in labour costs arising from increases in wages by investing in new machinery and equipment, devising new and more efficient production methods and altering the work organization. The selection of a suitable method of wage payment would fall into the last category. It seems reasonable to assume that employers attempt to arrive at some view of future market developments at least several years in advance and seek to obtain some advance understanding of the production techniques involved in various investment alternatives. It also seems reasonable to assume that the existing methods of wages payment and expectations of market developments play some part in the selection of marketing strategy and organizational choice. The transition from one method of wages payment to another can require a rather large-scale reform of the work organization. This is quite common for example when a system of wage payments based on time rates is discarded in favour of some form of piecework system. It is not at all infrequent, however, for this causal sequence to be reversed: successive technical and organizational changes can not only allow but also necessitate changes in the system of wages payment. At present, however, we do not have sufficient information to determine the extent to which or whether companies consciously attempt to control wage costs over the long term by their choice of different methods of wages payment. Wage increases seem to bear more directly on the choice of production techniques and work methods than the selection of the wages system as such. Thus, MTM techniques have been much more widely applied to the choice of production methods than to wage fixing. Perhaps, because the method of wage payment is a subject of collective negotiation, companies tend to regard it as less easily subject to their influence and have therefore failed to exploit it more fully as a variable in their decision-taking.

Within the overall framework of any system of wages payments, room must be created to allow for successive adjustment. Even systematic job evaluation—which may be thought to create a relative rigid system—is modified continuously by changes in the weighting, the addition of criteria or simply the expansion of coverage.

This flexibility probably accentuates the tendency of employers

Managerial Organization

to be more interested in rationalizing work methods than changing the system of wages payment as a device to hold down rising costs. For management tend to regard the method of wages payment largely or solely as a measure to induce greater productive efficiency on the part of employees.

THE STRUCTURE OF POWER AND INFLUENCE WITHIN THE BUSINESS ORGANIZATION

The introduction of highly advanced production and 'information' techniques can conceivably lead to changes in the process of decision-taking, i.e. either in the direction of centralization or decentralization, and consequently to shifts in the distribution of power and influence in the firm.[1]

Tendencies towards centralization appear to be closely associated with the introduction of automatic data processing. Access to computers and mathematical statistical methods of analysis makes it possible to rationalize and quantify information flows and decisional processes. The scope of decision can in this way be enlarged both in space and time.

If the traditional organizational form is retained, the decision-taking process shifts upwards along the hierarchy. Increased centralization is accompanied by a reduced freedom of choice and manoeuvre, i.e. less room for individual initiative, at lower organizational levels. The effects of this are felt particularly by those in the 'middle echelons' of management. For the number of technicians, systems analysts and other specialists tend to increase proportionately at the expense of the managerial staff. And, the new specialists are generally placed at a high level in the organization, both in terms of status and salary, and owing to their expertise are given a large measure of influence over the information-gathering and decision-taking processes without exercising 'direct' managerial functions. This process tends to relax some of the rigidities in the traditional authoritarian hierarchy and can frequently promote easier exchange and contact between different groups of personnel. At the same time, however, it can also create new sources of friction between other groups in the organization.

[1] This and the following sections are based largely on Dahlström, E., op. cit, *supra*, Chapter 3.

Technological change also has some influence on the number of levels in the organizational hierarchy of the firms though the exact effects are difficult to isolate and are not yet clearly understood. It appears that the number of decisional levels tends to increase as firms move from individual or craft production methods to a higher degree of mechanization. Moreover, there seems to be some tendency for firms at higher levels of technology and automation to experience a reduction in the number of decisional steps in the organizational structure. This appears to be attributable to the opportunities for centralized control offered by modern information techniques together with the increased resort to 'systems analysis' by firms operating at a highly advanced technological level. Consideration of the human factor as well as the acceptance of new administrative ideas have manifested themselves in conscious efforts to arrive at simpler organization forms.

Yet other factors bear upon the relationship. Thus, the availability of improved and more rapid information and control methods offers greater opportunities for delegating managerial decisions. And, as firms and workplaces grow in size they are often compelled to introduce some measure of decentralization to their processes of decision-taking: it is often a necessity as well as a theoretical administrative virtue to locate the decision-taking level as low as possible along the organizational hierarchy. Another complication is that the processes of centralization and decentralization can occur simultaneously in the same firm. Technological change as well as other changes make it possible and feasible to shift certain types of decisions to the higher echelons of management while simultaneously warranting the delegation of other types of decisions to subordinate levels.

As the company's level of mechanization rises, there is a noticeable increase in the interdependence of its component operations and departments. Even before automation, attempts are made in each area to co-ordinate the different operations of the firm, such as manufacturing sales and purchasing, into a smoothly functioning system. With the introduction of a more highly advanced production and information technique, however, the interdependence of these operations increases. In the event, the organization tends to be reformed so as to place the hitherto separate and independent areas of decision in one decisional and operational unit. Where modern information techniques are not accessible the increased awareness of the interdependence of operations leads to increased co-ordination, the establishment of permanent or temporary consultative groups, the creation of staffs with specialists whose function it is to achieve greater uniformity in or attempt to integrate as far as possible the various operations of the firm. Purely 'human' co-ordination groups seem to give rise to more friction between individuals in the organization than mechanical co-ordination by computers.

CHANGES IN JOB CONTENT

Technological progress is an undoubted agent of change at the workplace, disrupting traditional organizational patterns and simultaneously creating opportunities for new patterns to emerge. However, the organizational structure is also affected by other forces and must adapt to changes in conditions other than those which are purely technological in nature. It is reasonable to expect therefore that the lines of development will be diverse rather than uniform in content and direction. Any attempt to summarize the influence of different factors on the work environment necessarily involves a certain degree of simplification of reality's complicated patterns and inter-relationships. Fully aware of this limitation we shall nonetheless discuss certain trends in the development of work organization and job content that appear to be related to technological change. As in previous instances, we make no claims to completeness or even desirable comprehensiveness. Nor do we assert that the features in the work environment that we examine are necessarily connected with a particular production technique or technological level.

The point of departure for our discussion is craft production. This is characterized by a notable absence of job fragmentation, i.e. all or most operations of the job are performed by the same man.

The job is moreover performed relatively independently of supervision. Within fairly wide limits the individual worker has discretion to adjust his pace of work to suit himself; he is dependent on other operations only to a very limited extent.

Often, such work is performed in small firms or workshops. The relative independence of the work process allows contact and exchange with workmates or, in the case of the service sector, with customers. Where such jobs predominate, employers have increasingly attempted to secure a faster workpace and greater output by the introduction of some form of wage incentive system.

As the production process becomes progressively mechanized, the content of the job alters in several respects. The middle level of mechanization contains working conditions and job operations which differ radically from those found at the handicraft production level. Let us first take the case of firms in which only stationary machines are used in the production process. This level of technology is marked by an extensive job fragmentation, i.e. the set of formerly skilled work operations have been broken down into a series of short and relatively simple tasks. Since the bulk of employees perform only one or possibly several tasks, each job is highly repetitive. Machine tending and feeding are typical job operations. The movement of materials is largely mechanized with conveyor belts used to move goods between different work stations.

At this level of technology, the opportunities for the individual worker to influence various aspects of his job are considerably reduced. Work methods are often determined by specialists in methods planning. In many cases, the job is further limited because other personnel prepare, repair and set up the machines.

The assembly line, without buffer stocks between the different stations, is a common example of a high degree of external regulation of work pace. The margins left for individual deviations are extremely narrow. Moreover, social interaction is hindered by the way the job is tied to pace of the line and by the noise created by the machines.

The position of the foreman and relations between this front-line supervisor and his subordinates are also altered. Work study and payments by results systems are frequently applied to jobs at this level of mechanization.[1]

With the increasing use of machinery there is an increased

---

[1] See for example, *Den tekniska utvecklingens konsekvenser för arbetskraften vid Statens Järnvägär*, Stockholm 1960; and Erixon, I., *LKAB: s nya gruva i Svappavaara*. **Personalpolitik och personaladministration**, Stockholm 1966.

need for maintenance work, which bears some resemblance to handicraft operations. Yet even here there appears to be a trend towards increasing specialization within traditional occupational limits. The actual production is turned out largely by semi-skilled workers. There is a new group of workers who prepare, repair and set up the machines and layout work sites but do not turn out the production.

In the office, as well, there has been a similar trend towards increased division and specialization of functions, as we have already indicated in an earlier chapter. However, there has also been an increase in the number of salaried employees and hence a greater need for planning and co-ordination.

These changes in job content have certain implications in terms of changed job requirements. Thus, the transition from skilled to semi-skilled work is characterized by a decreased need for training, responsibility, range of knowledge, manual dexterity and performance capability. There is often less physical strain attached to the job, partly owing to more even muscle loading. However, the requirements of attention—even though only surface attention—and swift reaction are increased. For groups such as helpers and hands the shift from unskilled work to semi-skilled work involves increased training and responsibility requirements.

Set-up and layout men constitute an intermediate category. In general, such workers have higher qualifications than most semi-skilled workers. To compare set-up men with skilled workers in the traditional sense, however, is a difficult if not a meaningless exercise in view of the differences in the job content.

With the automation of production processes and the shift to a higher level of mechanization there is further change in job content. Now techniques are used such as program control where the machines react on their own and feed-back control where the machines modify the course of production to certain pre-registered quantities. Today only continuous flow process industries fall into this category, though certain partial operations in other types of production processes can be included.

In highly automated production processes the production job becomes one of monitoring the machines and reacting to production break-downs or disturbances. In so far as automation is applied to a sequence of previously separate work operations, there will be a net reduction in the workforce. This appears commonly to be the case despite the increase in maintenance workers that results where the more expensive machinery and equipment require extensive preventative maintenance.

The effects of technological change on worker qualifications are not quite clear. The shift from low and unskilled work to machine operating and tending might require increased qualifications. Greater physical effort and greater psychological stress too often accompany such a step; after a long period of fatiguing employment, the operator can suddenly be required to deal quickly with a complicated 'snag' in the machinery in order to avoid a production breakdown. When, at a higher level of mechanization, machine 'tending' is replaced by monitoring and reporting production breakdowns to the nearest supervisor, certain features of the job can appear remarkably similar to unskilled work.

The transition from machine tender to machine monitor involves an increase in specialization. The same is true of the shift from general machine repair to corrective maintenance employing methods such as 'plug-in fitting' and 'maintenance by replacement'. Yet it is also possible to note an enlargement of job content in the case of the change from machine tender to control room operator.

Responsibility as a job requirement is determined by each employer and varies for different personnel categories. This variation appears to be related more to the method of wage payment and type of work organization than to the level of technology as such. Despite the fact that control functions are increasingly being automated, there has been an enlargement of the production workers' responsibility because a production breakdown in one operation in the sequence can have extensive adverse effects in contiguous operations. Efficiency in such work is difficult to measure and the relationship between wage earnings and productivity is considerably weakened. Evaluation of the responsibility factor is essentially a subjective process.

At a high level of mechanization, we can anticipate that there will be certain constraints on internal job transfers because the job requirements for many positions will include a rather high level of formal education. At the same time there will be a tendency for the number of production jobs to decrease with increased mechanization. These overall trends indicate a need for continuous formal education to ensure greater opportunities for employees to transfer within the firm.

Another trend at this level of mechanization is the decreasing number of workers per unit of area by comparison with traditional industrial processes. This raises the problem of worker 'isolation' as opportunities for social interaction are greatly reduced. In the case of continuous flow process industries, personnel are gathered in centrally situated control rooms. This offers an opportunity for social contact as well as protection from machine noise and other environmental discomforts. Another feature of these industries is the improved contact and exchange between workers and technical supervisors. This is probably because the workers are few in number and each comprehends a larger part of the production process.

A final issue relevant to this discussion is whether job operations that are 'low on the mechanization scale' are tending to increase or decrease. An increase is indicated by the increased employment in the services sector, an area of notoriously low mechanization. At the same time, however, many service jobs can be expected to change as machinery is introduced, as new types of work organization are experimented with, as the average size of workplaces increases and the hours of work are reduced. Employment in agriculture and forestry have decreased as mechanization and division of labour have increased. The expected increase of 'industrialized' construction methods in the residential housing sector implies that many building sites will become more highly mechanized and take on more of the features of assembly industries. Job operations at the middle level of mechanization will tend to increase as a consequence of the above factors. The major proportion of job operations today, however, are on the low and middle level of mechanization.

In conclusion, it should be re-emphasized that in reality developments are not as uniform and clearly outlined as is suggested by the foregoing sketch. There are opportunities for organizational choices which take into account the needs of individual workers even while satisfying the general yardstick of efficiency. The essential task of the trade union movement will be to ensure that these opportunities are used to create forms of organization and work assignments that facilitate the adjustment of the individual to working life.

CHAPTER 5

Technological Change, Employment and Unemployment

Even if post-war economic developments in Western Europe in general—and in Sweden in particular—give no indication that rapid technological change results in unemployment, the experience and public debate in the United States alone would appear to warrant a discussion of the relationship between these two factors.

The social debate on this relationship is as old as the technological development itself. The arguments have perhaps not always been made with the same forthrightness as in the beginning of the 1800s—when unemployed workers attempted to solve their problem by physically destroying the labour-saving machines—but the history of industrialization contains many examples of technological changes resulting in the displacement of hundreds of thousands of workers from their place of work. By comparison the history of economic thought offers few attempts to analyse the relationship between these two factors, but it would be unfair to the economists of earlier times to assert that they wholly ignored these problems. Indeed, some of these thinkers can compete with many of the economists of today in terms of powers of observation as well as perspicacity, the latter group having tended either to predict a 'hurricane' of structural unemployment following in the wake of technological change or construct economic models designed to demonstrate that every technological change creates compensating employment opportunities for the workforce made redundant by its introduction.

A historical survey quickly reveals that technological change in the earlier stages of the industrial revolution had more extensive and far more dramatic employment effects than 'the second industrial revolution', automation, cybernetics, or whatever term one chooses to apply to the latest phase of technological change. In his article, 'Two centuries of Technological Change—Automation is Nothing New', Robert Lekachman reminds us of the upheavals in the English textile industry 150 years ago. In 1810, there were 100,000 machine weavers while 200,000 hand weavers were working outside the factory system.[1] By 1840 these proportions had been reversed and by 1860 the hand-weavers and their craft traditions had almost wholly disappeared. In a period that lies closer to us in time, the decade immediately after the First World War, a powerful wave of rationalization and modernization swept through Western Europe and the USA. This was plainly a result of the application of effective wartime manufacturing methods to civilian production processes. But the term 'structurally induced mass unemployment' obtained a new immediacy and greater apparent justification during the 1930s and succeeding decades.

THE CLASSICAL ECONOMISTS' VIEW

Curiously enough, economic theory has only peripherally and rather superficially examined the relationship between technological change and employment. The relative disinterest in this relationship evinced by the classical economists from Adam Smith to Ricardo and Marshall can probably be explained by the fact that technological unemployment by definition had no place in their economic system. Under the assumption of freely competitive product and factor markets, the pricing process would ensure a continuous adjustment to new equilibrium positions and unemployed workers would be 'absorbed'. This model assumed the validity of a 'compensation' theory, though Ricardo at least expressed some doubt on the issue. To the proponents of static economic theory, employment difficulties appeared to be inadequacies in the market adjustment mechanism rather than inherent forces which could disturb the long-term balance and ultimately undermine the entire system. This is, perhaps, the crucial difference between the thinking of the classical economists and Marx's theory of development, which viewed the long-term effects of technological change as disruptive for the capitalistic system as a whole. Since, according to

[1] *Challenge*, April 1963.

the Marxist system of assumptions, the only factor of production that created profit was labour, the continuous replacement of labour by machine capital would result in lower rates of profit. Under conditions of progressively stiffening competition, firms would be driven to new investment (higher 'organic composition of capital' in the Marxist terminology), but this in the long run could not prevent the lowering of the profit rate. The growth of capital, the falling profit rate and the increasing reserve army of unemployed would lead to the overthrow of the entire system. It is easy to criticize many of Marx's assumptions, but it is indisputable that a major tenet in his theory, notably the underconsumption hypothesis, has played an important rôle in modern discussions of the employment consequences of technological change. This idea has been 'borrowed' by several of the most extreme spokesmen for the view that a catastrophic increase in structural unemployment will follow in the wake of technological change. It is perhaps unnecessary to point out that many of these persons appear to be rather blissfully unaware of the doctrinal and terminological origins of their view and that their political conclusions do not coincide with those of the Marxists.

Those that assert the inevitability of an increasing level of technologically induced unemployment can also at first glance obtain a certain amount of support from Keynes, who successfully demonstrated that overall economic equilibrium was compatible with a significant proportion of unemployed resources. Keynes offers a good theoretical explanation for behaviour of the American economy throughout much of the 1950s, i.e. its constant high level of unemployment and low rates of growth. (As indeed the effects of the tax cut in the USA in the early 1960s may be seen as an empirical verification of Keynes' theory.) But Keynes displayed relatively little interest in structural economic problems in general or the structural aspects of unemployment in particular. Nor can one unearth in his theory any tendency towards a calamitous increase in unemployment, a central theme of the assertions of some American 'structuralists'.

But in general, economic theory has little to say about the relationship between technological change and employment. As Heilbronner states, we still lack a systematic and scientific analysis of the problem, '... we look in vain for an exposition in

THE COMPENSATION THEORY VERSUS THE THEORY OF UNDERCONSUMPTION

which technological change is organically incorporated as both a source of growth and disruption in economic evolution'.[1]

The only distillates from the often vague and ill-documented discussion are two broad lines of argument: one, which plainly has its roots in classical economic theory, is a kind of *compensation* theory, the other is linked, consciously or unconsciously, to earlier *theories of underconsumption* without, however, drawing the same disastrous conclusions for the capitalist system that were predicted by its originators.

The compensation model takes as its starting point a technological change that displaces labour. Such a change it is assumed cannot occur unless the measure lowers labour costs. (For the sake of argument, we shall disregard the fact that in the Swedish economy of today it is the shortage of labour that commonly compels rationalization.) A reduction in labour costs under conditions of perfect competition would be translated into a price decrease and hence lead to increased product turnover. In this way, new employment opportunities would be opened for the unemployed workers. Depending on the product's demand elasticity, there could be quite another sequence of events: the price reduction could leave the quantity of demand unchanged (or in any case result in an increase which is insufficient to absorb the unemployed workers). In the event, some part of consumer purchasing power will be released for the consumption of other products. Demand will then shift to new goods which in turn experiencing an increase in turnover, will display an increased demand for labour.

This simple compensation model is reinforced by another more sophisticated version which suggests—to the compensation theorists—that technological change actually tends to lead to an *increase* in employment rather than the opposite. This version adds another demand effect to the primary compensation effect and the effect of a shift in the demand mix. This is the increased demand for labour on the part of the industries that manufac-

---

[1] Heilbronner, R., *The Impact of Technology: Automation and Technological Change*. The American Assembly, Harvard University 1962.

ture the new labour-saving machinery. If one assumes that there is a certain multiplier effect stemming from this increase in employment, the prediction of the compensation theory—in its most extreme form—will be that technological change leads to a troublesome scarcity of labour. An oft-quoted empirical example is the increased use of computers in the USA. Currently it is estimated that the number of workers employed in the manufacture and production of new computers is increasing by more than 100,000 every year. We cannot help but note that the number of workers being declared redundant annually is higher.

The compensation model has been constructed on the basis of casual observation and arbitrarily selected empirical data. Its general validity has not been subjected to systematic empirical testing. It is not surprising therefore that it is marked by many serious shortcomings, a fact which its critics have been quick to point out. Let us examine some of the criticisms of the theory:

1. Cost reductions do not necessarily lead to price decreases. Under conditions of imperfect competition where pricing is subject to some control, a more likely consequence of reduced costs—at maintained prices—is increased profits.
2. If, under conditions of imperfect competition, the profits resulting from rationalization remain within the firm in the form of increased profits or are partly used to raise wages for the employees remaining, their cumulative propensity to consume (i.e. the sum of the workers' propensities to consume and the firm's propensity to invest) will possibly be lower than the original propensity to consume of the employed workforce before the technological change. Consequently, one would expect a decrease in overall demand.
3. Even if price decreases (whether absolute or relative) do result from reductions in costs, the compensation theory disregards time as a factor in the process. Thus, the cut in employment and individual income losses occur *before* the compensating effect and shifts in demand can make themselves felt. This loss in income would offset the compensation effect.
4. Even if one assumes, *arguendo*, that the time factor is not important and that overall demand will remain unchanged after a given technological change, it is possible that the released demand will be redirected to products from more capital-

intensive industries. In the event, the displaced labour would not be entirely absorbed.

5. The assumption of free mobility on the part of the labour force that underlies the compensation model is untenable.

The critics draw the conclusion that there are no forces in our economic system which guarantee that demand and hence employment will automatically adjust themselves to technological change. The practical implications of this view, which is only the old underconsumption theory in a new guise, vary from the need for public measures to maintain purchasing power at a level sufficiently high to ensure full employment, to the extreme position that our entire social system is threatened by an inexorably increasing structural unemployment which will subsequently spread to a large part of the labour force in industrialized countries with a highly advanced technology. In its most extreme form, with an almost metaphysical degree of belief in the potentialities of automation, not only to replace labour but to free itself entirely from human control, this view can lead to dire predictions indeed.

This entire discussion, admittedly presented in a very sketchy form, could be dismissed as irrelevant to employment conditions prevailing in most of Western Europe. The exceedingly rapid pace of overall economic growth and high rate of productivity increase characterizing the economic development of Western Europe during the post-war period, trends which are largely directly attributable to extensive technological improvements in the production apparatus, have not accompanied unemployment, structural or cyclical, to any appreciable extent. But this experience in itself constitutes no guarantee that such a situation may not arise when Western European industry reaches the technological level that industry in the USA currently occupies and which since the middle 1950s has been associated with a rather high level of unemployment. This is to assume of course that the relatively higher productivity of American industry is a symptom of its higher technological standard and more advanced position with respect to automation than the Western European countries. The question is thus whether the relatively high level of unemployment in the USA—high by Western European standards—can be attributed to the more rapid pace of technological change in the post-war period, or to other causes. This question—which has an interest transcending America's borders—has created much controversy in the past few years between the 'structuralists' (who assert that the high level of unemployment is largely structural in character), and the 'aggregate demand' school which maintains that unemployment is essentially a result of a lack of sufficient overall demand for labour to absorb all of those seeking work.

THE 'STRUCTURALISTS' VERSUS THE 'AGGREGATE DEMAND' SCHOOL

The old conflict between compensation and underconsumption theories no longer rages. Hardly anyone today asserts that workers made redundant by technological change are absorbed automatically due to the inherent workings of our economic system. Nor can a group be easily found that considers the labour displacement caused by rationalization to be so intractable that society using suitable measures cannot provide new employment opportunities in productive operations for the redundant workers. Today the controversy centres on the question of which measures are most suitable. Since this problem still has its greatest immediacy in the USA, we can link our presentation to the continuing American discussion. The question has been pursued there for many years and has created two distinct views. The first, the 'structuralist' view, whose foremost proponent has been Professor Charles Killingsworth, asserts that technological change has so transformed the structure of demand for labour that a hard core of unemployed persons has emerged with insufficient training and qualifications for available job opportunities.[1] The problem can only be solved by structural remedies such as retraining and further training programmes and measures to increase the geographical mobility of labour. An increase in the level of aggregate demand, the structuralists assert, would not succeed in substantially absorbing the unemployed workers given the need for higher skill levels, etc. The alternative view, the 'aggregate demand' thesis,

---

[1] Killingsworth, C., 'Automation, Jobs and Manpower' in *Exploring the Dimensions of the Manpower Revolution*. Volume 1 of *Selected Readings in Employment and Manpower*. Committee Print 88th Congress, 2nd Session, Washington 1964.

has had two members of the President's Council of Economic Advisers as its active spokesmen, Robert Heller[1] and Otto Eckstein,[2] as well as other noted economists, e.g. Solow.[3] This view has been influenced by Keynesian ideas which have been decisive for economic policy in Western Europe for several decades (in Sweden since the early 1930s) but have never achieved complete acceptance in the USA. The 'aggregate demand' thesis is that unemployment in the USA, whether technological or otherwise, could be significantly reduced by the expansion of total demand for goods and services, indirectly increasing the demand for labour through a tax cut. The extent to which these two views have succeeded in influencing the opinion of the administration or the public is still not altogether clear, though the recent tax cut suggests that the aggregate demand view is ahead on points. At all events, the points raised in the public discussion throw much light on the ways in which technological change can conceivably influence employment.

The structuralist brief which along with most of the discussion centres on conditions in the USA, contains the following points:

1. With few exceptions, unemployment has displayed a secular rise, i.e. in succeeding boom phases of the trade cycle the level of unemployment has been progressively higher, increasing in the following recession phases.
2. There have been shifts in the structure of unemployment; unemployment rates have been higher and unemployment shares have increased for the lowest and highest age groups, women, negroes and persons with a low level of education.
3. The emergence of this hard core of unemployed has appeared simultaneously with a considerable increase in productivity in American industry. The rapid pace of technological change is primarily responsible for this new unemployment development. This trend has been very much in evidence during the 1960–3 period and is considered by many to signal a new phase in the productivity trends in the USA.
4. There has been stagnation and even, at some time, a notice-

[1] *Economic Report of the President*, Washington 1964.
[2] Eckstein, O., 'The Relation of Aggregate Demand to Unemployment' in Ross, A. M., (Ed.), *Unemployment and the American Economy*, New York 1964.
[3] Solow, R., *The Nature and Sources of Unemployment in the United States*. Wicksell Lectures, Stockholm 1964.

able decline in the rate of increase of employment in the mining and manufacturing sector; the proportion of blue-collar workers has begun to decrease, while that of white-collar workers is rising. The unemployment statistics indicating that the less trained and educated members of the labour force have a relatively higher rate of unemployment is a symptom of the shift in the composition of the demand for labour. This trend has been referred to by Killingsworth as the 'growing imbalance in the American labour market'.[1]

5. An increase in aggregate effective demand would not—more than marginally—reduce unemployment among the poorly-trained and educated members of the labour force. Such an increase would merely intensify the demand for highly skilled workers who are already in short supply. It would thus only lead to more severe bottlenecks, excessive wage increases in the occupational sector experiencing excess demand and intensified inflationary pressures.

The opponents of the structuralist hypothesis question its basic premise, the assertion that productivity in the USA is increasing at an accelerated rate. Productivity in the USA during the 1900–63 period has in fact increased at a fairly constant rate. During the period 1957–62, productivity (measured as output per man-hour) for American industry as a whole increased by 3 per cent per year, but this figure was no higher than the average annual increase for the entire post-war period. The average increase for the 1957–62 period does exceed that for the 1910–47 period. However, the considerable rise in productivity in the period 1960–4 which was attributed by many to more rapid pace of technological advance, was plainly no greater than the average increase in the 1947–50 period and certainly contained a strong cyclical component. There are no known statistical methods that allow the researcher systematically to distinguish the effects of technological change from those of other changes. There seems, however, to be much evidence based on observation to support the view that technological change plays and will continue to play a fairly subordinate rôle in productivity trends. Thus productivity in American agriculture—where there has

[1] Killingsworth, C., *Structural Unemployment in the United States* (stencil), Geneva 1964.

been little or no automation but rather a rapid increase in mechanization in its more conventional sense—has increased by 6 per cent per year during the post-war period, a figure which exceeds the rise in industrial productivity by a factor of two, though, of course, agriculture is in many ways a special case. In general, however, it appears to be likely that the future rise in productivity will remain moderate, according to many experts, roughly on the same order of magnitude as previous increases. The weight of the constraints on the opportunities for rapid increases in overall productivity can be illustrated by the following observation. It would take more than thirty years for American industry as a whole to modernize to the standard achieved by the factories constructed in the 1950s at the current rate of industrial investment. Finally, it is worth noting that productivity gains are not solely a function of capital investment; they are also dependent on improvements in the training levels of the labour force.

In sum, productivity trends in the USA have not accelerated as swiftly as the structuralists argument would suggest and competent estimates indicate no radical increase in future trends. Moreover, an analysis of trends within different industries discloses no clear association between productivity and employment changes.[1] Nor can the structuralists assertion that unemployment is tending to become increasingly more structural in character, i.e. that unemployment is tending to concentrate more intensively among certain population groups, stand up under thorough analysis. In the 1965 *Manpower Report of the President* it appears that the structure of unemployment has not changed significantly during the post-war period; i.e. there are differences in the rates and shares of unemployment among different groups but these differences have not noticeably changed.[2] To be sure, the proportion of young people in the total number of unemployed has increased. But this increase is due less to exclusion of youths from jobs by technological change than to the effects of the 'baby boom' at the start of the 1940s still working their way through the American labour market.[3]

[1] Clauge, E., and Greenberg, L., *Employment*. In Dunlop, op. cit., supra.
[2] *Manpower Report of the President*, Washington 1965.
[3] *Technology and the American Society*. Report of the National Commission on Technology, Automation and Economic Progress, 1966.

This rather summary version of the discussion suggests that the evidence marshalled to support the structuralist hypothesis is rather meagre. Let us examine some of the counter arguments that have been put forward:

1. Admittedly unemployment has remained higher in each succeeding boom phase of former trade cycles, but this has not been the case in the most recent period of economic prosperity. In the spring of 1966, after successive tax cuts unemployment in the USA dropped to a level below that of any year since the autumn of 1957. The present period of high business activity which has continued for more than five years, is the longest of the post-war period.
2. The structure of unemployment has largely remained unchanged. Though there are differentially higher rates for persons with little or no vocational experience or training these differentials have not widened. The existing differentials are universal phenomena, and cannot be 'explained' by the greater demand for highly trained specialists in the automated industries.
3. The productivity in the USA economy during the period 1960–4 has not increased at a rate exceeding that of the 1957–60 period and has risen less rapidly than in the 'twenties.
4. The decline in the number of production workers, asserted by the structuralists to be an irreversible trend and an unmistakable symptom of structural change, has ended and at least temporarily reversed itself. The number of production workers has increased by 1 million from 1961 to 1964. The Bureau of Labour Statistics estimates that during the period 1964–75 there will be a further increase in the number of workers in the goods-producing industries to $4\frac{1}{2}$ million, though their relative share of the total labour force will decrease from $36 \cdot 3$ to $33 \cdot 7$ per cent during the period.
5. The assertion that there is an increasing number of vacancies that cannot be filled by competent workers is largely unproved and unprovable, since the USA with all its wealth of labour market statistics lacks comprehensive information about 'unfilled job vacancies'. The one relevant series that is available in the USA, however, a series based on the number of advertised job vacancies in a selected but large group of newspapers, indicates a reduction from 1955–65, which is the opposite of the tendency suggested by the structuralists.

TECHNOLOGICAL CHANGE CONSTITUTES NO THREAT TO FULL EMPLOYMENT

The controversy between the structuralists and the aggregate demand school is somewhat specious. Both groups are bringing an exaggeratedly narrow focus to bear on separate aspects of the same problem: namely that with a suitably weighted combination of demand-creating fiscal policy and an active national manpower policy, a balance can be created between supply and demand in the economy as a whole as well as in its various local labour markets. The USA has now passed the 'interim target' level of unemployment that was assumed to be compatible with relative price stability, notably 4 per cent. Now that this figure has been reached, the goal will be shifted to 3 per cent which is full employment according to current American opinion, or perhaps even a lower figure. The lesson to be learned by Sweden as well as Western Europe in general from the American experience is that economic policy even in a country with relatively higher productivity, a more advanced degree of technology and a rapidly increasing labour force is capable of dealing with the employment effects of technological change. To put this in another way, for every given increase in productivity there is a level of aggregate demand that will be sufficient to absorb the displaced manpower and lead to an increase in overall economic growth. This simple relationship must of course be modified to take into account the need for relative price stability and the fact that there is a functional relationship between the degree of effectiveness of overall demand and the flexibility of the labour market. But these complications do not change anything in principle, however important they may be for the formulation of practical policy programmes. As Silberman has observed, 'There are clearly no technological obstacles to full employment.'[1]

The preceding discussion has centred largely on the USA. For Sweden and Western Europe, the question of technologically-induced mass unemployment has not been an immediate one during the post-war period. In a study of certain economic trends in Western Europe, Per Holmberg found that increased productivity has been compatible with a *reduction* rather than an increase in unemployment. 'In an increasing number of Western

[1] Silberman, C., *The Real News about Automation*. Fortune, 1965.

European countries today, shortages of labour are being regarded as a far more serious "risk" than automation or structural unemployment.'[1] This statement is particularly applicable to Sweden.

EMPLOYMENT TRENDS FOR THE SWEDISH ECONOMY AS A WHOLE

The Swedish Long-term Economic Survey[2] has reviewed employment developments—for the economy as a whole and sectorally—during the 1950s and early 1960s and has made projections for the late 1960s and, in somewhat cruder terms, the 1970s. The most striking feature of both past and estimated future trends is the scarcity of available manpower resources. For the coming five-year period, it is estimated that there will be a drop in *the number of workers available for employment during the year* as well as *the number of working hours per worker per year* leading to a reduction in *the labour input* measured in working hours. This trend is expected to continue into the 1970s.

From Table 2 (opposite), which reproduces in a nutshell the important statistics of the Swedish economy during three decades, it further appears that the *input of capital equipment* has increased and is expected to continue to increase though at a somewhat slower rate. From our standpoint, it is interesting to note that the *capital intensity of production* (i.e. the quantity of capital input per unit of labour input or per working hour) has not increased from the 1950s to the first half of the 1960s, owing to the increment in the labour input. However, with an increasing input of capital equipment and a declining labour input, there will be a considerably higher capital intensity of production in the future. The Long-term Survey's projected increase in labour productivity appears to err on the side of caution. Considering that this productivity development will be the result of significant structural changes in industry as a whole, a continuously increasing capital input entailing an accelerated renewal of the capital stock and an almost revolutionary expan-

---

[1] Holmberg, P., *Förhållandet mellan full sysselsättning teknologiska förändringar i Västeuropa.* Arbetsmarknadsinformation, 1964:7. (The Relationship Between Full Employment and Technological Change in Western Europe.)

[2] Svensk Ekonomi 1966–70, Department of Finance.

Employment and Unemployment

TABLE 2

Production, Input of Capital and Labour,
Capital and Labour Productivity and Capital Intensity, 1950–65.
Percentage Change Per Annum

	1950–60	1950–65	1965–70	1970–80
A. *Input of labour*				
No. of whole-year workers	+0·4	+0·9	+0·3	+0·1
Annual hours per whole-year worker	−0·5	−0·3	−0·6	−0·5
No. of hours worked	−0·1	+0·6	−0·3	−0·4
B. *Input of capital*	+3·6	+4·2	+4·8	+5·1
C. *Capital intensity*				
Capital input per whole-year worker	+3·2	+3·3	+4·5	+5·0
Capital input per working hour	+3·7	+3·6	+5·1	+5·5
D. *Labour productivity*				
Production per whole-year worker	+3·0	+4·0	+3·9	+4·3
Production per working hour	+3·5	+4·3	+4·5	+4·8
E. *Capital productivity*				
Production per unit of capital input	−0·2	+0·7	−0·6	−0·7
F. *Production*	+3·4	+4·9	+4·2	+4·4

Source: The Swedish Economy, 1966–70.

sion of our entire educational system, the rise in overall productivity increase anticipated by the Long-term Survey (0·2 per cent of GNP per year for the second half of the 1960s and 0·3 per cent for the 1970s) appears to be unduly moderate and rather likely to be outstripped by actual developments. But even if the actual rate of growth of productivity is likely to exceed the Survey's estimates, there is no indication in the statistical series of a forthcoming technological revolution or productivity explosion. The estimated trends for labour input, capital input and productivity during the 1965–70 and the 1970–80 periods should moreover be seen in relation to the projected shortage of the supply of labour. For the period 1965–70, the demand for labour according to plans and expert assessments is estimated to rise to 165,000 persons (and an additional 100,000 to compensate for the planned reductions in the standard work week). To meet this demand, there will be an anticipated increase in the labour supply of little more than 100,000 persons, i.e. an estimated shortfall of 60,000. And the latter figure includes assumptions of a considerable increase in the participation rates of married women and an unchanged net immigration rate. The comparable set of calculations for the 1970s are of course a rather uncertain exercise but it appears almost indisputable that a gap between the demand for and supply of labour will continue to prevail during that decade. All this, however, rests on the assumption that there will be a continuous increase in demand, in the form of consumption and investment.

These overall calculations suggest strongly that even with a striking increase in the pace of technological progress, a more intensive structural transformation within Swedish industry, a rising input of capital equipment and a continuous increase in productivity, a scarcity of labour will be a far more likely condition in the foreseeable future than a net manpower surplus. Obviously, this reasoning is based on a great many underlying assumptions, the most important of which are the continued pursuance of a full employment policy by the government, no drastic decline in the international competitive powers of Swedish industry, and continued free international trade.

CHAPTER 6

Changes in the Structure of Employment

The employment trends for the economy as a whole treated in the preceding chapter disguise considerable differences in the employment experience of different industries, occupations and regions. By breaking down the data on employment (and unemployment) into these smaller categories, it is possible to illustrate the amplitude of these structural changes and thereby throw further light on the problems of increasing displacement of labour, which as we know is essential to economic growth and a rising standard of living.

EMPLOYMENT TRENDS IN MAJOR SWEDISH SECTORS

In Table 3, data are presented for observed and expected changes in productivity within and the distribution of employment among the major sectors of the Swedish economy from 1950–80. Their source is the Economic Long-term Survey's modified sectoral plans and 'illustrative calculation' for the 1970s.[1] The table as a whole presents a picture of marked stability. During the thirty-year period, there has been a movement of workers out of only two sectors, i.e. agriculture and forestry, both of which have experienced an accelerated increase in productivity. It is worth noting, however, that from the mid-'sixties on, there is a slippage in the rate of productivity increase in these sectors, a decrease in the number of persons leaving these sectors annually and the manpower from these sectors is satisfying a decreasing proportion of the labour needs of the other expanding sectors.

The table also gives a picture of marked stability in the size of labour movements out of sectors and changes in productivity

[1] *Svensk ekonomi* 1966–70, sou, 1966:1, Stockholm 1966.

TABLE 3

Changes in Employment and Productivity, 1950–80

Sector	Changes in employment in thousands				in percentages per year				Production per employer, annual increase in percentages			
	50–60	60–65	65–70	70–80	50–60	60–65	65–70	70–80	50–60	60–65	65–70	70–80
Agriculture	−185	− 95	− 70	−115	− 4	− 6	− 6	− 6	4	5½	5½	7
Forestry	+ 5	− 15	− 15	− 20	+ 1	− 3	− 4	− 4	2	7	7	7
Fishing	− 5	—	—	—	− 4½	− 1½	− 1	—	—	—	—	—
Total: agriculture, etc.	−185	−110	− 85	−135	− 3½	− 5½	− 5	− 5	—	—	—	—
Industry and crafts	+ 55	+ 80	+ 45	—	+ ½	+ 1½	+ 1	—	4	4½	4½	5½
Power stations	+ 5	—	—	—	+ 2	—	+ ½	—	3	6	6	5
Building and construction	+ 45	+ 45	+ 30	+ 20	+ 1½	+ 3	+ 2	+ ½	2½	3	3½	4½
Total: manufacturing and construction	+105	+125	+ 75	+ 20	+ 1	+ 1½	+ 1	—	—	—	—	—
Total: goods production	− 75	+ 10	− 10	−115	− ½	—	—	− 1	4	5	5	—
Transport communication	+ 10	+ 5	+ 5	+ 10	+ ½	+ ½	+ ½	+ ½	3½	4½	4½	5
Commerce	+ 65	+ 20	+ 10	—	+ 1½	+ 1	+ ½	—	1	3	3	3
Private services	+ 35	+ 15	+ 15	+ 20	+ 1	+ 1	+ 1	+ ½	1½	2	2	2½
Public services	+120	+100	+ 90	+290	+ 3½	+ 4½	+ 3½	+ 4	(½)	(½)	(½)	—
Total: services	+230	+145	+120	+320	+ 2	+ 2	+ 1½	+ 2	2	2½	2½	
All sectors	+140	+155	+110	+205	+0·4	+1·0	+0·7	+0·5	3	4	4	(4½)

Source: The Swedish Economy and the general outlook for the 'seventies. Ministry of Finance, Stockholm, 1966.

within sectors. Employment decreases were about 6 per cent of the labour force in the 1950s, about the same in the 1960s, and are estimated to fall to about 4 per cent in the 1970s. *About a half per cent of the labour force is thus affected annually by the process of urbanization* as this is expressed as the movement out of agriculture and forestry to other sectors. There has also been, and is estimated to continue to be, a significant shift in employment from the goods-producing industries to the service trades. During the past five years, manufacturing has been an expanding sector, responsible for 30 per cent of the total increase in the labour force. During the next five years, however, this proportion is expected to fall to about 23 per cent and continue to decline in the following decade. The most rapidly growing sector of employment are the government services. It is predicted that, by the 1970s, this sector will be increasing at a rate commensurate to the total labour movement out of the agriculture and forestry sectors plus the net increment in the labour force provided by shifts in age distribution, increased participation rates and immigration. The reasonableness of the assumptions underlying this prediction are open to question, but this issue shall not be further pursued here.

Clearly, the data in Table 3 do not allow firm conclusions to be drawn about the extent of or the trends in employment associated with these structural changes. For a start, the sectoral breakdown is crude and itself conceals significant intra-sectoral differences. Moreover, the table gives no information about 'stage by stage transfers'. For example, the movement out of agriculture and forestry goes to a large extent directly to the building and construction sector. At the same time, this sector contributes labour to manufacturing which in turn passes on workers to the services sector. The data presented in the table indicate that the increased rate of transfer away from the agricultural and forestry sectors results in a progressively smaller volume of transfers, that these transfers are channelled to the goods-producing sector to a lesser extent and that by the 1970s the services sector will be the only expanding sector of any consequence in the Swedish economy.

The productivity trends shown in the table are derived from data which are based on employment according to the census and are incomplete in many respects. Such significant factors as reductions in the hours of work, changes in the quality of the labour force and the increased extent of female part-time work have all been omitted from the calculations. This would suggest that the above data somewhat underestimate productivity trends. During the second half of the 1960s, the rise in productivity is expected to be roughly the same in all sectors as it has been in the past five years. The figures give no hint of an accelerating technological development, significant structural rationalization or of an industry in rapid transformation. Several rather modest rises in productivity are predicted for the 1970s. Agriculture, it is expected, will reach the point where unproductive small units will largely disappear and agricultural production will become more marked by modern techniques. In manufacturing industry, it is expected that the modernization of capital equipment will result in a faster growth of productivity. The industrialization of building and construction work is expected to continue as before and produce the same rate of productivity increase as during the 1950s and 1960s. That the productivity increase in the wholesale and retail sector should stagnate during the 1970s is a surprising forecast; goods distribution in Sweden is now in the midst of a significant structural transformation, which in the long run should produce a rising rate of productivity increase. For the large and burgeoning category 'government services', there are no known measures of productivity. The marked expansion in this sector—which is expected to employ 25 per cent of the population in 1980 or 10 per cent more than today—will offset productivity gains in other sectors and thereby considerably decrease the rise in total productivity. The Long-term Survey was careful not to forecast a larger increase in productivity of 4–5 per cent annually for the Swedish economy as a whole during the 1970s. The partially observed and predicted rate for the 1960s was 4 per cent.

The sectoral classifications are too crude and the data for productivity too patchy to allow conclusions to be drawn about the relationship between productivity and unemployment. Redundancies are most frequent in sectors with the greatest rise in productivity, and the growth in employment has been greatest in the services sector, which has a low rate of productivity increase. But these associations are not necessarily causal. The determining factors for changes in the structure of employment are changes in the structure of demand. The depopulation of the agricultural sector presupposes increased productivity but is a result of the low demand elasticity for farming products and the fact that export opportunities are limited by protectionist measures in many other countries. That the services sector is swelling is obviously not a consequence of low productivity growth but rather of long-term shifts in our social structure, which leads to a continuous expansion of the government sector. This trend is occurring in practically all modern welfare states.

In sum, it seems to be true that a sectoral breakdown does not significantly modify the general picture presented previously of the overall trends of employment and productivity during the 1950-80 period. Changes during the three decades follow a very similar pattern, the stream of workers from agriculture and forestry to other industries is fairly constant and net changes in employment among the major sectors consist of only a very small segment of the labour force. The growth in productivity is moderate. The overall picture tends to confirm that technological change is only a part of a process of continuing comprehensive transformation, whose character in spite of considerable technical progress has not essentially changed. The impact of such changes on employment as a whole, moreover, appears to be greatly limited; no dramatic changes are expected in the foreseeable future.

It remains to be seen, however, whether such findings remain applicable when the data are broken down into smaller categories. In the following section, the trends in the largest sub-sector, manufacturing industry, will be examined. The data for this sector are sufficiently extensive to allow some conclusions to be drawn. We shall then examine the structure of unemployment. In a concluding section, the major features of the regional distribution of the labour force will be described.

TRENDS IN EMPLOYMENT AND PRODUCTIVITY IN MANUFACTURING INDUSTRIES

Many different productivity time series have been constructed during the years and the results of these vary greatly depending on whether the value of sales, value of output, number of manual workers, number of employees, number of hours worked, etc.,

TABLE 4

Production (A), the Number of Employees and Productivity (C) within Manufacturing, 1950–65

		1950	1951	1952	1953	1954	1955	1956	1957	1958	1959	1960	1961	1962	1963	1964	1965
1. Mining	A	100	110	121	123	113	129	141	147	140	141	161	179	176	182	205	227
	B	100	104	110	116	118	122	127	133	135	127	132	133	121	110	105	105
	C	100	105	110	106	96	106	111	111	104	111	123	135	145	166	194	216
2. Metal works	A	100	112	126	123	135	153	168	173	164	186	218	243	257	274	314	346
	B	100	104	107	105	104	110	114	115	111	116	125	134	135	133	136	139
	C	100	108	118	117	129	139	148	150	148	161	174	182	190	206	231	249
3. Engineering excluding shipyards	A	100	110	113	108	120	127	136	147	153	166	187	208	228	242	264	283
	B	100	105	105	99	102	108	110	112	112	115	125	133	137	138	142	146
	C	100	105	107	109	118	118	124	132	137	145	150	156	166	175	186	194
4. Shipyards	A	100	104	109	113	116	124	131	140	149	143	144	150	174	165	177	181
	B	100	101	107	109	107	110	116	126	129	121	120	124	125	120	119	116
	C	100	103	102	103	108	113	113	112	115	118	120	121	139	137	149	156
5. Stone, clay and glass industry	A	100	105	108	108	116	124	126	124	126	140	149	161	170	185	211	227
	B	100	100	97	94	95	97	94	92	89	90	93	96	98	99	102	105
	C	100	105	111	114	122	128	134	136	142	156	161	168	174	186	207	216
6. Timber and wood industry	A	100	98	86	88	95	96	94	101	101	104	115	119	124	134	150	158
	B	100	100	95	94	99	101	95	93	92	92	96	96	95	97	100	103
	C	100	98	90	93	95	95	98	108	109	113	120	124	131	139	150	153
7. Paper and pulp industry	A	100	108	93	102	119	128	135	143	143	154	176	184	178	196	219	227
	B	100	105	103	102	106	110	113	114	114	117	121	126	125	123	122	122
	C	100	102	90	100	113	117	120	126	126	132	145	146	143	160	179	186

		1965	1966	1967	1968	1969	1970	1971	1972	1973	1974	1975	1976	1977	1978	1979	1980
8. Printing	A	100	102	97	99	103	110	113	116	120	125	134	141	149	171	173	189
	B	100	103	104	103	107	111	112	112	114	115	119	123	124	126	129	134
	C	100	99	94	96	97	99	101	103	105	109	112	115	120	127	134	141
9. Food manufacturing	A	100	98	98	100	101	103	107	109	110	117	123	128	134	137	—	—
	B	100	99	96	95	96	98	99	98	98	99	102	104	107	107	108	108
	C	100	100	101	104	105	105	108	111	113	118	121	122	126	128	—	—
10. Beverages and tobacco industry	A	100	102	107	109	110	122	127	121	131	132	136	136	138	144	—	—
	B	100	98	101	100	98	101	101	92	93	92	94	92	93	88	88	91
	C	100	104	106	109	112	121	127	130	141	144	144	149	148	164	—	—
11. Textile industry	A	100	102	83	95	95	90	93	100	94	105	114	115	117	123	127	127
	B	100	101	90	91	87	81	78	74	70	70	72	69	68	66	66	—
	C	100	101	92	104	109	112	120	135	136	152	160	169	173	187	193	—
12. Clothing industry	A	100	105	91	99	96	98	101	98	97	99	108	121	126	133	137	137
	B	100	103	97	99	97	98	98	95	90	89	91	93	89	89	88	—
	C	100	102	94	100	99	100	103	104	107	110	117	129	139	148	156	—
13. Shoe and leather industry	A	100	94	85	99	99	98	98	102	98	103	101	102	106	114	113	108
	B	100	98	87	88	86	82	83	83	79	78	78	74	72	74	72	—
	C	100	96	98	113	115	119	118	123	124	133	131	140	148	157	160	—
14. Rubber industry	A	100	108	104	109	131	139	141	149	164	157	176	190	190	202	237	260
	B	100	103	97	102	111	117	115	119	120	128	139	145	141	138	146	—
	C	100	104	107	107	118	119	123	125	137	123	127	131	135	146	162	—
15. Chemical industry	A	100	103	104	109	116	122	130	137	139	152	162	171	183	199	222	240
	B	100	102	104	103	103	105	108	109	109	109	112	114	114	115	116	120
	C	100	101	100	106	113	116	120	125	128	139	145	151	161	173	191	200
16. Total: manufacturing	A	100	105	104	105	113	119	125	131	134	143	157	169	179	190	208	221
	B	100	103	101	99	100	104	104	104	103	104	110	114	115	115	116	117
	C	100	103	103	106	113	116	121	126	130	138	144	150	157	167	179	187

Source: Bentsel—Beckeman Framtidsperspektiv för svensk industri, 1965–80, Stockholm, 1966

have been chosen as indicators. Our series is one which has been worked out by the Swedish Institute of Industrial Research, and based on government statistics for industry. It was published as an appendix to the Long-term Survey. One of its limitations is that it follows the traditional practice of relating the volume of production to employment without taking into account the fluctuating and growing capital input. As a measure of productivity therefore the series is incomplete and in some respects misleading. The lack of data on the capital input in specific industries and the absence of time series of the necessary length makes it impossible, however, to complete the index series used by the Long-term Survey. Another somewhat more technical weakness of the series is that it is based on the number of employees, an indicator that does not take into consideration changes in the hours of work. For our purposes, however, this omission is not crucial. For the reduction of hours of work has probably been fairly uniform throughout the various industries and will therefore not affect inter-industry comparisons. The statistics are summarized in Table 4.

The starting point for our analysis is the distribution of employment by industry. There is a wide dispersion of the percentage increase around a mean of 17 per cent, which indicates the moderate nature of the employment increase during the period 1950–65 in industry as a whole. As is evident from the table, about half of this increase occurred during the years 1959–61. Engineering, iron and metals and rubber industries experienced the greatest growth in employment with a cumulative increase of about 40 per cent during the period of observation. Employment in the textile industry declined in absolute terms; more than one-third of the workforce in textiles was lost in the early 1950s. This experience was shared by the shoe and leather industry, which lost one-quarter of its workforce, and the beverages and ready-made clothing industries which each lost about one-tenth of their workforces. For the mining industry, there was a change in trend in employment during the period. A relatively marked increase during the 1950s was followed shortly by a decline of the labour force almost to the level at the start of the decade. The trends were less dramatic for the wood industry which also finished the decade with a net increase of about 3 per cent.

The question of greatest interest in this context and one that has long exercised economists in many countries is whether there is a significant association between changes in productivity and employment. The prediction flowing from the most common economic model is that the growth in employment should be weakest in industries with above-average increases in productivity. A glance at the table indicates, however, that there is no clear-cut association of this type between the two variables. True, the marked decline in the number of workers in the textile industry coincided with a favourable productivity trend, but many industries with contracting employment, e.g. shoe and leather and ready-made clothing, registered only a very weak productivity increase. Moreover, a number of other industries have experienced an above-average increase in employment in conjunction with a marked rise in productivity. Irons and metals for example have led the league table in productivity growth while simultaneously experiencing an above-average increase in employment.

Even when the series are broken down into smaller time periods there is no evidence of a close association between changes in productivity and employment in these sub-industries (cf. Table 5). For manufacturing industry as a whole, productivity trends are sharply upwards from period to period with particularly high growth values for the most recent years. At the same time, however, employment has expanded at an even more rapid pace, with the exception of 1963–5 when the labour force reserves appeared to have reached the point of near depletion. This pattern repeated itself in many industries, notably iron and metal, engineering and paper and pulp. The two exceptions were mining, which registered an exceptionally high increase in productivity, particularly during 1963–5, together with a rapid decline in employment and shipbuilding.

While it is difficult to find a unique relationship between changes in productivity and employment, there seems to be a significant association between changes in level of output and employment. Industries with an absolute decline in their number of workers during the period—i.e. textiles, shoes and leather, ready-made clothing and beverages—were at the same time the least expansive. As well, many of the most expansive industries display the largest increases in employment, mining being the outstanding exception.

TABLE 5

Changes in Production, Number of Employed and Productivity in Industry During the Periods 1951–54, 1955–58, 1959–62 and 1963–65, Annual Averages in Percentages

Branch	Production				Employment				Productivity			
	51–54	55–58	59–62	63–65	51–54	55–58	59–62	63–65	51–54	55–58	59–62	63–65
Mining industry	+3·4	+5·7	+ 6·2	+ 8·9	+4·2	+3·4	−2·5	−4·5	−0·8	+2·2	+8·7	+14·2
Metal works	+8·0	+5·3	+11·9	+10·5	+1·1	+1·6	+5·1	+0·9	+6·7	+3·5	+6·4	+ 9·4
Engineering, excluding shipbuilding	+4·9	+6·3	+10·5	+ 7·4	+0·5	+2·5	+5·3	+2·1	+4·4	+3·7	+5·0	+ 5·3
Shipbuilding	+3·7	+6·5	+ 4·2	+ 1·4	+1·8	+4·7	−0·7	−2·5	+1·9	+1·7	+5·0	+ 4·0
Stone, glass and clay industry	+3·9	+2·1	+ 7·7	+10·1	−1·3	−1·7	+2·4	+2·5	+5·2	+3·9	+5·1	+ 7·4
Wood industry	−1·1	+1·7	+ 5·3	+ 8·4	−0·2	−1·8	+0·7	+2·9	−1·1	+3·6	+4·7	+ 5·3
Pulp and paper industry	+5·1	+4·8	+ 5·7	+ 8·5	+1·4	+1·9	+2·3	−0·6	+3·5	+2·8	+3·3	+ 9·2
Printing and associated industry	+0·8	+4·0	+ 5·6	+ 8·1	+1·6	+1·8	+2·2	+2·5	−0·6	+2·2	+3·4	+ 5·5
Food industry	+0·2	+2·1	+ 5·1	—	−1·0	+0·4	+2·3	+0·3	+1·2	+1·8	+2·8	—
Beverages and tobacco industry	+2·5	+4·5	+ 1·3	—	−0·4	−1·3	±0	−0·8	+3·0	+5·8	+1·3	—
Textile and clothing industry	−0·7	±0	+ 6·4	+ 3·2	−2·1	−3·6	−0·3	−1·6	+1·2	+3·7	+6·7	+ 5·0
Shoe and leather industry	+0·2	−0·1	+ 2·0	+ 0·7	−3·7	−1·8	−2·4	—	+3·9	+1·8	+4·7	—
Rubber industry	+7·3	+5·9	+ 3·9	+11·2	+2·8	+1·9	+4·3	—	+4·3	+3·9	−0·3	—
Chemical industry	+3·7	+4·7	+ 7·2	+ 9·4	+0·7	+1·4	+1·2	+1·7	+3·1	+3·2	+5·9	+ 7·6
All industries	+3·1	+4·5	+ 7·6	+ 7·3	+0·1	+0·8	+2·8	+1·0	+3·0	+3·7	+4·8	+ 6·2

Source: The Swedish Economy, 1966–70.

The Structure of Employment

Further, there appears to be a weak association between changes in output and productivity in the sense that some of the most rapidly expanding industries—iron and metals, engineering, and chemicals, also have favourable productivity trends. The textile industry constitutes a noteworthy exception.

The conclusion from this rather summary survey is that changes in employment are 'explained' by changes in produc-

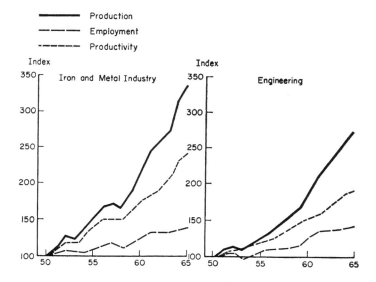

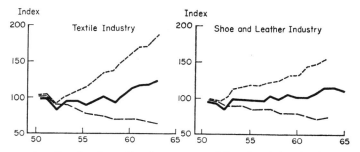

FIG. 1. Production, Employment and Productivity in Several Industries, 1950–65

tivity only to a minimum extent if one disregards the obvious relationship that an industry with a favourable productivity trend can turn out a given level of output with a smaller labour input. The level of output, however, is ultimately determined by effective demand. A low rate of increase of productivity therefore constitutes no guarantee of increased employment. Indeed, in the long run, the opposite outcome is more likely to be the case. Similarly an exceptionally large rise in productivity need not necessarily constitute a threat to employment.

Finally, it can be worth while to examine in greater detail the industries that deviate from this general pattern. The *mining* industry is indisputably—if one judges from the above index series—the most marked exception. It conforms most closely to the model of a rapid rationalization causing decreasing employment even in an expanding industry. The reduction in the number of employees in the mining industry has been closely associated with an above-average increase in production and a rise in productivity that was exceptionally high (see Table 5).

This decrease could conceivably have created certain employment problems. Indeed registered unemployment for the mining workers which was well below the national average in the 1950s has in recent years risen above it, though it has never exceeded 2 per cent of the membership of the unemployment insurance society.

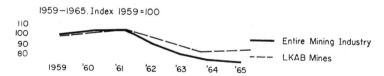

FIG. 2. Employment in the Mining Industry as a Whole and in LKAB Mines, 1959–65

A closer study of the figures indicates, however, that employment in mining firms has contracted by less than the amount suggested by the industrial statistics. Figure 2 shows that the employment decrease in one large mining firm as a whole is less than for the part which is registered under the mining industry because of a shift of employment from mining work to main-

The Structure of Employment 101

tenance (engineering) and construction work. This can be assumed to apply to the mining industry as a whole (cf. Figure 2).

Given the relatively less favourable overall labour market situation in the northern regions of Sweden, one would expect that released workers would have particular difficulties in finding new employment. In fact, as Diagram 2 shows, the decrease in mining employees for the period 1960–5 was less in the Northern (i.e. LKAB) mines than in the mining sector as a whole. As well, the productivity increases in the northern mines were somewhat lower than those of the industry as a whole. This is probably related to the shift from surface mining to underground mining in Kiruna. Changes in productivity for the mining industry as a whole and for the LKAB mines are shown in the following table (in index numbers).

	1959	1960	1961	1962	1963	1964	1965
Total Mining Industry	100	111	122	131	150	175	195
LKAB	100	109	121	136	152	177	191

From the studies of LKAB that were carried out in conjunction with the present report, it emerged that the contraction in personnel up to 1964 could be managed in such a way that serious employment problems for employees could be avoided. The firms' measures for retraining, etc., as well as the relatively high labour turnover have been contributing factors. It is interesting to note moreover that the rate of decrease in employment was lower in the North than in Middle Sweden which offers greater opportunities to find jobs in other industries.[1]

For the textile industry, too, a favourable productivity trend has coincided with a marked decrease in employment. This was accentuated by the relatively small increase in production. These trends have, however, been fairly constant throughout the period, a factor which has facilitated adjustment. This is supported by the observation that registered unemployment in the industry has been lower than the industrial average. That a certain amount of unemployment, particularly among women, was concealed from the statistics is an issue which shall be examined more closely in a later chapter (cf. Chapter 8).

[1] *Teknisk utveckling och arbetskraften i gruvindustrin*, Stockholm 1966.

TECHNOLOGICAL CHANGE AND THE STRUCTURE OF UNEMPLOYMENT

The data presented in the previous section suggests that there is little likelihood of a close association between productivity and unemployment. This is supported by a time series (Table 6) of roughly comparable production and unemployment statistics for a number of industries.

TABLE 6

Productivity Increases and Unemployment Levels for Certain Industries. Index: All industries = 100

Industrial sector	Productivity increase 1959–63	Unemployment during 1960–63
Mining industry	123	160
Clothing industry	112	90
Textile industry	102	125
Wood industry	102	160
Metal manufacturing and metal works	100	80
Paper and pulp industry	100	65
Shoe and leather industry	98	150
Food industry	89	135

In general, if there is an association between changes in productivity and unemployment, it is extremely weak. In several of the industries with a high rate of increase of productivity, unemployment lies somewhat above the average and paper and pulp, which has had a slight productivity increase during the period, registers the lowest level of unemployment. In all cases, there is very little deviation from the mean. The only surprising finding from the table is the fact that even in industries with a combination of a marked rise in productivity and contracting employment (notably textiles, ready-made clothing and mining) unemployment is so low. There seems to be little (if any) evidence of 'technologically-induced' unemployment in Swedish manufacturing.

The unemployment problem in Sweden is largely one of workers in industries other than manufacturing. Of the average

17,000 registered unemployed during 1964 only about 4,450, i.e. 25 per cent, belonged to manufacturing unemployment insurance societies. More than 6,000 were building workers and 1,700 farming and forestry workers.

TABLE 7

Unemployment in Selected Industrial Unemployment Insurance Societies, 1956–64, as a percentage of Total Insured

	1956	1957	1958	1959	1960	1961	1962	1963	1964
Manufacturing	1·0	1·2	1·8	1·5	0·9	0·8	0·8	0·9	0·7
Building and construction	5·5	6·3	7·4	5·5	4·4	4·0	4·3	4·6	3·3
Forest workers	2·5	3·8	6·6	5·8	4·1	3·9	4·7	4·6	5·1
All Unemployment Insurance Societies	1·7	1·9	2·5	2·0	1·4	1·2	1·3	1·4	1·1

The above-average unemployment rates among building workers (see Table 7 above) are more a product of seasonal fluctuations than technical progress in the building sector. Winter unemployment among building workers has always been high. Changing technology and organizational innovations in recent years have resulted in a more even distribution of construction work throughout the year. Consequently, unemployment has greatly declined.

There is a strong seasonal component in unemployment in the forestry sector, with high rates during the late winter months. That this pattern has not greatly changed over the years is shown in Table 8.

TABLE 8

Unemployment Among Forestry Workers in April and May in Relation to Annual Averages 1956–63

	%		%
1956	236	1961	218
1957	229	1962	209
1958	191	1963	176
1959	160	1964	182
1960	193	1965	189

Growing unemployment among forestry workers, who for a

number of years have displayed the highest unemployment rates, is undoubtedly a consequence of the swift technological change in the sector. The explosive increase in productivity from 1950 to 1960 (compare Table 3) has created redundant manpower which has not been absorbed by other industrial sectors. Technological progress together with a weak trend of demand for forestry products, the lack of alternative employment opportunities and a certain degree of sluggishness or immobility on the part of the workforce—related to their age structure—have all contributed to the emergence of a relatively high rate of unemployment.

The concentration of unemployment in seasonally sensitive and non-manufacturing industries also has a regional aspect.

TABLE 9

Unemployment Among Insured Workers in Different Regions, 1961–64, *as a percentage of Total Insured*

	1961	1962	1963	1964
Largest cities	0·7	0·8	1·0	0·6
Forestry regions	2·4	2·9	2·7	2·7
Other regions	1·0	1·2	1·2	0·9
Total Sweden	1·2	1·3	1·4	1·1
Forestry regions in per cent of all Sweden	200	222	193	245

That unemployment in the counties of intensive forestry is more than twice the level for the country as a whole and that this differential is widening are both expressions of the fact that the labour market structure of the northern counties is dominated precisely by those industries which are the subject of intensive rationalization.

REGIONAL SHIFTS IN THE DISTRIBUTION OF THE POPULATION

The continuous structural changes in Swedish industry during the twentieth century have been reflected in the main by the distribution of population among different industries.

The Structure of Employment

TABLE 10

The Swedish Population Distributed According to Major Sector of the Economy, 1900, 1930 and 1960, in %

Main Sector	1900	1930	1960
Agriculture, forestry, etc.	55	39	17
Industry	28	36	45
Commerce and transport	10	17	21
Services	7	8	17

Economic growth has meant that a growing proportion of the population is employed in manufacturing industry or the services. This trend has been accompanied by a significant geographical adjustment to the new requirements of industry for the distribution of manpower and capital. The transition from an agricultural to a highly industrialized economy has entailed significant shifts in the geographical distribution of the population.

There are two major features in this development: the movement from rural to urban areas and the population transfers among various urban regions.

The relationship between economic growth and geographic adjustment has expressed itself in a continuous movement from rural to urban areas. At the start of the 1930s the populations of rural and urban areas were roughly equal. By 1960 this balance had been altered to the point where 73 per cent of the total Swedish population were living in metropolitan areas. With the development of communications the employment significance of the urban areas has been greater than the statistics indicate. The spread of the automobile and the increased opportunities for commuting between work and home over long distances has facilitated structural adjustment.

The urban areas have not developed uniformly. From Table 11 (p. 106) it is evident that assertions that the three conurbations, Gothenburg, Malmö and Stockholm, have had the greatest growth are somewhat exaggerated. Their rates of growth lie somewhat below the average for urban areas throughout the country.

During the 1950–60 period, the smaller towns (i.e. less than 1,000 inhabitants) experienced a lower growth rate than the

TABLE 11

Demographic Changes During Decades, 1910–60,
in Percentage Figures

	All Sweden	Urban areas	Stockholm area	Gothenburg area	Malmö area	Rural area
1910–20	7	25	19	22	27	− 4
1920–30	4	15	21	13	11	− 5
1930–40	4	18	18	10	17	−10
1940–50	11	31	29	26	26	−16
1950–60	6	17	17	16	19	−14

Source: Aktiv lokaliseringspolitik Bilaga II, SOU 1963:62.

others. In fact, many of these small towns had a decreasing population. The highest percentage increase in the total population in all inland areas occurred in the size group 2,000–20,000, i.e. in the middle-sized cities rather than the three giants.

But even if Stockholm, Gothenburg and Malmö have not grown swiftly by comparison with other urban areas in Sweden, the population trends have involved a distributive shift to these major cities. In the event, all other regions (Counties) have had a declining share of the population. It should be noted, however, that expanding industrial regions are found in practically every county. In these towns, one has to contend with basically the same kind of problems as exist in the three major cities.

Employment in areas with a declining population base has been maintained and displacement and re-deployment difficulties have been lessened by the increased practice of commuting to work. In many cases, however, there has been some geographic migration. The latter applies largely to the northern counties. Within these fairly heterogeneous counties, labour has always been employed largely in agriculture, forestry, hunting and fishing. During the 1950s, there has been a particularly swift shakeout of labour due to the dying out of the smaller farming units and comparable trends in forestry. The displacement, though following the common pattern, has taken place over a shorter time period than that of other parts of the country. Because the population is spread thinly throughout the regions, the opportunities for commuting have been relatively few.

Employment increases in industrial operations have been roughly equal or slightly lower than the average for all regions. The expansion has not been sufficiently great to absorb the surplus labour from agricultural and forestry sectors. The result has been emigration to other regions and relatively high unemployment.

CHAPTER 7

The Impact of Changing Technology on the Occupational Structure

The way in which technological change alters the nature of job requirements and thereby transforms the occupational composition of the labour force has been a provocative question for many studies of the manpower consequences of technological change. All analysts concur on the point that technological change has some effect on the occupational mix in the individual firm and the industry, as well as the economy as a whole. Opinions greatly diverge, however, concerning the pace and direction of the shifts, their employment and income effects and their implications in terms of opportunities for improved occupational adjustment.

The lack of available data on these questions means that any position taken must be based on a fairly shaky empirical foundation at certain points. Subject to this qualification, we shall present some of our own views and conclusions in the present chapter. The first section discusses changes in the occupational mix of the labour force in general. The second section examines the shifts in the skill structure that can be observed, i.e. whether the occupational mix has in general shifted upward or downward in terms of education and training requirements. Finally, an attempt is made to estimate future trends and spell out their implications for training and retraining policies.

CHANGES IN THE OCCUPATIONAL STRUCTURE

Let us define an occupation as a type of work performed by an individual over a long time period with only marginal variations in its content. The acquisition of skills or qualifications for a particular occupation requires a given mix of training and practical experience. A job (a position) is characterized by its functions, tasks and responsibilities. The occupational structure can for practical reasons be defined as the relative number of persons in each type of work at a given point in time. Changes in the occupational structure would thus consist of changes in the proportions of individuals employed in existing occupations or the emergence of new and disappearance of old types of work. Where a discrepancy exists between the occupational structure —as defined above—and the training and vocational experience of the labour force, certain frictions are created.

As with other changes in the economy, shifts in the occupational structure can arise from other than purely technological causes. Thus, changes in the composition of consumer demand for goods and services affect the growth rates of individual firms and industries and thereby alter the relative shares of different occupations. Population growth rates and the age distribution of the labour force, and government policy with respect to education, training and research, are also influential factors. Finally, the wage structure and its evolution and personal employee goals are significant agents of change, creating occasional scarcities or surpluses in the supply of persons in different occupations.

Our knowledge of how the occupational structure changes in Sweden is as indicated exceedingly limited. The information contained in the Swedish population census cannot be adapted for this type of analysis. The labour force investigations currently carried out in Sweden are of too recent vintage to allow a meaningful time series analysis. Moreover, they are based on samples which are too small to be representative for such purposes. In other industrialized countries, however, there have been some recent studies of changes in the occupational structure.

In the USA and Canada for example, two statistical studies have measured the relative impact on the occupational structure of two factors: differences in the rate of growth of different industries and shifts in the occupational composition of each industry (the latter being due largely to the forces of changing technology).[1] The data indicate that the varying pace of growth

---

[1] Clauge, E., *Effects of Technological Change on Occupational Employment Patterns in the United States, The Requirements of Automated Jobs.* North American Joint Conference, Washington D.C. December 8–10, 1964. OECD,

in different industries has had a relatively greater effect than shifting occupational patterns on the overall change in occupational employment. Technological change may have contributed to shifts in the occupational distribution but these findings suggest that it is not the sole or even the major factor in the transformation of the occupational structure.

As far as changes in different occupational groups are concerned, it was established that the white-collar groups in general are growing faster than manual occupations. In particular, there has been a marked increase in the relative growth of professionals. This development, however, is largely attributable to changes in the structure of industry. The service occupations have also greatly increased. According to one study, blue-collar workers as a group (i.e. craftsmen, operatives and labourers) have increased at the same rate as the increase in the total labour force. A similar study in Canada, however, indicates that the blue-collar share has decreased. The unskilled worker has declined markedly in both countries. The primary cause for this, according to the USA study, is the changed industrial structure, but the Canadian investigation suggests that shifts within industries are the key factor. The greatest decline for any occupational group in both countries was that registered by the agricultural occupations, largely owing to the changed structure of the economy.

It is not possible to apply these findings directly to Swedish conditions, though the broad trends should not be dissimilar. As is evident from Table 3, the number of workers employed in Swedish agriculture and forestry has rapidly declined since 1950 while employment in manufacturing has increased at a rate exceeding that of total employment. The most expansive sectors with respect to employment have been building and construction and government. This table gives no indication of changes in the occupational structure, but we can deduce that the occupations typically associated with each individual industry have changed at roughly the same rate as overall employment in that industry.

Paris 1965; Schonning, G., *Effects of Changing Industrial Structure on Occupational trends, The Requirements of Automated Jobs.* OECD, Paris 1965; *see also* Meltz, N. M., *Changes in the Occupational Composition of the Canadian Labour Force* 1931–1963. Department of Labour Economics and Research Branch, Ottawa 1965.

If we restrict ourselves solely to mining and manufacturing, we can divide industrial employment statistically into white-collar and blue-collar groups. The data indicate that the white-collar sector has increased its share fairly rapidly during the post-war period. This shift appears to have accelerated somewhat in recent years (see Table 12).

TABLE 12

Changes in Administrative Staff as a Proportion of Total Employment in Swedish Manufacturing, 1946–63

Industry	Administrative Staff as a percentage of employment					Change in % over entire period
	1946	1950	1955	1960	1963	1946–63
Mining	10·2	10·7	12·8	17·5	21·2	11·0
Metal and Engineering	18·8	20·8	22·7	25·0	27·4	8·6
Stone Quarrying	9·3	12·1	13·4	15·6	18·0	8·7
Wood	9·5	10·7	11·6	13·0	14·4	4·9
Paper and Pulp	10·7	12·6	13·2	14·7	17·2	6·5
Printing and Allied	27·8	29·6	30·5	32·6	34·9	7·1
Food	18·1	19·1	19·2	22·0	23·6	5·5
Beverages and Tobacco	17·0	16·9	18·0	20·7	23·6	6·6
Textile and Ready-made Clothing	12·5	13·9	15·4	15·0	15·8	3·3
Leather and Rubber	14·1	16·5	18·2	19·2	20·1	6·0
Chemicals	27·0	28·1	30·3	33·8	35·3	8·3
Total Manufacturing	16·0	18·1	19·8	22·0	24·2	8·2

Source: SOS Industri, Central Bureau of Statistics.

QUALITATIVE CHANGES IN THE OCCUPATIONAL STRUCTURE

It thus appears rather likely that significant shifts have occurred in the occupational structure in Sweden as well as in most other industrial countries in recent decades and that factors other than technology have been instrumental in such shifts. This observation, however, is not the only one of interest. It is also important to note how the skill structure has been altered. Have there been shifts within each occupational family in terms of educational or training requirements and have old occupational classifications obtained new content owing to technological progress, without these changes being directly expressed in the occupational employment statistics.

If we disregard momentarily the fact that the very broad and unclearly defined occupational groups can disguise considerable internal shifts in skill requirements, the available statistical data allow certain conclusions to be drawn with respect to changes in the overall skill structure.

Robert L. Raimon has analysed the effects of technological progress on the changes in the occupational structure from 1950-60 on the basis of material in the USA census and the extent to which these changes resulted in a net increase or decrease in the overall level of skill requirements.[1]

Raimon's study indicates a fairly weak statistical association between productivity changes and changes in the average skill level. It should be noted that a somewhat unfavourable employment change was experienced by those industries registering the highest productivity increases. Consequently, the observed increase in the average skill level of the occupational structure was probably due more to the fact that employment increased at a relatively faster rate in sectors traditionally requiring a high level of skill and education—such as teaching and professional services—than to the phenomenon that productivity rose at a faster rate in these sectors. The effects of shifts in the occupational structure of industries appear to be fairly unimportant. These trends have clearly not been uniform. Several important industries, such as motor car accessories and repair, banking and transport, printing and weaving display a falling average level of skill requirements.

One should perhaps refrain from drawing more extensive conclusions about the transformation of the occupational structure from the above studies. Yet it seems fair to say that the findings rather effectively demolish a great many of the over-simplifications and generalizations of the consequences of mechanization and automation in industrial life. The greatly optimistic assertion, occasionally encountered in public discussion, that machines

---

[1] Raimon, R., 'Changes in Productivity and the Skill-mix'. *International Labour Review*, Vol. 92, No. 4, October 1965, ILO, Geneva 1965; *see also* Wickham, S., 'Future Demand for Vocational Skills of Different Levels'. *International Labour Review*, Vol. 93, No. 2, February 1966, ILO, Geneva 1966.

will release men from tedious and repetitive work and result in an upward shift in the skill and training requirements of jobs is scarcely borne out by the statistical data.

It is exceedingly difficult to determine the extent to which the American experience is applicable to Sweden. We may reasonably assume, however, that the Swedish development will not differ radically from that in the USA and other industrialized countries. We can for example point to the rapid expansion of the absolute and relative number of employees in the public sector, which entails a significant increase in highly qualified occupations in education, research, the medical and health services, and public administration. Similarly, employment in agriculture and forestry is rapidly declining and while this affects many workers with a high level of skill and long practical experience it also means that large groups of workers with little or no vocational training are being 'phased out' of the labour force. The upwards shift in the educational and training qualifications observable for the occupational structure as a whole, is thus attributable largely to changes in the overall structure of the economy. Probably, however, there are significant deviations from this pattern within particular sub-sectors.

In the industries listed in Table 12 the proportion of administrative employees in total manufacturing employment has markedly increased in recent decades. Within this broad occupational sector, certain categories such as higher executives, technicians and managers have increased quite rapidly while the clerical workers, a rather large group, have increased at a somewhat slower pace than the rest. Thus, there has been an upward shift in terms of education and training qualifications in this occupational sector as a whole. It is interesting to note, too, that the increase in employment has generally been most pronounced in those industries which had the largest proportions of white-collar personnel at the outset. The rule seems to apply here as well that relative changes in inter-industry employment are major factors in the evolution of the occupational structure.

The industrial statistics do not allow a comparable breakdown of blue-collar workers by occupational group. From a recent LO Study of the engineering industry[1] it is possible to

[1] Almgren, H., op. cit. *supra.* Svenska metallindustriarbetareförbundet, Stockholm 1966.

extract a picture of the trends within different occupational groups during the past decade from the jointly produced statistics of the Swedish Metal Workers' Union and the Swedish Metal Trades Employers' Association. Unfortunately, the occupational classifications used in these data make it rather difficult to draw any safe conclusions with respect to the qualitative aspects of the changes in the occupational structure. Nor can one estimate with any degree of certainty whether the relative growth rates of the various occupations depend on the expansion of the sub-sector or are an expression of productivity changes caused by technological progress. Even given these reservations, the engineering statistics offer much of interest.

While the total number of workers covered by the data increased by 32 per cent from 1955 to 1965, the group of 'unskilled and semi-skilled workers' (labourers and operatives) increased by 40 per cent. In contrast, the 'skilled workers' (i.e. craftsmen) increased by only 20 per cent. These statistics cover only male workers. If one takes into account the fact that the proportion of female workers in the industry has increased and that with few exceptions women belong to the 'unskilled and semi-skilled' group, the impression is strengthened that there has been a downward shift in the general level of training and skill during the period. This shift, however, could have been due to the great increase in the proportion of younger workers in the industry, a large segment of whom enter the low skill categories. It appears likely that other factors, notably technological and organizational change, have also affected these trends. Finally, it is conceivable that the great scarcity of skilled workers has operated as a constraint on the growth of that occupational group in engineering.

The relationship between 'production' and 'non-production' workers has not noticeably changed during the period. The number of 'qualified' non-production workers (e.g. tool-workers, machine maintenance men, instructors, set-up men, inspectors and testers) has increased almost twice as fast as the 'less-qualified' non-production workers (e.g. warehousemen and storeroom workers, transport workers and dustmen). Instructors and set-up men increased by as much as $+80$ per cent. Interestingly enough, the share of 'unskilled workers' in the 'qualified' non-production occupational category increased, while at the same time the proportion of skilled workers increased in the 'less qualified' occupational groups.

Any attempt to summarize the results of this and other studies of changes in the occupational structure and skill requirements in relation to technical improvements in the firms would encounter the difficulty that few unambiguous tendencies evidence themselves. Plainly, there is little evidence that technological change in general dramatically raises training and skill requirements. To be sure, several industry studies found that new jobs with significantly higher education and training requirements were created. But at the same time there were many new jobs and an increase in employment in old jobs requiring little or no formal vocational training. In several cases, changes consisted of expanded work assignments, greater responsibility and increased opportunities for personal initiative and control over the pace for work. At the same time, however, there was a tendency in other cases for increased specialization and division of work into simpler job operations, often with increased control over operatives.

The difficulties of establishing any direct relationship between technological change and shifts in the skill and training requirements within different occupations (i.e. 'upgrading' and 'downgrading') appear to be almost insuperable. The occupational statistics that are presently available are exceedingly crude and undifferentiated with respect to varying technical levels or work environments. Moreover, there are inherent ambiguities in the concept of skill. One is often compelled to compare and weigh such non-comparable and non-additive elements as 'knowledge', 'attentiveness', 'responsibility' and 'physical strain'. In the event, a rather unfortunate degree of subjectivity finds its way into the calculations. To avoid this pitfall, many researchers have taken the alternative course of linking the level of skill and training requirements to the average length of training in different occupations (i.e. the time required to complete the formal course of training plus on-the-job training to the point of normal performance).[1]

Finally, attention is called to a study carried out a couple of years ago by the IFO economic research institute in Munich. The study covered thirty firms, representing different industries and

---
[1] Lindahl, S., op. cit., *supra*.

different size groups, all of whom had experienced large technological changes during the period 1951–7. Only in a few cases, however, had these changes consisted of the introduction of automated systems.

The study found that the occupational structures of the investigated firms had changed in the following way. The fraction of *Hilsfarbeiter*, i.e. unskilled workers, had decreased, while that of the *angelernte* workers, i.e. semi-skilled workers, had increased. The proportion of skilled workers had declined, particularly those craftsmen whose skills were related only to one particular industry. Several firms had adopted a policy of hiring as few skilled workers as possible because they felt that specialized training was an undesirable burden. The only noticeable increase in skilled workers occurred amongst those groups associated with production maintenance, notably electricians, etc. A similar tendency was found in the case of clerical workers; there was a decreased demand for highly skilled labour and an increased demand for the medium skill ranges with good vocational training. A rather small increase occurred in certain new occupations, e.g. technicians, punchcard operators.

The study concluded that 'the great growth in the number of skilled workers without vocational school training makes a traditional vocational training largely superfluous. In a large proportion of the mechanized production processes studied, it was evident that training in a specialized craft was less useful than the ability to acquire certain new skills. Plainly, a broadly based elementary and vocational education has become more important than an apprenticeship training of the traditional sort.'[1]

SOME CONCLUSIONS AND A PERSPECTIVE FOR THE FUTURE

The shortcomings of the available statistical data and the gaps in our knowledge with respect to the relationship between technological change and shifts in skill requirements make it impossible to give a more precise picture of the transformation of the occupational structure in the past 5–10 years. We may assume, however, that significant shifts in different occupational cate-

[1] *Soziale Auswirkungen des technischen Fortschritts.* IFO-Institutet für Wirtschaftsforschung, Duncker & Humblot, Berlin/Munich 1962.

gories have occurred and will continue to occur in the future. The trends of the past few decades offer no basis for expecting a radical rise in the skill and training requirements of all or even most occupational groups. Certain occupations for which the acquisition of skills or qualifications requires long periods of training or specialized education such as managers, administrators, teachers of all types and doctors, will increase their share of overall employment. The demand for unskilled labour will probably decrease relatively but not absolutely. As far as the skilled occupations are concerned, the trends will be more diversified. Presently, there is a severe shortage of certain types of highly skilled labour. The likely explanation for this, however, is that certain industries and firms are still operating at a relatively low technical level and therefore require greater inputs of labour with long experience and varied know-how. But while technological advance may well result in a decreased need for skilled workers in some such sectors it will probably create a greater demand for craftsmen in others.

What are the probable employment effects of changes in the skill mix? Plainly it has been possible to maintain full employment in Sweden in the post-war period in spite of significant changes in the occupational mix during these years. This suggests that it has been possible for labour to adapt to the changed composition of demand in the sense that they have been able to meet the new job requirements and find new employment. We have also gained the impression from interviews with representatives of various industries, study visits to firms and from the literature, that it has proved possible to a large extent to transfer already employed personnel to new work assignments even in firms experiencing fairly drastic technological reorganizations. The *caveat* here is that such reorganizations must be carefully planned and employees given adequate opportunity for further training or retraining.

There is scarcely any indication that these conditions will change in the forseeable future. Even if changes in the occupational structure as a whole do take the form of a continuous moderate increase in educational and training requirements, this conclusion need not be radically modified. We must keep in mind that the labour force itself is undergoing a gradual and continuous increase in qualifications as a result of the expansion of the educational system. The latter trend includes not only the increase in coverage of the universities, grammar schools, vocational secondary schools, etc. It also encompasses the extensive on-the-job training programmes and further education for adults carried out within the firm at both public and private expense. Recent trends and projected plans suggest that the labour force will have a significantly higher average length of education in the forseeable future, i.e. the next ten to fifteen years. This does not mean that a considerable expansion of present adult education and training programmes is not essential to a balanced labour market. Indeed, quite the contrary, the requirements of manpower adaptation, i.e. the need to change occupation or acquire additional training, are often felt most keenly by workers in the higher age groups. The continuous expansion of basic education at various levels and future plans for this sector will probably lead to a more rapid change in work techniques and thereby an increased need for the training of adults whose early education was deficient in that regard.

Changes in the occupational structure are a result of an interplay between the firm's demand for labour inputs of various types and the supply of labour that is forthcoming. We have centred on the *ex post* occupational structure—but we know too that there have been areas of acute long-term labour shortage where employers have been unable to obtain sufficient new recruits to satisfy their manpower needs. An unsatisfied demand for labour means a loss of potential output and forgone productivity gains. At the same time, difficulties have arisen for certain types of workers to find new employment after being displaced because of their lack of training. We also must reckon that there is a fair amount of concealed unemployment for similar reasons.

These and other problems will not be solved simply by a general expansion of the educational system. True, the current and proposed school reforms will promote a greater diversity aud thereby greater adaptability on the part of the workforce. But systematic long-term planning in vocational education has yet to become a reality.

To accomplish this, more and better information is required of changes in the occupational structure and skill and training requirements. Systematic and current employment statistics with an occupational classification that allows comparisons to be made between firms and industries would appear to be an indispensable pre-condition. Hitherto, our national manpower policy has been pursued on the basis of rather short-term forecasts. Work is already in progress to produce more long-term forecasting data but this is far from completed. It is significant that the recently submitted Long-term Survey practically entirely disregards the question of how the occupational structure will change during the coming period and only estimates the overall demand for and supply of labour.

The rate of expansion and changing orientation of the education system must be more closely co-ordinated with expected developments in different sectors of the labour market. We wish once again to stress LO's approach to training and education policy, namely that vocational training as well as basic general education should be given a broad and diversified character in order to facilitate future retraining, adjustment and skill improvement.

CHAPTER 8

Labour Mobility

The advance of technology in post-war Sweden has taken place in a labour market characterized by a manpower scarcity of hitherto unknown severity. The projections of the Long-term Planning Commission for the period 1965–80 indicate that this shortage of labour will continue and probably intensify. Registered unemployment has been exceedingly low, apart from that in several occupations highly susceptible to seasonal fluctuations and in a few isolated regions, though of course when the aggregate figure is broken down by industry and sub-industrial sector, we obtain a more varied picture. The highly diversified economic development, with considerable expansion in some industries and stagnation or contraction in others, reflects the process of dynamic growth working its way throughout the economy.

It is no more than an assumption, however, that this process will accelerate in the future. Indeed, if we view it in a historical perspective, the acceleration hypothesis is somewhat dubious. The transformation of the rural society and the household production and consumption patterns of the pre-industrial economy into the production apparatus and market economy of an industrialized society was a lengthy process. Its earlier stages were marked by events of greater dramatic impact and repercussions for many more people than technological change has had in recent years. The enormous wave of emigration that swept through Sweden in the latter half of the past century was a symptom of the abject failure of society at that time to master its economic and social problems. The crucial difference between the present situation and conditions seventy-five years ago is that expanding sectors in today's economy are capable of absorbing manpower at a rate commensurate with the growth in the labour force and redundancies in the contracting sectors.

Another important difference is that the personal difficulties for an individual adjusting from a rural to an industrialized job environment are probably greater than the problems involved in the transfer from one industry to another.

The continuous structural transformation of industry, presupposes that the labour force will adapt itself through extensive job and occupation changing as well as inter-local migration. The substantial net changes in the numbers employed in different industries and occupations must be viewed against the background of significantly greater gross labour flows—or turnover—the nature and scope of which are still imperfectly known and understood. We are probably safe, however, in maintaining that the movement of workers that is directly or indirectly attributable to technological change is significantly smaller than the total quantum of labour turnover. We occasionally encounter the view in the literature of automation that increases in productivity constitute a measure of the number of 'discontinued jobs'. Surely, however, in a progressive economy, work methods can change and job content can be altered without jobs being discontinued. But even were one to take the overall increase in productivity as a starting point—the average annual rate of increase for the country as a whole has been in the order of 3-4 per cent—the labour turnover generated by technological and structural change would constitute only a small fraction of the total mobility of labour.

It would be somewhat over-hasty, however, to conclude from this that the labour turnover generated by technological change can be accommodated relatively easily in the overall mobility patterns of a full employment society, however lively these patterns may appear to be. For the propensity of individuals to move—which is a symptom of their desire for better work adjustment, can easily conflict with the requirements of manpower adaptation inherent in the process of technological change. A current manifestation of this conflict in the Swedish economy is the phenomenon of labour turnover in local labour markets which is excessive in relation to the levels necessitated by increased productivity, combined with an overall pattern of sluggish inter-local movement. Predictably this has resulted in islands of unemployment and underemployment in a full employment economy.

This conflict between the inclinations of individual workers and the overall manpower needs of a changing economy has another aspect; the costs associated with the fraction of labour turnover that is not 'voluntary' on the part of the individual worker, not only the actual costs of removal but also the losses sustained in the process of disposing of old and acquiring new housing, the interruptions in the children's school attendance, forgone non-wage benefits, reductions in income or additional periods of training. To these must be added the social and psychological sacrifices often involved in a change of environment and adjustment to a new social setting. At the same time, there are costs incurred by society, both by the depopulated local authorities in the form of lost economic and population bases for their social services, and for the recipient local authorities which—often in a situation of scarcity—must create new services. It is primarily when the productivity gains attached to labour mobility are in line with the total 'costs' of the individual and society that the movement of manpower is justified from the welfare economics viewpoint.

The following section describes the magnitude and composition of gross labour turnover which can be useful to illustrate in greater detail the scope of the problems.

STATISTICAL DATA ON LABOUR MOBILITY

In Sweden the available statistical data on labour turnover consist of an unbroken series since 1947 of the number and percentages of weekly job separations and new employee accessions. During the 1947—58 period this data was presented quarterly and covered selected industries. In 1958, the series was changed in two respects: the data were reported monthly instead of quarterly and coverage was extended to all manufacturing industries. Also, the breakdown of total job separations into voluntary and employer-initiated cessations of employment was discontinued. The major results of these series (with weekly statistics multiplied by 47 to obtain an approximate measure of annual labour turnover) are reproduced in Table 13.

The data indicate considerable cyclical variability, with a high rate of labour turnover in periods of business prosperity and

Labour Mobility

TABLE 13

Annual Average Number of Job Separations as a % of Employed Workers

Year	Separations	Employer-initiated cessations	Year	Separations
1947	51·2	—	1958*	23·5
1948	42·3	—	1959	28·2
1949	37·6	—	1960	35·7
1950	37·6	—	1961	41·8
1951	37·7	13·5	1962	45·6
1952	32·9	15·5	1963	46·1
1953	37·6	17·5	1964	53·1
1954	23·5	10·0		
1955	32·9	8·0		
1956	28·2	14·3		
1957	23·5	13·0		
1958	18·8	25·0		

* New Series.

Source: National Central Bureau of Statistics.

greatly reduced turnover rates in periods of recession (i.e. 1953—4 and 1958—9). In contrast, the proportion of employer-initiated cessations of employment, i.e. largely layoffs, vary inversely with the trade cycle; its highest point was the recession year 1958. The wide cyclical fluctuations in labour turnover rates are *prima facie* evidence that factors other than continuous technological change determine the extent of gross labour flows.

Further evidence in support of this proposition is offered by the data on labour turnover in individual industries. The turnover rankings disclose that separation rates in the food and kindred products sector are high while those in metal working—an industry subjected to relatively rapid technological change—are below the average. The lowest separation rates of all industries are those displayed by the mining industry. (They are less than one-half of the average separation rates of all industries.) Low labour turnover in the mining industry is plainly not a reflection of an exceptionally slow pace of technological change. It probably stems from the isolated position and undifferentiated industrial structure of the mining towns. There appears to be no indication of a causal relationship between the size of gross labour turnover and the degree of technological change. It is interesting to note that the separation rates for 1964 are almost the same as the high turnover rates of the immediate post-war years. Among industrial workers, the number of separations in relation to the total number employed at the beginning of every week is currently above 50 per cent. This statistic, however, should not be interpreted to mean that more than one-half of all industrial workers change jobs annually. Several investigations in selected industries allow us to analyse in greater detail the composition of labour mobility.

The Swedish Textile Industrial Association carried out a statistical study in 1964 attempting to determine the extent to which labour mobility among textile workers was concentrated amongst a small segment of workers who change their jobs relatively frequently. They found that about 80 per cent of all male workers employed in the textile industry did not change jobs during the year studied. The corresponding figure for female employees was 79 per cent. The number of new recruits during the year was 40 per 100 employees working at the start of the year. About half of the new recruits ceased work during the course of the year. Those workers who had been both newly recruited and had ceased employment during the year had an average length of service of two months.

The results indicate fairly clearly that an extremely mobile group of workers who changed jobs at least twice during the year accounted for about half of the total number of job shifts observed, i.e. the figure represented by the separation rate of 40–50 per cent per year. The preponderant part, i.e. 80 per cent of the labour force, were 'stable' in the sense that they did not change jobs for at least one year. The results correspond fairly closely to the findings of other studies of labour mobility[1] and to the experience of the local employment exchanges.

The component of total job departures most closely related to technological changes, plant shutdowns and cut-backs in production is that covered by the category 'employer-initiated cessations'. This category includes job termination for disci-

---

[1] Meidner, R., *Svensk Arbetsmarknad vid full sysselsättning*, Stockholm 1954. (The Swedish Labour Market under Full Employment.)

plinary reasons but disciplinary discharges constitute an almost negligible fraction of all employer-initiated cessations. This latter Swedish statistical category is almost synonymous with suppression of the job by the employer for economic reasons. Employer-initiated cessations appear to constitute about 15 per cent of all job changes but this figure has probably declined during the business boom of the past few years. During the period 1951–8, it varied between 3 and 5 per cent of the total labour force. The findings of the LO Membership Survey correspond fairly well with these results. Thus, 13 per cent of those workers who responded to the LO survey indicated that employer-initiated cessations were the cause of their most recent change of jobs. Not less than 10 per cent were directly related to reductions in personnel for economic reasons.

Further light was thrown on job changes by the results of a study conducted by the National Labour Market Board in conjunction with one of its regular quarterly labour force surveys.[1] The study, conducted in May 1964, found that 14·2 per cent of male workers and 15·7 per cent of female workers had changed jobs at least once during the preceding twelve months. If we keep in mind that the labour force survey covers a representative sample of the entire labour force and therefore in all likelihood shows a lower figure for labour turnover than the tables of the National Central Bureau of Statistics (which include only labour turnover in mining and manufacturing industries), the results appear to correspond reasonably closely. According to the findings of the LO Membership Survey, 16·5 per cent of the men and 15·5 per cent of the women indicated that they had obtained their present position (December 1965) during the course of the 1965 calendar year. According to the findings of the Central Bureau of Statistics and the textile industry study, about half of the labour turnover rate of 40 per cent, i.e. 20 per cent, was accounted for by workers who changed jobs at least once a year. The labour force survey found that at a somewhat lower total labour turnover (i.e. perhaps about 30 per cent) about 15 per cent of those who worked changed jobs more than once during the preceding year. The statistical findings with respect to the number of persons who began a new job during the preceding year were somewhat higher (22·6

[1] *Anställningstid och anställningsbyte*. Arbetsmarknadsinformation, 1965:4.

per cent for men and 29·6 per cent for women), because this survey included new entrants to the labour force. Married women in the age group 35–54 display a particularly high new accession rate. The difference between the fraction of the total number of workers who began a new job during the preceding year and the frequency of job changes constitutes an approximate measure of 'labour force' mobility, i.e. mobility into and out of the labour force. The figure is 8·4 per cent for men and as much as 13·9 per cent for married women. These estimates may appear to be rather high but they are significantly affected by the high figures for the lower age groups and the return of married women to work in the middle age groups. One should also remember that the entry of the new age group of young people to the labour force each year alone accounts for a gross increment of 3·5 per cent.

The difference between the total labour turnover rate of 40–50 per cent and the significantly lower 'technological' turnover rate represents inter-industry and inter-occupational mobility, an activity that is particularly significant for our report. There are no statistical data available to measure inter-occupational mobility. But we can obtain some idea of the extent and nature of inter-industry mobility from the membership statistics of industrial unions affiliated to LO. For the latter part of the 1940s gross transfers between LO member unions were about 5 per cent annually while 'net transfers' (the sum of the union's balance of exchange disregarding sign) amounted to approximately 2 per cent of total membership. In the mid-'fifties this series was discontinued and subsequent analyses have had to content themselves with data from selected industries. At our request, the Swedish Textile Workers Union carried out an analysis of entries into and withdrawals from its organization during the period 1961–5. The major findings are summarized in Table 14.

As is evident from Table 14, the union's gross transfers for the observed period were of the same order of magnitude as that figure observed for Swedish industry as a whole, i.e. about 4–5 per cent annually. From the union's commentary to the study, it appears that the statistics should be viewed as a minimum for the actual turnover in union membership. An extremely large segment of the total membership, about 5 per

TABLE 14

Entries into and Withdrawals from the Swedish Textile Workers Union, as a Percentage of Total Membership

	1961	1962	1963	1964	1965
Entries	4·8	4·0	5·6	4·8	3·7
Withdrawals	9·0	7·0	8·0	8·5	8·1
Net Change	−4·2	−3·9	−2·4	−3·7	−4·4

Source: The Swedish Textile Workers Union.

cent annually, left or were excluded from the union. About half of this group consisted of those workers (primarily women) who ceased employment altogether. Among those giving up membership were a number of older members, who had been made redundant and after receiving unemployment insurance had failed to request withdrawal. The majority of the other half of those leaving the union consisted of workers who had changed jobs without notifying their union local. A comparable situation arises in the case of 'new entries'. These circumstances could increase the transfer figures given above by as much as 50 per cent.

In the group, 'requested withdrawal', there were members who left the labour force entirely for one reason or another (notably women who discontinued gainful occupation, members who reached pensionable age, etc.). The annual number of members requesting withdrawal as a percentage of total membership was respectively:

1961	1962	1963	1964	1965
%	%	%	%	%
4·4	6·3	6·8	5·7	5·1

or an annual average of 5·7 per cent for the period of observation. It is worth mentioning at this point that the Central Bureau's statistics for 'labour force' mobility, gathered in a totally different way, indicated a figure of 8 per cent for men and 14 per cent for women in 1963–4. These two results are not incompatible if we take into account the fact that an uncertain number of those resigning from union membership (estimated by the union to be about one-half of the total) have discontinued gainful employment. If we incorporate that estimate, the fraction of total union membership that withdrew from the union during that year would rise to 9 per cent. This corresponds fairly well with the findings of the Central Bureau.

From the preceding discussion, it appears that the statistical data available for an analysis of labour mobility is incomplete and inadequate. The basic source of information today consists of material, undifferentiated with respect to sex or age groups, recording monthly the total number of separated and newly recruited employees. The findings of the different sources used are summarized in Table 15 which also includes the comparable figures for the early post-war years.

TABLE 15

The Mobility of Workers in Manufacturing Industries During the Periods 1945–50 and 1960–65 (separations during one year as a % of total employed workers)

	1945–50	1960–65
1. Job changes (with no change of industry)	35—40	30—40
(a) local	30—35	—
(b) inter-local	5	—
2. Inter-industry mobility	7	5—7
3. 'Labour-force mobility'	3— 8	7—10
Total mobility	approx 50	40—50
Total No. of Workers Moving in per cent	—	20—25
Employer-initiated cessations as a percentage of total separations	—	8—12

Source: 1945–50: Meidner, R. *Svensk arbetsmarknad vid full sysselsattning* (The Swedish Labour Market Under Full Employment), p. 159.
1960–65: The National Central Board of Statistics; The National Labour Market Board; The Swedish Textile Workers Union; The Swedish Textile Industry Employers' Association (cf. text).

There is considerable stability in the pattern of labour mobility —as this is measured by these exceedingly approximate statistics —during the post-war period. Total labour turnover in recent years is at about the same level as that during the early post-war period, which was one of transition from a wartime to a peacetime economy, and hence conducive to high mobility in the labour market. It is still the case that job changing in local labour markets is frequent while inter-industry mobility is relatively limited. The observed slight increase in 'labour force mobility' is probably related to the increased activity rates of female workers and the increased prevalence of individuals who combine gainful occupation with study as required lengths of education and training increase. Voluntary separations—in a formal sense—dominate the labour turnover figures. Less than one-tenth of all job changes are employer-initiated. If Table 15 is taken as an approximately correct indication of the major features of the composition of labour mobility, it suggests that the Swedish labour market is fairly flexible. Such a degree of flexibility should greatly facilitate the vocational adjustment of individual workers. In a number of studies, it has been shown that the choice of first job often occurs 'blindly', i.e. in an unplanned manner, after which the individual corrects his originally arbitrary selection through several job changes. The small rôle played by the public employment exchanges in establishing contact between employer and job-seeker—in the LO Membership Survey only 15 per cent had obtained their present job through the labour exchanges—and the high proportion of vacancies filled through 'friends and relatives' (35 per cent), gives an impression of rather random job changing. None the less, this process appears to be largely rational in the sense that job changes are often thought by the worker to entail an improvement in conditions of employment, particularly with respect to pay, the type of job and supervision. This degree of freedom which often leads to improvement in individual adjustment in stages, is one of the more important virtues associated with the full employment economy. It should have the effect of easing many of the difficulties associated with manpower adjustment to technological change. Yet, in many cases, the change does not lead to improvement. A further consideration is suggested by the findings of a recent study that a large proportion of those currently employed—more than 50 per cent according to the LO Membership Survey—have no desire to change their job or work assignment, and that this proportion rises with increasing age.

I

REDEPLOYMENT DIFFICULTIES AND LOSS OF INCOME ASSOCIATED WITH PLANT SHUTDOWNS

Our attention, however, should be concentrated on those areas where the effort to secure a continuous increase in overall productivity will openly conflict with the need of individual workers for security. At first glance, one could assume that this conflict will be confined largely to that small segment of job changes that result from redundancies. In the LO Survey this group amounted annually to one-tenth of all job changes, or 2 per cent of total LO membership. That this figure corresponds to the average annual rise in productivity is perhaps something more than a mere coincidence, but without access to more systematic evidence on this point, one is reluctant to jump to conclusions. For many of the redundant workers, job changing can be a fairly straightforward process. However, many persons, even prior to receiving formal notice, can be confronted with a problem of choice requiring a careful weighing of the arguments for and against a change of job or occupation.

As our examination shifts to the marginal groups who are affected or who will soon be affected by changes in industrial life, our discussion alters its focus from the question of how technological change affects employment to that of how labour turnover affects the individual. Our stock of knowledge in this area is exceedingly limited; our sources are primarily case studies of plant shutdowns.

The Swedish Labour Market Board has recorded the total number of employees covered by notified cut-backs in production and plant shutdowns for a period of years.[1] This time series is reproduced in Table 16.

The uncertainty of these statistics is considerable. In some cases, advance notice has not been followed by actual cut-backs in production, in other cases men have been made redundant without advance notice. If the data are accepted as the basis for a rough estimate of the proportion of the workforce made redundant each year, the fraction would vary between 0·5 per cent and 1 per cent annually. The metal-working industry displays particularly wide variations, but the figure never greatly exceeds 1 per cent in any one year. The precarious

[1] Notice is required only of firms with at least 10 employees.

TABLE 16

The Number of Employees Covered by Advance Notice of Curtailed Production, 1960–65

	1960	1961	1962	1963	1964	1965
Total	6,732	8,271	9,993	8,108	4,312	8,890
Of which: Iron and metal	955	1,856	4,255	3,623	1,287	2,012
Forestry	896	2,185	1,825	984	743	599
Textile and clothing	2,718	2,571	1,204	608	578	2,774

Source: National Labour Market Board.

position of the textile and clothing industry is reflected in its high notification statistics, which occasionally have risen to 3 per cent of total employment.

A few studies have been made in an attempt to assess the results of efforts to redeploy redundant manpower. Two such studies were included in a recent Swedish publication.[1] In one, the shutdown of a textile plant in Malmö in 1958, the situation with respect to placement one year after the shutdown was as follows:

TABLE 17

Distribution of the Total Workforce One Year After a Plant Shutdown

	Men	Women	Combined
Unemployed	3	14	9
Withdrew from labour force	2	13	7
Ill	6	4	5
Undergoing retraining	4	—	2
Total not re-employed	15	31	23
Total re-employed	85	69	77

Source: *Näringsliv i omvandling* (Industry in the Process of Transformation), SNS, Stockholm, 1964.

Similar results were suggested by the findings of a study of a plant shutdown in Norrköping several years later. Two years

[1] *Näringsliv i omvandling*. Studieförbundet Näringsliv och Samhälle (SNS), Stockholm 1964.

after the shutdown about 23 per cent of the redundant workforce were without a new job.

LO has made a study of the shutdown of a ready-made clothing factory, also in Norrköping, in 1965.[1] Six months after the shutdown, 10 per cent of the men and not less than 27 per cent of the women were without a new position. The fraction of the total workforce of the plant was 25 per cent, which corresponds fairly closely to the results of the previous studies.

Plainly, the results of these studies must be interpreted with great care. The skew of the age distribution towards the higher age groups was unquestionably a factor in the number of workers unable to find new employment; workers in this group were classified as ill, unemployed, retired or simply withdrawn from the labour force. On the other hand, the highly differentiated industrial structure of the Norrköping and Malmö areas together with the fact that the plant shutdown occurred—in two out of these cases—during a period of prosperity militated in favour of the redundant workers. One cannot help but gain the impression that a considerable segment, primarily the older and female workers, are not 'redeployable' given the current magnitude of national manpower policy efforts and resources. It is no consolation, but rather a serious harbinger for the future, that only a fraction of this unredeployable group registered as unemployed. To the extent that future plant shutdowns will affect industries that are less 'female-intensive' than the textiles and clothing sector, the departure of redundant workers from the labour force will be a less quiet procedure than that of the elderly women in Malmö and Norrköping.

The slow pace with which individuals adjust to a new job situation stands in ready contrast to the high turnover figures reproduced above. One should remember that almost all studies of labour mobility have found a functional relationship between age and the propensity to change jobs. Thus, in his study of labour mobility in the town of Norrköping,[2] Bengt Rundblad found that the average number of job-shifts for men who were 45 years old in 1958 was 0·57 each in the preceding five-year period, the figure for the men 35 years old was 0·88

[1] *Vargen-undersökningen.* En företagsnedläggning och dess konsekvenser för arbetstagarna. LO Research Division, Stockholm 1966.
[2] Rundblad, B., *Arbetskraftens rörlighet*, Uppsala 1964. (Labour Mobility.)

job-shifts each while that for men 25 years old was 1·61 job-shifts. The figure for the 25-year-olds was thus more than treble that of the 45-year-olds and double that of the 35-year-olds.

The LO Membership Survey offers further evidence that the tendency to change decreases with increasing age and that this is true with respect to occupational shifts as well as job shifts. 75 per cent of LO members who were 60 years old desired no change, the corresponding figure was 66 per cent for those in the 40–50 age group, 66 per cent in the 30–40 age group and 64 per cent in the 25–30 age group.

For a variety of reasons, it is likely that the relatively immobile categories of workers will be more highly concentrated in the workforce of plants that shut down. For a start there is the upwards shift of the age distribution in the population as a whole, an unfavourable development from the standpoint of labour mobility. Further, industries with a high rate of shutdown often have a workforce that is relatively indisposed to move. An industry with a contracting workforce is generally compelled to decrease or even halt recruitment. Where there is a risk of shutdown, the most highly mobile workers will have often left prior to the event. At the time of shutdown, therefore, frequently the only employees remaining are elderly employees with long periods of service and a low capacity for job change. This tendency will be accentuated as industries and firms with unfavourable age distributions increasingly enter the risk zone. A further complication is introduced by the fact that plant shutdowns usually begin in highly differentiated industrial sectors where the low wage firms are pushed out by contiguous competing high wage firms in expanding industries. When the structural malaise spreads to the heart of the industry, those industrial sectors which are less highly differentiated and even dependent on the particular industry will be hit. This can lead to a consequent aggravation of redeployment problems. The textile industry appears to be moving into this critical phase. Another tendency, particularly marked in the case of the ready-made clothing industry, is the shutdown of subsidiary plants established during periods of prosperity in less densely populated areas with a good supply of female labour.

The difficulties and inconvenience accompanying a plant shutdown, however, are not confined solely to that segment of the workforce which is subsequently unable to find new employment. A compulsory job transfer is entirely different in character from a voluntary job change. An unwanted job change often results in economic as well as social and psychological sacrifices. For, even when followed by re-employment, redundancy in practice often entails a reduction in pay for a considerable proportion of the workforce. Thus, in the above study of the shutdown of a Malmö plant, it was found that 26 per cent of the men and not less than 45 per cent of the women experienced a drop in income from their new job compared with that from the old. In the Norrköping case the results were even less favourable: the group experiencing a reduction in income were women in all age groups and men in the age group 36 and over. And, in the LO study of the clothing firm in Norrköping, it was found that 37 per cent of the men and 41 per cent of the women had experienced reductions in pay as a result of job change due to redundancy.

These figures are plainly higher than the corresponding figures for voluntary job changes. Thus Rundblad found in his Norrköping study that amongst three age groups of job changers i.e. 40–50 years, 30–40 years, and 25–30 years (undifferentiated with respect to voluntary and involuntary changes) the fraction of men in each group experiencing a drop in income was respectively 19, 10 and 19 per cent.

A worsened financial position, however, is not the only inconvenience suffered in connection with a shutdown. There is little systematic evidence on this point, but the LO study of the Norrköping clothing firm suggests that a majority of the female employees tended to take new jobs that were less skilled. Also, there was a feeling among a particularly high proportion of the female employees that they were generally 'worse off' in their new jobs.

Though the data available have many shortcomings, they do indicate that the favourable overall figures for employment and unemployment tend to disguise significant problems of adaptation for workers made redundant by plant shutdowns. To a surprising extent, these individuals tend to leave the labour force. We consider this rejection of workers desiring jobs in the midst of a so-called full employment economy to be a seriously disturbing development. Yet we do not conclude that the structural transformation of industry should be halted or slowed down. We urge instead that our national manpower policy programme, which is at present ineffective in dealing with this problem, be expanded to the point where it can have a significant impact. Moreover, we feel that the fact that a large segment of the redeployed workers experience a drop in income as a result of redundancy should be recognized not only as a series of personal misfortunes but also as a failing of the system. In the above cases of plant shutdowns, a significant proportion of female employees were transferred to domestic work and other service occupations and non-specified jobs. One cannot help but suspect that an emergency situation has led to many emergency solutions, which have in turn resulted in not only a worsened financial position for the individual, but also an under-utilization of his or her vocational abilities and experience. In so far as such *ad hoc* solutions involve shifts of manpower to less productive employments, the overall economic value of the rationalization step will be diminished. The responsibility for this diminution squarely rests with society.

The labour market administrative authorities should devote far greater resources than hitherto not only to the procurement of productive and suitable employment for redundant workers but also to the procedure of following up the results of such redeployment. It has happened that the new job has proved to be unsatisfactory to the redundant individual and has led to a flurry of job changes with successively increased obstacles to a durable adjustment to working life. Early warning and advance planning of redundancies and plant shutdowns by the employer, trade union and labour market authorities, greater activity by the public employment exchanges on behalf of those workers 'less attractive' to the job market, generous removal and retraining grants and subsidies, even for elderly workers, and increased resources allocated to vocational rehabilitation for those workers who are difficult to place are some of the measures that are urgently needed to avoid the personal and social tragedies presently associated with plant shutdowns and redundancies. We do not accept that there is a valid cost argument for limiting the efforts of society to redeploy labour who have the greater part of their productive life behind them. Full employment is an objective that applies to everyone, irrespective of sex, age or training.

INTERNAL TRANSFERS

The adjustment problems associated with plant shutdowns, however grave, are like the visible part of an iceberg, only a small fraction of the whole. A plant shutdown is always a dramatic and closely observed event, often followed by concentrated and co-ordinated measures by government authorities attempting to solve the accompanying problems. A far more extensive process of adjustment takes place away from the glare of publicity and confronts many more individuals with problems of a similar nature. While, in a fair amount of cases, transfers require a move to another place of work, a great many entail only changed work assignments or displacement to another job within the same plant. In the LO Survey, 18 per cent of all those queried stated that they had been transferred within the firm in the previous three years and about half of these transfers were in conjunction with large reorganizations. This suggests that the frequency of such internal transfers amounts to about half that of *inter*-firm changes. Our industry studies offer another example of the problems associated with large reorganizations.[1] Swedish Railways, which is the largest firm in the north of Sweden but could equally be regarded as itself an industry, is presently having serious problems of adjustment in conjunction with its continuous reduction in staff. (Swedish Railways is cutting down its workforce every year by an amount equal to the total number of workers employed in a large Swedish factory, i.e. about 1,500 to 2,000 men.) These problems are aggravated by the unfavourable age distribution of its workforce. An 'attrition' rate in the order of 1,000 men annually together with a reduction in recruiting has hitherto facilitated the process to some extent, but extensive inter-operation employee transfers have been needed to even out scarcities and surpluses of staff in various sections.

Little is known about the process but there is no reason to

[1] Erixon, I., *LKAB: s nya gruva i Svappavaara*, Stockholm 1966; and *Den tekniska utvecklingens konsekvenser för arbetskraften vid Statens Järnvägär*, Stockholm 1966.

Labour Mobility

minimize the individual difficulties and inconvenience accompanying this redirection of labour. According to the LO Survey, there were not many (10 per cent) who indicated that taking everything into account they were 'worse off' after an intra-firm job transfer, but the picture becomes less reassuring when the evaluations on specific aspects of the change in jobs by workers undergoing an intra-firm transfer are compared to those by workers transferring *between* firms. Of the thirteen aspects of the job change that the subjects of the survey were asked to evaluate, there was not one in which a larger number of intra-firm transferees felt they were better off than the inter-firm transferees. Particularly noteworthy was the difference in the assessment by both groups of such factors as the supervisor, hours of work, fringe benefits and workmates. On all points, more than twice the number of external transferees indicated that they were better off than the internal transferees. Clearly, internal displacement can create problems of adjustment for individual workers. There is good reason to investigate the problems encountered by the older and partly disabled workers given the increasing share of our population in the middle-age groups and the decreasing number of 'retreats' in industry for employees past their prime.

CHAPTER 9

Worker Adjustment and Technological Change

The adjustment of the individual to his working situation is the outcome of a complex process involving many factors interacting in a great variety of ways. One group of factors is linked to the individual himself, notably his physical and mental constitution, general state of health, personality type and characteristic behaviour. Another group of factors consist of the existing norms and values within the groups to which the individual belongs. The experiences of the individual in his childhood environment, social groups, trade union organizations and earlier jobs help to form the expectations he brings to and claims he makes of his job.

The third group of factors relevant to the individual's adjustment are the features of his work environment. The key factor here is the content of the job, but others such as the type of supervision, the degree of social interaction, the quality of equipment and machinery, the degree of skill required to perform the work assignment, wage earnings and the system of wage payment are not without influence. Technological change can and often does alter these elements in the work environment and the effects of such change 'on the shop floor' have repercussions on the worker's adjustment to the job.[1]

NEED ADJUSTMENT

Successful worker adjustment is closely related to the extent to which the job succeeds in fulfilling certain human needs. All

---

[1] The chapter is based largely on Bolinder, E., *Individen och den industriella miljön*, Stockholm 1966; and Dahlström, E. (Ed.), *Teknisk förändring och arbetsanpassning*, Stockholm 1966.

Worker Adjustment and Technological Change 139

such needs cannot be listed here; we shall confine our list to those factors to be discussed in the present chapter. The more conspicuous omissions, notably the need for job security, freedom of job choice and a certain level of income and amount of leisure, will be discussed separately in other chapters.

The individual worker requires on-the-job protection of health, life and limb. This need falls within the traditional sphere of worker protection and includes such questions as safety, accident prevention, industrial illness, and disorders arising from long-term exposure to physiologically unsuitable job operations or work environments.

Other needs, which can be termed 'psychological', are linked to the nature of the job and working situation. Typically, such needs are less susceptible to registration and measurement than 'physical' needs. It is therefore more difficult to quantify the requirements that they pose for the work situation and the firm. But this does not mean that psychological needs exist to a lesser extent or can be excluded from consideration.

One of these is the need for variety and achievement. This would include the need for change of pace, diversity and variability in the job as well as the opportunity to display one's ability and develop one's capacities through its performance. This would also encompass the need to perform a job that earns external respect and internal self-esteem and provides an opportunity for greater self-realization. Currently, working life consists of many job operations characterized by either extreme monotony or extreme variability and in consequence offering relatively little opportunity for workers to fulfil many of their needs. One such extreme case is repetitive assembly work that only engages a small fraction of the individual personality. Another case is the type of job that continuously changes its content and/or confronts the job-holder with excessively difficult work assignments, perhaps with extensive overtime and resultant stress.

As well, the individual requires some degree of autonomy in and influence over his work situation, that is, some say in the determination of his work pace and method and mode of co-operation with work associates and supervisors, and some opportunity to participate in decisions affecting the work environment and conditions of employment. Again, we can readily find extreme cases in contemporary industrial life. There are, for example, a great many job operations which are very narrowly constrained by the pace and location of machinery and by previously planned and rigorously detailed instructions regarding work methods. Another extreme case is a job in an authoritarian managerial system under which no attempt is made to consult with or inform employees about forthcoming changes before such changes are implemented.

The worker also has the need to obtain a reasonably clear picture of the way in which his own rôle and work effort fits into the overall production process. Job and occupation are capable of giving the individual a sense of identity and are potential sources of esteem and prestige. This would indeed be desirable, for the sense of identity derived through work can lead to increased self-confidence and greater self-realization for the individual worker. But it presupposes a modification of existing norms and values, which as we know can be instrumental in shaping the individual's expectations. There is, for example, a traditional tendency to regard manual work as an inferior form of labour. And this social attitude considerably reduces the opportunities for the individual manual worker to experience increased self-esteem. There are, moreover, marked differences even among manual workers, depending on the training and qualifications required by the job. Jobs consisting of simple work tasks, capable of being performed efficiently after a relatively short period of 'programmed' training, offer little scope for the individual to develop self-esteem.

The individual requires some degree of social contact and communication in his work. Social interaction at the workplace is of great importance too, because it can compensate the individual psychologically for the lack of influence over his own work task and the absence of opportunity for stimuli from and involvement in the actual performance of the job.

Empirical research has taught us that employees attempt to safeguard themselves against the requirements of technical systems and shortcomings in the formal organization of the firm by the formation of informal work groups. Trade union organizations are also important in this context; an effectively functioning union organization offers opportunities for members to enjoy greater social contact and exchange and a higher degree

Worker Adjustment and Technological Change 141

of responsibility for and influence in the moulding of the work environment.

PHYSICAL ADJUSTMENT

Changing technology has generally entailed a lowering of the requirement of physical strength in job operations. Materials handling, work consisting of lifting and transporting goods, has become largely mechanized. Of course this trend has not been uniform throughout all sectors. Some industries still require the ability to perform physically heavy work despite extensive technological changes. A case in point would be felling operations in forestry work.

Moreover, even within other industries where changing technology has been accompanied by an extensive decline in heavy manual work, within each firm new work assignments can be found that require considerably increased physical effort. For example, new job operations may have to be performed at higher temperatures, increasing the physical strain associated with the operation, because new equipment has been installed in existing and not entirely suitable sites. As well, the higher speed of operation of new machinery necessitated by cost considerations may increase the physical load on the operator.

Further, even if job operations with relatively high degrees of total 'muscle' effort are tending to decline, there are still many operations characterized by individually burdensome movements integrated into a sequence of otherwise physically light tasks. These are much more difficult to identify and assess but they lead none the less to problems of adjustment particularly for those individuals who may be well qualified to perform the other, less physically demanding elements of the job. Work assignments of this sort are especially unsuitable for elderly workers and others of limited physical strength.

At the middle stage of mechanization, there appears to be a tendency for jobs to require a different type of physical qualification. The greater fragmentation and increased mechanical control of the job at these stages combine to reduce the individual's degree of freedom to choose his own work method and pace of work. There is little evidence that the rhythm of exchange of muscle activity and muscle relaxation that is natural to the individual has been taken into account in the job design. The pre-planned work positions, work motion and materials handling methods that are associated with job operations at this level of mechanization consist of repetitive motion patterns that increase the risk of overloading certain muscle groups by concentrating strain on certain parts of the body.

A fast work pace in conjunction with repetitive and sometimes complicated motion patterns can in certain cases create new physiological problems. These stem from the interplay between the body's motor organs and its central nervous system. This is particularly noticeable in cases where the requirement of speed is combined with the need for acute attentiveness and precision in the performance of the work task. The early external symptoms are fatigue and declining or intermittent attentiveness. These soon lead to an increased frequency of industrial accidents. Given that there are wide variations in the capacities of individual workers, more effective methods of 'matching' employees with job tasks should be incorporated in the worker placement activity of personnel departments.

At a higher level of mechanization, where the bulk of work tasks consist of instrument monitoring and maintenance work, the problems of physical adjustment are almost the reverse. Thus, it is sometimes necessary to compensate for the physical inactivity associated with the performance of such work by introducing special physical exercises to maintain worker fitness and vitality. The direct physical requirements of the job are related to the interplay between information intake and motor organs, i.e. the individual's reaction time. What is the capacity of the individual to apply prescribed measures acting on the basis of information provided by instruments? The individual's physiological and psychological make-up constitute the constraints on his ability in this sphere.

Changing technology also results in changes in the overall work environment. For example, mechanization has been associated with a considerable increase in industrial noise. Many industrial workplaces tolerate noise levels that exceed safety limits as far as the hearing of employees is concerned. Hearing tests of industrial employees have found defective hearing due to industrial noise among more than half of the workers tested. There are admittedly certain difficulties involved in insulating

Worker Adjustment and Technological Change 143

workers from noise when the problem is tackled only after the machinery and equipment have been installed. However, if attempts are made at the planning stage to estimate the probable noise risks and apply preventive measures, the likelihood of an acceptable solution would considerably increase.

In certain cases, hygienic risks can also increase as a consequence of changing techniques. More efficient production equipment can result in increased toxic contamination. Thus, in the quarrying industry, improvements in the efficiency of manufacturing methods have increased the density of silicate dust in the work atmosphere and have led to a rise in the number of silicosis victims amongst the workforce. And, in the production of textiles, a new technique in cotton harvesting, in conjunction with the introduction of more efficient equipment in cotton processing, as led to an increase in the number of cases of 'cotton dust lungs'.

New products and new materials have tended continuously to bring in their wake new vocational hazards. This is particularly true of the chemical industry where developments must be closely attended. For there has been a disturbing increase in the incidence of allergic illness in that sector. Moreover, the launching of new products has been accompanied by an increasing contamination of the physical surroundings by industrial gas and liquid wastes. This has grown from what was originally a problem of industrial hygiene to a consideration of overriding social importance.

Radioactive materials have been increasingly used in industrial processes, particularly in control and the measurement operations in conventional industries. The use of such materials should be regulated to prevent over-exposure of workers and worker protection in this sphere should be co-ordinated with general worker protection programmes.

Unresolved problems of physical adjustment for workers lead progressively to problems of physical health and express themselves in different forms of illness. Excessive loading of the skeletal-muscular systems has resulted in a high incidence of back illness among mining and manufacturing, building and construction, and forestry workers. This is a consequence of the vicious cycle between a weakened and vulnerable back and continuously excessive work loads. Changing technology has, as we have indicated, altered the physical load requirements of many work tasks. In the event, there has been a noticeable shift in the pattern of industrial illness. One trend has been the marked increase in throat, chest and shoulder ailments, caused by unvarying work positions and physiologically straining motions in work assignments. Another development is the increase in psychosomatic illness, reflecting the increased strain, and fatiguing nature, of job requirements. One fact that should not be forgotten is that unresolved problems of physical adjustment lead to a lowering of productivity; they are expressed in the form of an increased absence rate due to illness or a higher rate of turnover in personnel. Preventive measures are therefore justified not only by the need to improve the health and welfare of the individual but also the need for increased efficiency in industrial life. From both standpoints, it is imperative that the findings in the field of ergonomics, the bio-technological study of ways of designing the job and its requirements to 'fit' the physiology of the individual, be incorporated more systematically in job design.

PSYCHOLOGICAL ADJUSTMENT

A discussion of psychological adjustment to work could readily encompass the entire complex process of interaction of factors within and without the work environment. Such a discussion, however, would be too extensive for our purposes. We propose to confine ourselves in the present discussion to those psychological factors that are directly related to job requirements and the work situation, though other problems will crop up in later sections of this chapter.

The public discussion of stress in working life has increased apace with technological advance. This is undoubtedly a reflection of the increased psychological strain experienced by many in their working situation. In the discussion, however, it is often difficult to distinguish the experiences related to technological change as such from those linked to the more lasting conditions of the working situation. The fact that changes are continuously occurring is itself of importance in this context.

The way in which changes are planned and carried out is often instrumental in shaping the individual's understanding and perception of his position in the work situation. Psychological disturbances are often based on anxieties and fears about the consequences of changes for the individual. Doubts can be had about how the individual's job operation will be altered, how the individual's work-group will be changed or how his relationships with supervisors will develop in the future. Industrial doctors have almost invariably found that the stream of patients with psychosomatic illnesses increases with the internal reorganizations of the firm. The crucial preventive measures would appear to be advance warning and comprehensive information of impending changes together with continuous consultation during the period of implementation. In a later chapter, Chapter 14, we shall discuss in greater detail how such changes are and should be administered in the enterprise.

In the case of psychological adjustment to the more lasting conditions of the job, the chief source of concern appears to be work tasks in the middle stages of mechanization, i.e. job operations characterized by the repetition of a sequence of simple work tasks with the work pace dictated by the machinery. In this connection, it has been established that the requirement of a fast work pace in combination with unvarying and fatiguing physical loads can create a severe threat to mental health, particularly for individuals with low psychological tolerances. It is well worth noting that many of these job requirements are particularly incompatible with the psychological equipment of elderly workers. These workers are particularly vulnerable because of the progressive ageing of their central nervous systems.

The findings of a USA study indicate that there is a close association between the degree of mental health and the type of work task.[1] This study covered partly workers in the motor-car industry in the Detroit area and partly workers in other industries. The group of workers employed at repetitive and non-independent work, requiring little vocational training, had a significantly larger number of individuals with a low degree of mental health than the group of workers employed in skilled jobs. There were, to be sure, a number of deviant individual cases in both groups, but the overall results were fairly unambiguous. It was felt that the controlled nature of the experi-

[1] Kornhauser, A., *Mental Health of the Industrial Worker*. A Detroit Study, 1965.

K

ment had eliminated the possibility that the result might be due to another factor. One conclusion of the study was that repetitive work with mechanically controlled work pace was riskier from the psychological standpoint than work of a more highly skilled nature with a greater degree of autonomy.

The results of the USA study cannot be generalized to the extent that one can assert that *all* such job tasks are risky for *all* individuals. But they are sufficiently disturbing to warrant a closer look at the problem. They suggest the paramount importance of selecting a job design—at the methods study and planning stage—that allows scope for individual differences. For this is a pre-condition to a satisfactory psychological adjustment by the worker.

Job tasks in a highly automated process have quite different requirements and therefore pose quite different problems of psychological adjustment. In many cases, they require a continuous state of readiness to react and attentiveness over a sustained period of time, i.e. they entail considerable mental strain. The increased need for shift work associated with such processes raises its own problems of adjustment. Another disadvantage is the frequent combination of social isolation and extensive economic responsibility. At present the direction of the overall development is still a matter of speculation. Yet this if anything would appear to warrant more careful attention to safeguard against the adverse effects, in terms of poor occupational adjustment, of increased discrepancies between job requirements and the mental capacities of individual job holders. This constitutes a serious and standing challenge to present personnel administration programmes.

Significant changes are carried out in the administrative system and social organization of the firm simultaneously with, and relatively independently of, technological change. There appears to be some tendency for such changes to create an increasingly impersonal work environment; scant consideration is being given to certain fundamental human needs for social interaction. As a result employees tend to experience loneliness, uncertainty, anxiety and a diminished sense of identity. Such effects only accentuate the problems of achieving satisfactory psychological adjustment.

We have previously mentioned that factors outside the work

situation can be influential in the process which we have termed psychological adjustment. Without clarifying their rôle in greater detail, we should merely like to observe that the importance of such extra-vocational factors appears to be increasing with rationalization and structural change. The progressive 'urbanization' of the population, i.e. the migration of the working population and dependants to the larger cities, entails a movement away from accustomed environments, residence in isolated dormitory towns, and long and harrying travel to work. These factors are also relevant to a successful psychological adjustment of the worker.

JOB SATISFACTION

As we indicated in Chapter 2, in our discussion of job satisfaction, our starting point is the individual's conscious and expressed attitude to the job. The individual's attitude may vary along a continuum from enjoyment to outright dislike of the job. In the USA there have been many attempts to study the level of job satisfaction in American industry. The findings indicate that only a relatively small number of employees claim they find their work distasteful. In the LO Membership Survey, about 4 per cent of the members stated that they were not happy with their present job in response to a general question about their job attitude.

This figure can be interpreted as an expression of man's natural ability to adjust to and accept the conditions in which he finds himself. Enjoyment of the job is largely a function of the individual's expectations and demands. Many persons pitch their expectations and demands to a level which is consonant with their estimation of the realistic possibilities. This can involve a certain measure of resignation or a search for compensation in leisure pursuits. That women trade union members in the LO Survey appeared on the whole to be more content with their present jobs than men suggests that there are differences in the level of expectations of the two groups. Married women in particular tend to have lower expectations in so far as they view their vocational rôle as ancillary to their family rôle.

By the expedient of adjusting his expectations, the individual can adapt to and become quite satisfied with working and living conditions even of a very transient nature. But as a matter of empirical observation certain recurrent factors in the work environment appear to have an important bearing on job satisfaction. This emerges from a number of studies of job satisfaction of workers in industries at the middle stages of mechanization.

It is possible to distinguish two broad types of situation depending on the degree of mechanical regulation of the job. Thus, it has been found that workers employed in repetitive work where fairly low qualifications are required but the work pace is mechanically controlled only to a limited extent display a relatively high degree of job satisfaction. This is related to the fact that the work task does not take up the entire attention of the individual and/or allows a fair amount of social interaction. In firms with such a work environment, measures to improve supervision and the external job conditions can greatly affect job satisfaction. Wage increases can also have an important effect here.[1]

Another work situation that is not at all uncommon at the same level of mechanization is the assembly line where products move between stations without buffer stocks. Among workers in such an environment, it has been found that adjustment to the job is often unsatisfactory. High labour turnover and negative feelings about the job and the firm are symptomatic of such a situation. It appears likely that it is the type of work—the mechanically controlled work pace, the repetitive nature of the work, and little training required—that creates dissatisfaction. In one investigation it has been found that adjustment is not noticeably more satisfactory among workers with long periods of continuous service in such a working situation. The relatively high wages paid for work performed 'on the line' make it particularly difficult for such workers to move to other jobs, but they do not create satisfactory worker adjustment. A study of persons who quit after ten years of continuous service indicated that all had chosen jobs which were quite different in character from the one they left.[2]

[1] Gardell, B., *Arbetsanpassning och teknologisk miljö*. Handbok i Ergonomi 1966, p. 551, Uppsala 1966.
[2] Walker, C. R., and Guest, R. H., *Man on the Assembly Line*, Harvard University 1952.

In sum, at the middle levels of mechanization—where most Swedish firms find themselves today—there are several typical features of the work situation that appear to be detrimental to the job satisfaction of employees, notably where the pace of work is mechanically regulated and at the same time quite fast; where the job operation consists of the continuous repetition of work tasks and at the same time requires close surface attention on the part of the operator; where these conditions taken together or individually lead to isolation at the work place by precluding social exchange with work associates, i.e. where noise levels are excessive or there are long distances between work stations in the plant.

Our information about the job satisfaction of employees in firms at the highest levels of mechanization, i.e. in firms employing automated systems, is more limited. There appear to be certain factors associated with the working situation under automation that could create the preconditions for a more successful worker adjustment than in middle levels of mechanization. Monitoring work involves the observation of instruments and machines, the reading and registration of the indicated values. With such a work assignment the employee is not subjected to constant pressure from the production process. He has more say in regulating his pace of work and working rhythm—apart from the times when production disturbances arise. He has a fair degree of freedom to act according to his own judgment and on his own responsibility. From these standpoints the work tasks associated with automated systems would appear to offer greater opportunities for a higher degree of job satisfaction.

A third point of departure for a discussion of job satisfaction could be the assessment by employees of the importance of various factors in the job and the work environment. A large number of studies have centred on just this type of data. A survey of the literature in this field indicates that the factor rankings in one study of 11,000 workers are fairly representative of almost all other such studies.[1] The most important factors, according to the subjects of this study, were job security and the design and content of the work assignment. Of lesser importance were the welfare benefits and external job conditions.

[1] Hertzberger, F., *Job Attitudes*. Review of Research and Opinion. Pittsburgh, Pennsylvania, 1957.

In the LO Membership Survey, LO members were asked about their attitudes to certain aspects of their jobs. Twenty-five per cent indicated they were largely unable to determine their own pace of work and 18 per cent stated that they felt too constrained by the technical equipment or job instructions. About 25 per cent thought that their opportunities to have some say in the layout and design of their job operation were inadequate. Seventeen per cent said that they had a job where interruptions in the form of rest periods and shorter breaks were regularly required. The answers to these questions indicate that a rather large segment of the total membership of the unions affiliated to LO feel that they work under conditions involving some degree of coercion, and that they do not have much influence over their work situation.

A comparison between the answers on these points and the answers to the general question of enjoyment of work indicates that there are a considerably greater number of members who have severe problems with individual aspects of their jobs than those who indicate that in general they dislike their jobs.

JOB INVOLVEMENT

Contributions to the discussion on job satisfaction are increasingly recommending that the analysis be intensified in order to widen our understanding of this phenomenon. One response to this has been the recent concentration on the issue of job involvement, a phenomenon closely related to psychological adjustment. A high degree of job involvement implies, as we pointed out in Chapter 2, that the individual derives much satisfaction in performing the work effectively and that he identifies with the work organization and its goals. The opposite case is when the worker views the job largely as a means of earning an income, and otherwise finds it meaningless and uninteresting and, in extreme cases, distinctly repugnant.

The factor determining the degree of job involvement appears to be the extent to which the job and the work organization fulfil various needs of the individual worker. The following needs and their fulfilment are thought to affect crucially the individual's attitude to his job:

(a) the need for some degree of independence and control over the job; frustration leads to a feeling of powerlessness;

(b) the need for an interesting and meaningful job; frustration leads to feelings of meaninglessness;
(c) the need for social interaction and the opportunity to accept and identify with existing rules norms and patterns of behaviour; frustration leads to feelings of social isolation and lack of normative guidelines.

A feature common to all these needs is that they are relevant to and often instrumental in the development of the individual's self-confidence and self-esteem. In cases where such needs are left entirely or largely unfulfilled, the individual will display a low degree of job involvement. For the job is unable to give him a sense of his own worth.

At the middle-high levels of mechanization, job operations and the work organization are not auspicious foundations for the fulfilment of worker needs. This appears largely to be owing to the separation of the planning function from the actual performance of the job. Changing technology has entailed certain advantages for employees, such as better job placement, more correct assessment of work performance, and an increased degree of job security. But the repetitiveness and the simplified nature of the work tasks, the loss of awareness of the overall organization and production process more than offset these advantages. Increased trade union influence in the firm—through works councils, suggestion committees, joint application of work study and job evaluation measures—has not meant joint participation in the planning process for *every* individual. Employee feelings of powerlessness have not been eliminated.

The feeling that one's own job is meaningless and insignificant is a factor that reduces the need-fulfilment effects of the job. The experience tends to be a function largely of certain aspects of the firm and work organization. Thus it is more common in larger than in smaller firms, in individual assembly work than in stock work, with unskilled and semi-skilled work than with work that requires vocational skills and experience, with repetitive and monotonous work than with work that includes a change of pace and task and requires a variety of capacities and skills.

A third factor is the degree of isolation created by the job and work organization. Informal work groups are particularly important to the individual's social experience in the middle-high levels of mechanization; they often provide the experience of group membership with its communication and solidarity. Consequently, the disruption of such work groups by technical and organizational changes and subsequent difficulty in reviving new groups can be a critical point in the development.

In the LO Membership Survey there was a question relating to job involvement. The answers of 47 per cent of the membership indicated that they experienced some degree of involvement in their work, while 29 per cent indicated that their attitude was more one of indifference. The remaining 24 per cent stated that they had not thought much about the problem. Even a careful interpretation of these figures suggests that a large proportion of the membership works at a job without any particular feeling of involvement. For a rather large group, employment consists of exchanging work effort for a reasonable wage. A somewhat larger group places some value on their present job, at least in so far as that encompasses the overall work situation (work associates, trade union, supervisors, and other factors).

We found that the changes in the structure of work organizations and jobs associated with the level of mechanization that characterizes large sectors of Swedish industry today—and can be expected to continue to hold sway during the period of time this report is designed to cover—entail a decreasing degree of worker influence over the job design, an increase in work assignments that are less meaningful to operatives and less likely to develop worker personalities, and an increase in the extent of social isolation at the work place. True, trade union organizations are gaining increasing influence over various aspects of firms' activities. The benefits of this latter change, however, do not entirely filter down to all trade union members, though the situation would be significantly less favourable without the expanded trade union participation in enterprise affairs. In firms operating at a higher technological level there appear to be several features that hold out a hope for greater job involvement and more complete need-satisfaction in work, notably the increased interdependence of different groups of personnel and integration of job operations. As the focus of control shifts from the output of the individual to that of machinery, there is an increased degree of freedom for individuals in the work situation. In the event, there is a greater

Worker Adjustment and Technological Change

likelihood that the individual's need for self-esteem will be fulfilled. The extent to which this will occur in practice, however, will depend on the values that influence the shaping of the work organization and environment. This is a question that will be discussed in greater detail in a later chapter.

INDIVIDUAL CAPACITY AND THE PRECONDITIONS FOR ADJUSTMENT

In discussions of the need for job requirements to match human abilities the mistake of viewing the labour force as a number of individuals with the same or roughly similar qualities is easily made. In many different contexts, concern with the problems of worker adjustment finds expression in assessments of the 'normal effort' of an 'average worker'. The problem with such concepts, however, is that they are often mean values of an array of individual observations with an exceedingly wide variance.

Thus, many studies of industrial workers have shown that there are wide deviations from the mean for various aspects of worker capacity. This has been found to be true for physical factors such as height and strength as well as psychological factors, the degree and extent of illness limiting working capacity and the ageing of motor and sensory organs.

These studies also show that only a small fraction of the workforce is sufficiently physically and/or mentally capable to perform all work assignments in a firm. A significant proportion of employees—varying in different investigations from 15–50 per cent—have somewhat limited vocational capacities. The reasons for this observed variation lie partly with the use of varying definitions by the investigators; discrepancies were found in the definitions of job requirements and the concept of 'partially disabled' used in the different studies.[1]

According to the findings of medical diagnoses, there are four ailments that clearly predominate as causes of limited occupational capacity. These are defects of the skeletal system, defects of mental health, malfunctions of the heart and circulatory

---

[1] Bolinder, E., *En inventering av hälsotillstånd och arbetsmässighet inom en industris manliga arbetskraft*, Socialmedicinsk Tidskrift 39:7/62:276; and Heijbel, C. A., *Medelålders och äldre arbetskrafts anpassning till högmekaniserat arbete*, SNS-skriften 'För gammal?', 1963; *see also* Samordnad rehabilitering, del III, SOU 1965:57.

system and stomach and intestinal disorders. In one industrial medical study it was found that 12 per cent of the workforce could be classified from the medical viewpoint as having a limited working capacity. Another study of the members of an unemployment insurance group of comparable size and age and sex found practically the same proportion.[1] These findings underline the need in industrial life to reduce job requirements to below the level of the 'average worker'. Otherwise, employers must recognize that their recruitment base will be considerably narrowed.

In the same study, an attempt was made to record the performance of industrial workers designated as having a limited capacity for work. More than half of this group performed their jobs equally effectively as those who had no comparable occupational disability. The output and performance of another 20 per cent were lower by less than one-seventh. One can perhaps conclude from this that those workers having a limited capacity for work will not suffer from a lack of job opportunities. There are several factors, however, that militate against this conclusion. First, is the requirement commonly laid down in modern industry that workers should be able to change jobs upon short notice. Such change can entail a decrease in job adjustment for a certain proportion of those workers with limited capacities. Such an outcome can be avoided only if firms adopt a personnel policy that as a matter of routine assesses the individual's qualifications and capacities to match the requirements of the new job. The LO Membership Survey's findings of a clear difference in adjustment improvement between those who changed employers and those who were internally transferred indicate a need for more effective personnel evaluations.

The greater uniformity of work assignments and the increasing tendency to base job requirements on the capacities of the 'average worker' have been accompanied by a tendency to disregard the task of placing individual workers according to their particular limitations. This can lead to job changing which is voluntary in appearance but which in reality disguises a coercion stemming from adjustment difficulties.

All investigations have found that working capacity decreases

[1] Lundgren, A., *En studie över de villkorligt arbetsföra och deras problem vid en norrlandsk storindustri*. Festskrift tillägnad Carl Kempe 80 år, 1884–1964.

with increasing age. Moreover, there is an accompanying increase in the risk of ill-health. In Sweden, the mean age of industrial workers is rather high, and in the near future there will be an upwards shift in the age distribution of the working population. The problem of adjusting job requirements to the middle-aged and elderly worker is therefore taking on a note of urgency. Firms planning to use elderly workers alongside younger workers will find it necessary to increase their application of ergonomic methods and eliminate unnecessary task loads in work assignments. The application of ergonomic research findings should be complemented by a systematic assessment of the capacities of individual workers. The results can be used to increase the information base for personnel policy decisions and make possible more effective methods of transferring employees within the firm.

Such programmes would also help to reduce absenteeism. The decision of an employee to visit his doctor and obtain sick leave is not always prompted primarily by a change in his state of health. His ailment may have remained constant while the job requirements have changed. A chronic ailment that has not hindered the individual in his performance of a given job can make it difficult for him to adjust to a new job or even to changes in the old job if such changes involve increased requirements. A damaged back can function without causing difficulty where the work assignment does not strain it beyond a given point. In another job where the loads are so high that this point is exceeded, the same back will prevent the individual from performing the job. A natural tendency to insomnia or ulcers under sustained tension may never create difficulties to individuals working the day shift. Put the same persons on a night shift and these tendencies may develop into symptoms leading to an inability to perform the job.

This point can be illustrated by the results of a study carried out by the public insurance companies in larger Swedish cities.[1] It was found that among workers as a whole long-term illness increased in frequency with rising age. But this tendency was noticeably stronger in the case of certain groups of insured persons who were subjected to constantly changing job re-

[1] *Långtidssjuka i våra storstäder* 1962. En socialmedicinsk tidskrifts skriftserie nr 32, 1965.

quirements because they worked in industries undergoing rapid technological change.

The follow-up studies of employees made redundant by plant shutdowns also found that older workers and others with limited working capacities not only experienced the greatest difficulty in finding new employment, but even when they obtained a new job they had greater difficulties in adjusting to the new work assignment.

In this chapter, we have sought to present the problem of manpower adjustment in two lights. First, we have attempted to show that adjustment is a multifaceted concept that can be viewed from many different angles. Secondly, we have emphasized the need to take greater account of the fact that workers have widely differing abilities and capacities. In the discussion, we have viewed adjustment largely as a question of the ability of the job to fulfil certain needs of the individual.

If we regard the work assignment as a given factor as far as its requirements and content are concerned, the employee's needs can be summed in the catch-phrase 'the right man for the right job'. We have found that this need has not been fulfilled to a sufficient extent, particularly in the case of workers who have limited working capacities because of age or ailments. It is a matter of some urgency that measures be taken to improve their situation.

Obviously, however, work assignments cannot rightfully be regarded as fixed, immutable elements in the working situation. They continually change in content, requirements and output in response to changing technology and changing organizational arrangements. We therefore examined the needs that had to be fulfilled to allow satisfactory worker adjustment in order to provide a more solid foundation for the conclusions and recommendations presented at the end of this report.

There has been some experimentation with changes in organizational arrangements designed to improve worker adjustment. The modern study of ergonomics has great potentialities as a spur to improve physical adjustment. Moreover, there have been several notable attempts to devise methods to improve psychological adjustment. A most promising avenue in Sweden is the new system of works councils. In Norway, experiments have been started with self-regulating work groups. LKAB has introduced in its new mines new forms of work supervision. Another example is offered by the experiment with job enlargement in the USA. The so-called general rating—a category of worker who performs services on deck as well as in the engine rooms—in highly automated ships in the Swedish merchant navy can also be mentioned in this context.

Neither the design of the job nor the layout of the work environment are uniquely determined by technological and economic factors. There is a certain range of possible organizational arrangements and job designs that take into account the needs of the individual. As we pointed out in Chapter 2, we do not think that there is an inevitable conflict between the needs of better worker adjustment and the dictates of increased productivity in industry. We suggest that measures designed to improve worker adjustment will also frequently entail measurable gains in productivity, by decreasing absenteeism and labour turnover, the symptoms of poor adjustment. Such measures can have a considerable cost-reducing effect. There are certain firms, however, that are tending to move in the opposite direction by breaking down and simplifying job operations into limited work tasks partly to lower the costs of training. We consider it a matter of the utmost urgency that research findings and experiments be incorporated more frequently in the design of work arrangements in order to ensure that they better fulfil the *psychological* needs of the individual worker.

CHAPTER 10

Hours of Work

What is the nature of the relationship between technological change and changes in the length and disposition of hours of work? What are the implications of this relationship in terms of the opportunities of the individual to adjust to his overall environment, to work, to family life, to his housing, to his relationships with other persons, to the consumer services of different kinds in the community and to leisure?

The relationship between changes in the hours of work and technological advance can be discussed as a problem of how a balance is struck between work and leisure. The huge increases in productivity that have been realized make it both possible and desirable to take out some part of the increased product of industry in the form of increased leisure. Over the post-war period, about 15 per cent of the entire increase in productivity has been taken by workers working shorter hours.[1] This trend can be viewed as the value placed on leisure by employed workers in relation to an increase in their real consumption opportunities as well as those of the unoccupied population. The average weekly hours of work per full-time employee decreased by about 10 per cent during the period. But the total average weekly hours of work per family remained fairly constant because of the increased participation rates of married women.

Only 'individual bargaining' over hours of work, i.e. negotiations between each individual worker and employer, would allow greater consideration to be given to individual preferences for leisure than is given by current institutional arrangements. Legislation and collective agreements create the necessary general and non-selective rules while leaving some scope for the adjustment of leisure and hours of work to the manning needs

[1] *Individen och arbetstiden.* SNS, Stockholm 1965.

Hours of Work

of production processes in different plants as well as the needs and preferences of individual workers. For the legislative provisions and collective contract rules on hours of work, holidays, shift-work and overtime are often applied locally by agreement between the parties.

CHANGES IN HOURS OF WORK AND CURRENT CONDITIONS

For most of the working population, the average weekly hours of work per individual employee have progressively declined during the post-war period. In 1952–3 the paid annual holiday was increased from two to three weeks. During the period 1958–60, the standard work week was reduced from 48 to 45 hours. In 1964–5, annual holidays were increased again to four weeks and the standard work week will be reduced by another $2\frac{1}{2}$ hours during the period 1967–9. On the whole, these reductions mean that average weekly hours of work have fallen by $7\frac{1}{2}$ hours over a period of less than two decades.

The increase in annual holidays has spread itself fairly evenly throughout the labour force, while the fall in the standard work week has tended to have a greater effect amongst those working a relatively longer work week. Nevertheless, both changes have helped to even out the differences between hours of work in different jobs. This effect was perhaps more obvious in the case of the reduction of the standard work week. For example, the fall of the standard work week in 1958–60 reduced the work week of more than 90 per cent of the blue-collar workers in Swedish industry by three hours, while only 30 per cent of the white-collar workers experienced some cut in working hours.

Owing to the limitations of the available data, we can only give a rough idea of the proportions of the workforce currently putting in different hours of work per week.

In Table 18 the occupied population in 1965 is broken down into groups of individuals working different average working weeks. The data was obtained from the combined results of four labour force surveys conducted during the year (February, May, August and November).

According to these findings, more than half of all employees and more than two-thirds of all male employees have an average working week of forty-five hours or more. These

TABLE 18

Proportions of the Occupied Population Working Different Average Weekly Hours of Work

Hours/week	All	Percentages Married women	Single women	Men	Employed men and women
Less than 34*	18	52	19	8	18
35–44	27	26	38	24	28
45 and above	55	21	43	68	54
Total	100	100	100	100	100

Source: Labour Force Surveys, 1965, National Labour Market Board.

* It should be observed that 1–2 per cent of the labour force were involuntarily working a shorter average work week. This proportion was largely the same for men, married and single women and which corresponds to about one-tenth to one-twentieth of those working less than 34 hours per week.

TABLE 19

Proportions of LO Membership Working Different Hours of Work per Week

Hours/Week	All	Percentages Men	Women
Less than 37·9	9	1	36
38–44·9	14	12	21
45	70	79	38
More than 45·1	7	7	5
Total	100	100	100

Source: LO Membership Survey, 1966.

figures may be compared with the results of the recent LO Membership Survey (Table 19), although it should be observed that the data in the LO Survey covers only regular working hours which are not fully comparable with the statistics of actual hours worked in the labour force surveys. Nevertheless, it does appear that a considerably larger segment of the membership of trade unions affiliated to LO, particularly men, put in a longer working week than other groups in the labour force.

It would be erroneous to look upon these variations in average weekly hours of work as a reflection of the range of possible choices open to the individual worker. Admittedly, the figures suggest that conditions of production allow some flexibility in the length of the working week for the individual worker, but this degree of choice is restricted to those workers in regions with a fairly highly differentiated industrial and occupational structure. There is some variation from workplace to workplace and job to job, notably in the clerical sector, but the chief differences are those between manual and salaried employees.

Overtime
The industrial statistics on hours of work present no evidence that on the whole overtime work has increased since the start of the 1950s. However, there are considerable differences among industries in the amount of overtime worked. Thus, in 1965, overtime work varied between 1–8 per cent of total hours of work respectively in the textile industry and the paper and pulp industry. Overtime work tends to be greater in the continuous process industries. Seasonal fluctuations are related to conditions of production, changes in fashion, seasonal swings in sales, etc. Industries with relatively wider seasonal variation tend to rely on high overtime to meet their manpower needs in the peak season. There are exceptions to this, notably in industries that are located in areas with access to a reserve of temporary employees during spring and autumn seasons, though these do not preclude a slight seasonal swing in overtime work.

Cyclical fluctuations too can affect the amount of overtime worked before they begin to result in additional recruiting or lay-offs. Also, structural change, such as a long-term decline in employment in an industry, can manifest itself in a low volume of overtime work. The textile industry currently presents a case in point.

LEISURE—HOURS OF WORK

The disposition of working hours is as important to the occupational and overall adjustment of individual workers as the length of the work week.

As the material standard of living has increased, leisure has acquired a new meaning independently of its function as a period of respite and relaxation from working life. One expression of this changed attitude is the rapidly rising demand for leisure-time consumer services of various types. With the increased annual holiday and the shift to the five-day week for a great many workers in the early 1960s, the increased length and concentration of periods of leisure have tended to aggravate the conflict between the demand of workers in the service sector for reasonable hours of work and the wants and preferences of consumers. But this tendency has been partly offset by other factors. Thus, some services are now 'offered' under conditions resembling the 'production' of goods, notably tinned and pre-packaged foods. Other services, moreover, have acquired a self-service element, e.g. laundromats, self-service stores and restaurants and transport. Further, with the advent of the four-week annual holiday, there have been conscious attempts to 'stagger' leave amongst larger sectors of the workforce. The rationale for such attempts has been twofold: to meet the manning needs of modern production techniques; and to attempt to utilize the capacity of the consumer service sector more efficiently by evening out the distribution of demand for services.

Holidays
Before the widespread introduction of four-week annual holidays, the manning problems of continuous process industries were resolved by dividing the workforce into groups taking their annual holidays in turn, a practice which had long prevailed in the communications sector. The advent of the three- and four-week annual holiday has spurred on attempts to develop new methods of approach. In one pulp mill the question of the distribution of hours of work during the whole year has been looked at afresh, and in many cases attempts have been made to distribute holidays over more than one period and during more than one season in order to take into consideration the intended uses of the holidays, e.g. travel abroad, holidays in the mountains, stays at the summer cottage, etc.

National legislation as well as collective agreement provisions on holidays give the employer the prerogative of determining the disposition of holidays, but employees have the right to obtain their four weeks of annual holiday in succession. In the event, there has been some give and take between the two parties on both issues, and plans have been evolved that take into account local conditions, the manning needs of the production process and employee preferences.

In expanding capital-intensive industries a slight increase in leisure in relation to overall hours of work results in a considerable increase in labour costs. It has proved profitable to work out a compromise between the manning needs of a firm and the needs and preferences of the workforce by planning organizational arrangements and investments with this problem specifically in mind.

Holiday Work
The production and organizational problems created by the public holidays too have stimulated management in such industries to change hours of work and experiment with increased leisure during periods other than holidays. Thus, in one Swedish pulp mill, to allow the extension of continuous production over public holiday periods, the workforce has been increased by a fifth shift and hours of work and leisure have been distributed in intermittently shorter and longer intervals throughout the whole year.

In several sectors other than manufacturing industry, particularly in communications, and for many individuals in all industries, holiday work has long been an accepted practice. In the shipping and railway industries holiday work is an integral production requirement. Hotels, restaurants and other services operate under the same conditions. But there are some cases where changing technology appears to be decreasing the incidence of holiday work, notably in the case of the automation of the telephone system.

The Five-day Week
With the fall in the standard work week to 45 hours in the 1958–60 period, the number of working days was often reduced to five.

The LO Membership Survey gives a rough idea of the extent to which the five-day week has spread throughout the labour force. Broadly, about two-thirds of the membership of unions affiilated to LO now labour under this condition of service. The incidence of the five-day week is highest in the building sector —100 per cent—and the printing and graphical industry, and lowest in the post office. State hospital system and railways, 10–15 per cent. The five-day week is enjoyed by 70–80 per cent of the membership of trade unions in the goods-producing sectors but only by 20–40 per cent of trade union members in the service sector. Within many service sub-sectors and in the paper and pulp industry, where the five-day week is not an established practice, time off is generally given during the weekdays.

Those workers for whom the work week consists of five days, labour as a rule nine hours per day, exclusive of mealtime breaks and travel to and from the job. For employees, however, the relevant time period is usually the time of absence from the home, i.e. hours of work, including travel and breaks during day. The difference between these measurements of 'gross' and 'net' hours of work varies greatly from urban to less populated areas. In many cases, lunch and mealtime breaks were reduced in conjunction with the introduction of the nine-hour day.

Shift Work
While examples of shift work systems can be found in manufacturing industry, such systems have been long the rule and are more extensively used in communications. The trend of shift work has an upward slope: the practice is increasing in those industries in which such systems have already been introduced and is spreading to new sectors, notably computer work.

The increased application of shift work systems has been motivated largely by the high, or rising, amount of capital invested per worker. The reduction in hours of work has in many cases provided the necessary incentive for reorganizations to be undertaken which had long been warranted.

Unfortunately the opportunities to illustrate these changes are few, due to the limitations of the available data. The existing figures cover only the number of industrial workers with a 42-hour work week, which corresponds fairly well to the number of workers employed in continuous-process industries but does not cover workers in intermittent three-shift or two-shift systems which have 45-hour work weeks. During the period 1953–65, the fraction of workers in continuous three-

Hours of Work 165

shift systems increased from 2·5–7 per cent. Much of this increase stemmed from growth in the continuous-flow process industries which have long had a relatively high proportion of their workforce in shift work.

The increase in shift work in industry as a whole was attributable mainly to increase in paper and pulp and iron and steel. The data support the findings of the LO Membership Survey that only a small segment of the workforce is engaged in continuous production systems.

TABLE 20

The Proportions of LO Membership in Different Systems of Shift Work

Systems of Shift Work	LO Membership in %
Day-shift	78
Two-shift	8
Continuous three-shift	3
Intermittent three-shift	2
Other systems	10
Total	100

Source: LO Membership Survey, Appendix 1, *Trade Unions and Technological Change* (1967).

Table 20 indicates that continuous shift systems are relatively rare but that this category, together with the categories of workers working under shift systems other than day shifts, are so large that the problems stemming from this disposition of working hours warrant greater attention. Two-shift systems have spread to most sectors but are highly concentrated in printing and graphical trades, textiles, mining and metal-working, and hotel and restaurant work. Three-shift work is concentrated largely in power plants, paper mills, chemical plants and iron and steel-works but can be encountered in most service sectors and particularly in the railway industry, real estate and medical and health services. The category 'Other systems' includes primarily certain service sectors, such as the railways, post office, transport, and medical and health services.

The trends to date indicate that the length and disposition of hours of work are largely organizational questions, to be decided within the broad framework of legislation and collective agreements. Changing technology can provide an incentive for a more systematic reorganization of hours of work in a firm or industry. Interestingly, however, the introduction of automation in an enterprise does not necessarily mean that a greater number of employees will change over to continuous shift work. The shift work effects of automation appear to be limited largely to temporary intervals when, say, new machinery is being 'broken in'. There appears to be a closer association between increased capital-intensity and a changeover to shift work. Often a scarcity of labour has delayed or prevented a changeover to shift work even where such a step has been warranted from a cost standpoint, notably in the case of an increased demand for output during a business boom.

The strongest association of all, however, is that between hours of work and the overall production conditions of the industry (which are affected by changing technology only to a small extent) such as those prevailing in communications, medical and health services and other services. This does not preclude the possibility that changes in organizational arrangements can create better conditions of employment for individuals, though the supply of labour would appear to be of crucial importance in this context.

OCCUPATIONAL ADJUSTMENT AND HOURS OF WORK

The opportunities of individuals to select jobs because of their hours of work are closely related to their opportunities to choose occupations, i.e. professional, clerical, service or industrial.

But the range of choices confronting the individual job seeker cannot be described in general terms since this range is often a function of the relationship between the supply of and demand for labour in the local labour market. It is the overall scarcity or surplus in the local labour market in the short or long term that shapes the enterprise demand for and workers' supply of hours of work. Where there is a scarcity of labour, favourable hours of work are viewed as an instrument to attract workers to a given type of work. This has undoubtedly been true in the case of many married women, who have returned to the labour market largely because they have been able to obtain part-time work. For obvious reasons, the disposition of working hours has always been particularly important for women.

Differences in hours of work are also of importance in the vocational choices of youths, who tend to value leisure consumption more highly than the older generation. Thus it appears that the policy of greater equality of hours of work cannot be viewed in isolation from the question of greater freedom of choice for working individuals.

For individuals who are gainfully occupied, there are certain constraints operating on the choice between work and leisure. Hours of work are usually fixed and part-time work is only infrequently available as an alternative. The collective agreement gives the employer a right to require a certain amount of *overtime work* and often the circumstances do not allow the employee to refuse. In many contexts, notably on the assembly line where production is dependent on an entire shift working overtime simultaneously, problems arising from overtime work have been tackled in local negotiations on collective overtime work. This practice can spread to sectors where, as in the metal-working industry, industry-wide negotiations have set out a framework agreement with higher wage earnings for overtime applicable during a given time period according to local negotiations. This can help to reduce existing inequities in the distribution of overtime work between different employees, but it also has the effect of reducing the individual's degree of freedom.

With shorter hours of work there are greater opportunities for individuals to take on second jobs, or to 'moonlight'. Again we must acknowledge that our information of this labour market phenomenon is extremely limited. In general, it appears to be true that the individual attempts to use a second job to compensate for shortcomings in his permanent position, either in terms of job satisfaction, social contact and exchange or wage earnings. Second jobs in such cases can be beneficial for the individual's job satisfaction. Clearly, they can also have other less beneficial and possibly detrimental effects, such as the deterioration of the individual's physical and mental health over a protracted period, due to pace of work, length of working hours, inadequate rest during free time, etc.

Any number of working hours can be too many depending on

the strain they impose in relation to the individual's physical or psychological equipment. Where worker expectations and ambitions exceed the limits of what the particular job can offer, the individual can find the job distasteful and the desire for the working day to end can become overwhelming. An assessment of the length of hours of work must be based on many different considerations, viz. the individual's physical and psychological condition, social circumstances and working conditions. For certain types of work, hours of work can be limited by such factors as the physical load of work tasks and other job characteristics such as noise, heat, cold, toxic risks, traffic, safety, etc.

Part-time work has increased in recent years as employers faced by the pressure of labour scarcity have attempted to bring married women back to the labour market, who often will not return under other than part-time conditions. This is one form of adjustment of hours of work to social and family needs. There are many different forms of part-time work, a shorter work day and hourly employment—which predominate, but also a shorter work week, duty system and seasonal work. A form that has become increasingly popular is 'partnership work', where two employees share a full-time position. Workers are offered part-time work in fields such as music, transport, post office, sales, municipal and real estate work. According to the estimates of trade unions, there is a clear need to increase the range of choice as far as full- and part-time work is concerned, in trade, hotel and restaurant work, hospital work, post office, textile and ready-made clothing, manufacturing, metal-working and wood and wood products. In trade unions where the proportion of part-time workers is relatively high, notably in real estate, insurance and the unions of entertainment firm staffs, there is no apparent need for further part-time work. Within most industries and occupations, the need for part-time work varies with the local area. Some demand for part-time work is 'concealed'. This could be unearthed and satisfied if managerial attitudes with respect to part-time work and division of hours of work were to be changed.

Attitudes to the question of a divided or undivided *annual holiday* appear to have become more flexible on both sides with the advent of the four-week annual holiday. The problems that arise for the family where both parents work and the children attend school appear to be soluble in local negotiations between unions and employers, particularly where vacation preferences are simultaneously taken into account.

Certain firms have subsidized holidays during the spring and autumn. It is also conceivable that where new annual holidays require a redistribution of hours of work as a whole, leisure time can be given in larger regular periods. Moreover, regular overtime work, such as that now allocated under local collective bargains in the metal-working industry, could conceivably be compensated by leisure during other parts of the year instead of extra pay.

Holiday work has been considered a problem from the standpoint of overall adjustment. Experiences in this context are varied, however, and are related more to the general problem of the working week. Production during the public holidays constitutes a special problem, but here, too, the experiences vary depending on whether the number of shifts has increased allowing a radical reorganization of annual hours of work or organizational arrangements.

In the majority of cases, *shift work* too is a problem from the standpoint of overall adjustment. The family must adjust at least in part to the rhythm of the shift. Residential conditions are often decisive factors in the attempts of the individual shift worker and his family to make an adjustment. Also, relations to other persons and families can be disrupted by a reorganization that requires of workers a daily rhythm that differs from the common pattern of the family, the circle of friends, and of the opening hours of various consumer services. We have still insufficiently explored the question of how social and residential conditions in large cities and rural areas can be adjusted to create an overall environment that corresponds to the rhythm in shift work or compensates for the inequalities in hours of work.

Shift work and hours of work other than the typical day shift also have certain medical implications.[1] The predominant problem here is physiological adjustment. When the daily rhythm of society and that of the shift worker are out of line, the worker often suffers from a lack of sleep owing to the noise of the family's necessary daytime activity, traffic, children playing,

[1] Bolinder, E., *Individen och den industriella miljön*, Stockholm 1966.

etc. Loss of appetite and indigestion can also result from the difficulties of dealing with the problems of meals and generally coping with the daily rhythm of shift work.

In any assessment of shift work the length of the shift cycle is an important factor. It is thought in Sweden that a well balanced alternation of shift and days off constitutes the best solution to avoid a clash between the rhythm of society and that of the shift worker. Our experience with permanent shifts is rather limited in Sweden. The practice occurs largely in newspaper production, textile manufacturing, night work in hospitals and amongst night watchmen. It is imperative that firms study more regularly workers on permanent night shift work for signs of adverse effects. Detrimental effects among the younger family breadwinners should particularly be attended to by increased social and housing measures. Within the service sector, where shift systems are characterized by complicated time-tables, there is a need for systematic study of the disposition of hours of work and a more concentrated individual and trade union effort to ensure that consideration is given to social conditions and the physical and psychological needs of the individual.

Many problems are limited to particular families or persons. It would be worth while to take stock of these problems and attempt to assess locally the costs and benefits associated with practices such as continuous production, holiday work, irregular length of work intervals, taking into account the costs that are not readily measurable in terms of money.

In general, and during reorganizations of working arrangements in particular, health checks should be made regularly and periodically as a matter of course. The shift work system must be so planned as to allow the best possible adjustment for the individual vocationally and socially. Public measures such as child care and supervision centres, shops and local government services can be more easily adapted to immediate needs in smaller communities, but in larger cities there seems to be a serious need for trade unions to clarify the problems and secure appropriate measures through firms and local government authorities.

CHAPTER 11

Systems of Wage Payment

Systematic job evaluation, merit rating and various methods of wage payment are important managerial administrative aids. Employers have always sought to operate systems of payment that stimulate employees to greater and more effective work effort. The selection of particular systems depends largely on employer views of the average worker, his values, structure of needs, attitude to work and reaction patterns. One finds that commonly managers assume that the most important motivating force in the employee's make-up is the desire to maximize earnings. Given this basic assumption, it follows that wage earnings should in so far as possible vary in accordance with output.

Moreover, since work assignments in an enterprise can vary greatly, it has been generally accepted that different jobs can command different rates of pay irrespective of the performance of the individual job holder. As a rule, a more 'difficult' job involves a higher rate of pay than an 'easier' job. Such a pay structure can provide an incentive to employees to take on jobs with increased responsibility and more difficult content. The abilities and skills of different employees can also vary considerably, and from the employer's viewpoint such differences can justify differences in pay. For the firm must be able to attract and retain individuals with particularly valuable qualifications.

Since employees, through their trade unions, participate directly in the determination of rates for different jobs, the choice of the system of payment is also affected by the values and attitudes of employee representatives. The early approach of the trade union movement to attempts to differentiate pay was to insist that age and length of continuous service should be the key criteria for wage differences. Subsequently—when the wages policy of solidarity was first introduced—the objective was altered to one of narrowing and levelling out wage differences between workers in different industries. That aim is still prominent amongst the overall objectives of current trade union wages policy, but it has been refined somewhat to take into account the fact that the wage structure must also reflect such factors as differences in the nature and degree of difficulty of the job.

To a large extent, the Swedish trade union movement too appears to have accepted the idea that financial incentives are key motivational factors. The membership display a preference for various types of wage incentive systems. This attitude has been shaped by the employers' wage policy ambitions, and the experience that piece rates generally result in higher wage earnings than hourly rates. It could be added that piecework systems are more prone to wage drift. Yet workers also want a system of payment that provides a relatively stable and predictable level of earnings and is sufficiently easy to understand to allow operators to have some measure of control over its application. A certain degree of security is of paramount importance to the employee.

Although the Swedish trade union movement's wages policy of solidarity implicitly accepts the idea of job evaluation, the reaction to various forms of systematic job evaluation within many trade union circles has been less accommodating. Trade unionists also appear to have been unreceptive to merit rating, though the practical experience in this sphere has been much more limited.

WORK STUDY AND WORK MEASUREMENT

Once it is accepted that variations in employee performance, job content or relevant individual qualifications constitute appropriate bases for differentiating pay, it becomes necessary to devise effective methods to analyse and measure such factors.

Management has long invested considerable resources in methods research and with good result. The procedures and techniques of work study have greatly progressed from the time

Systems of Wage Payment

when the foundations of the field were laid down by Taylor and Gilbreth almost ninety years ago.

Today, work study consists of the systematic examination of the interplay between the worker and the task he is expected to perform, the equipment, materials, process, machine speeds and feeds, working conditions, etc., with the objective of defining clearly and evaluating all the factors in this interplay that are relevant to, and significantly affect, output. The object of the exercise is to determine how better results can be achieved. The original narrow focus on performance of the job has been widened to encompass the human operator and environmental factors, such as job security and the worker's physical adjustment in the wider sense. New fields have emerged such as ergonomics and occupational physiology which focus on the physical aspects of the job, i.e. the physical relationship between the man and the job and the physiological requirements of different jobs.

Work study comprises a number of different procedures and techniques. The two most important techniques are methods study and work measurement. Methods study procedures typically consist of a sequence of steps leading to the development and definition of the best method of performing a given task in the existing circumstances. First, the relevant data are selected and assembled for study. Then, the existing method is recorded and analysed using such methods as interviews, direct observations, process charts, films, chronocyclographs, etc. Finally, a new and improved method is devised by eliminating, combining, changing or simplifying operations and sequences, and defined using the same methods as in the recording stage: process charts, films, etc.

Work measurement procedures, in contrast, attempt to measure the human effort involved in the job. Since the measurement of energy expenditure requires bulky and cumbersome equipment, a variety of procedures have been developed to measure work effort in terms of time. The work task is broken down into its constituent elements and 'normal' times are established for all basic movements involved in the task by studying the times of a large sample of operators. Where such a detailed time study procedure cannot be justified economically, other methods have been devised using *synthetic time standards*, based on time study values for different work elements which frequently recur within a given plant, or *elemental time data* obtained from research on elemental movements of fingers, hands, arms, etc., which are basic to many industrial tasks. Work measurement procedures are often used to provide a basis for cost calculations, planning, and piecework systems.

Elemental time data systems are a particularly important ingredient of work study techniques. In Sweden, the Methods-time Measurement System (MTM) is a clear favourite. The use of this system, however, has long been confined in the main to larger Swedish firms and as an aid to methods study. In recent years, however, MTM has begun to enjoy wider currency as a basis for setting piece rates. Today there is much development work in Sweden attempting to simplify and reduce the costs of the MTM technique. It is extremely likely that this research will result in the discovery of new and expanded uses for the MTM system.

Currently, work study is used mainly in production engineering in industry, though it is gradually finding increasing application in the administrative sector. According to a study carried out by the Swedish Employers Confederation[1] work study systems are now used in all large industrial firms in the country and have also been installed in the majority of firms with less than fifty employees. According to the same study, 60–75 per cent of the volume of wage incentive systems operated in industrial firms with at least fifty employees are based on work study techniques. This means, on the other hand, that 25–40 per cent of payment-by-results schemes are still based on fairly crude estimates founded on earlier experiences or on calculations which are made after the job has been finished.

The quality of work study probably varies greatly from firm to firm. The SAF study shows that the number of work study personnel per worker is significantly higher in the larger firms than in the smaller. As far as the use of work study as a basis for payment-by-results systems is concerned, differences in the size of the firms are less important. Direct work measurement, a relatively primitive and costly method to provide a basis for

---

[1] Eskilsson, S., *Löneutveckling under kontroll.* Svenska arbetsgivareföreningen, Stockholm 1966.

wage incentive systems, is the favourite of small firms and popular among many of the larger firms. But elemental time data systems and other standardized time data systems are also used to an appreciable extent.

The Swedish Employers Confederation, SAF, and its members, are actively developing and diffusing the techniques of work study. The bulk of all basic training in work study, as indeed in all production engineering techniques in Sweden, is carried out by the Industrial Rationalization Institute (RATI) which is administered by SAF. SAF, as well as its member employers' associations, have also employed experts in work study techniques to provide advisory and other services to affiliated firms. During the Autumn of 1965, SAF established a technical division to encourage research and development and to promote work study techniques. This division incorporated sections of the Work Study Institute of the Metal Workers Employers Association. For Swedish employers, work study is essentially a potential key to greater managerial control over wage earnings in the workshop.

Swedish trade unions also carry out a fairly extensive programme of training in work study procedures. LO, as well as certain national industrial unions, have acquired groups of staff with expertise in this field. Recently, LO has established a work study co-ordinating body with its member unions.

From its early highly controversial origins, work study has become gradually accepted as a sphere of industrial relations to be jointly administered by employer and trade union. Through different collective agreements, the trade unions have secured a fair degree of influence over the way in which work study techniques are applied. In so far as such systems are used to provide a basis for wage earnings, their installation and operation are regulated by collective agreement.

With the installation of MTM systems in industry, special rules have been negotiated at the national level and inserted in the collective agreements governing the application of this system and its relationship to systems of wage payment.

The rules in the national agreement have been complemented by domestically negotiated agreements, i.e. plant-wide MTM agreements, which allow firms to change over during the term of the contract to payment by results under an MTM system or some type of standard time rates system approved by the employer and the union branch or club.

In addition to money factors, the collectively negotiated rules also cover: the extent of the MTM reorganization in the plant, the classification of workers in wage categories, excessively controlled work, the piecework compensation rate for jobs having no piecework target, pay during the training period, the breaking-in period and production stoppages, the job layout, distribution increments (lost-time allowance), the training of and information for worker representatives, installation and operation plans, guidelines for the transition period, etc.

Yet despite the wide coverage of these agreements, there is no real equality between trade union and employer in negotiations over the issue of work study. For the employer is free to select whatever system he chooses for production planning and methods study. And this gives him an advantage in terms of superior knowledge of job content and processes in domestic negotiations over wage earnings.

PIECEWORK AND TIMEWORK SYSTEMS

The pay a worker is to receive for his work effort can be computed according to a variety of different methods. A simple—perhaps the simplest—method is to link the wage to a unit of time, such as an hour, week, month or year. Such a system is termed a time rate system. As has earlier been mentioned, the feeling has long and widely prevailed that a worker can be stimulated to greater and more effective efforts to the extent that such efforts result in higher pay. This would suggest to some that wage earnings should not be related to the amount of time the worker spends on the job but rather should vary with his output. This type of system of wage payment, commonly termed a wage incentive system, enjoys wide use throughout Swedish industry. Such a system can be cast in many different forms. In so far as it is designed to create an immediate mathematical relationship between the size of the wage earning and the degree of effort or quantity of output of the worker, the system is referred to as piecework or payment by results. Piecework systems can be based entirely on the individual's output (pure piecework) or contain a greater or lesser fixed element (mixed piecework). Piecework prices can vary in the same proportion as output, proportionally more or less than output (differential piecework systems) or in proportions which differ at different levels of output. Finally, piecework systems can apply to the measurement of work done by an individual or by a group or working unit. Figure 3 shows graphically how workers' earnings vary with output under different types of piecework systems.

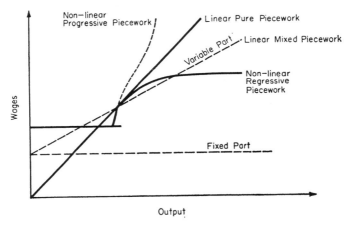

FIG. 3. Examples of Different Piecework Systems

A precondition to any form of payment-by-results system is that the performance of operators can be defined, isolated and measured in a reasonably uniform manner. Some tasks, however, do not lend themselves to such measurement and therefore present what would appear to be at least a logical limit to the opportunity to operate such systems. The choice of wage system, however, is a complex process encompassing many different interests and considerations. The process can result in the selection, installation and operation of payment-by-results systems for 'political reasons' even in cases where the employer has little or no control over the quantity of or quality of output. On the other hand, wage incentive systems have by no means been applied in all situations where they are technically feasible.

According to the LO Membership Survey, about half of the

members of unions affiliated to LO are paid according to a time rate system, i.e. fixed hourly, weekly or monthly rates. The other half are paid according to some form of payment-by-results system, such as pure piecework, mixed piecework, bonus pay system, premiums piecework, tips, etc.

The overall distribution of different systems of payment is shown in Table 21.

TABLE 21

The Proportion of LO Members Paid According to Different Systems of Wage Payment

System	LO Members in %
Monthly rates	21
Fixed hourly rates	25
Fixed weekly rates	7
Individual piecework according to standard time allowance systems, MTM, etc.	9
Individual piecework according to other systems	11
Group piecework, etc.	20
Fixed pay with bonus or room or board	4
Other	3
Total	100

Source: LO Membership Survey.

Amongst manual workers in industry, however, piecework is the most prevalent system of payment. In manufacturing, the proportion of total hours worked by manual workers on payment-by-results systems is about 65 per cent. In construction, the piecework proportion is 67 per cent. The piecework percentage appears to be particularly high in paper and pulp (about 85 per cent for men). It is about 71 per cent among male local authority workers in the Swedish Union of Local Government Employees as a whole, but over 80 per cent for workers in Stockholm and Gothenburg. In contrast, the piecework percentage among warehouse employees and drivers in private trade is as low as 20 per cent and in the co-operative sector about 60 per cent.

These examples indicate that there is considerable variation in the proportion of piecework throughout different sectors of the labour market and among different groups of workers. Plainly, the piecework percentage also varies among firms and industries. According to the SAF investigation mentioned above, piecework systems were operating in one form or another in 95 per cent of all workshops in Swedish industry. The size of the firm appears to be related to the prevalence of piecework. Thus in the largest-size group all firms operated some type of piecework system. Almost 45 per cent of the total number of hours worked by manual workers in Swedish industry were worked on pure piece rate systems. Pure piece rates tended to be more prevalent among the smaller firms than the larger ones. The smaller undertakings also operated hourly rate systems to a greater extent than the larger firms. The larger firms, however, had more than twice the percentage of mixed piecework systems as the smaller firms.

JOB EVALUATION AND MERIT RATING

The varying qualifications required by jobs in terms of training, skill, experience, responsibility, physical effort, etc., are often used as the basis for determining differences in pay. Through systematic job evaluation it is possible to assess the relative requirements of jobs and in this way facilitate the development of an equitable relationship among the rates for different jobs. By systematic job evaluation we mean the systematic assessment and comparison of the requirements of whole, partial or combined job operations to measure their relative degrees of difficulty. The systems of job evaluation used in Sweden vary from relatively simple ranking schemes based on rather general job descriptions to quite detailed point systems carefully comparing the point values of particular jobs. The fact should always be kept in mind, however, that whatever the degree of subtlety or refinement of the system, the number of factors that depend on a subjective assessment is always sufficiently large to colour the overall result. This is largely the import of the term 'evaluation'.

The earliest practical application of systematic job evaluation in Sweden occurred in the early 1940s. Since that time, its use has grown perceptibly. In 1957, an LO study estimated that job evaluation schemes were used in eleven industrial unions' jurisdictions as a basis for differentiating pay and covered about 40,000 workers, i.e. 3 per cent of the membership of unions affiliated to LO.

A new study in 1962 indicated that this number had increased to 150,000 or about 10 per cent of LO membership. Since 1962 job evaluation has spread still further. A contributing factor here has been the issue of equal pay for equal work performed by men and women.

The classification of different positions and jobs in national agreements, a frequent subject of negotiation, is often based on the industry's evaluation of the relative degree of difficulty of the job. Thus, in a sense, the job categories in collective agreements are based on a rough system of job evaluation.

In the white-collar sector job evaluation schemes have been installed among the staff of a number of industrial firms, notably AB Svenska Shell, and applied in several public authorities, e.g. to accounting clerks in the National Power Administration, clerical positions in the Swedish Forest Service, and foremen and supervisory posts in the larger engineering workshops and machine stock-piles, etc. On the whole, however, the pay of salaried employees is based only exceptionally on systematic job evaluation.

Yet a job evaluation scheme based on the job classification principle is now found in the national civil service and local government salary scales, and an occupational nomenclature is now used for salaried staff in industry.

Whenever a systematic job evaluation scheme is to be introduced in an area, it is essential that the trade unions and employers agree at the outset on the rules regulating its installation and operation. The construction of the job evaluation system is often done jointly by union and employer through a special committee established for the purpose with an equal number of representatives for workers and management. These job evaluation committees continue as standing committees to evaluate new jobs and constantly re-assess existing jobs and requirements changes. The worker representatives in such committees are often entitled under the terms of the collective agreement to obtain subsidized training in job evaluation techniques. The manner of assessment of jobs is usually regulated by collective agreement. Whether job evaluation is administered nationally or locally, however, depends largely on the structure and conditions of the industry.

Job evaluation is in principle quite distinct from wage negotiation. The number of categories into which jobs are divided and rates at which payment for these job groups is graduated are subjects of collective bargaining. The views of the parties on 'reasonable' wage differentials will, however, colour the formulation of the job evaluation scheme as well as the extent to which the assessment of jobs bears on wage setting. It is generally laid down in the special agreements governing the installation of job evaluation schemes that during the transition period the procedures of translating job evaluation results into differences in pay will not result in wage reductions. It has thus become a generally accepted practice to hold the wage line for the lower-ranked job groups and make upward adjustments over a lengthy period of transition to bring differences in pay in line with the findings of job evaluation schemes.

Job evaluation is essentially an assessment of the qualifications required by the job and a gradation of pay in accordance with job requirements. But it is also possible to appraise the performance of the individual worker and align pay accordingly. Such a system would be based on some form of merit rating. By merit rating we mean the systematic assessment and comparison of employees to determine their relative ability in terms of experience, quantity and quality of work, initiative, versatility, care of equipment and materials, etc. In addition to its use as a means of differentiating pay among workers, merit rating can also be helpful in assessing training needs and facilitating employee transfers.

Merit rating can be used as an aid to wage determination by providing a basis for differentiating pay between employees in positions with the same relative degree of difficulty. It is primarily a means of setting a rate for an individual employee. A higher rate is given to an individual who is found to be particularly skilful and useful. Merit rating as such is quite distinct from the determination of the rate at which payment for different individuals is graduated. To date, the use of systematic merit rating has been extremely limited in the LO sector.

In the process of wage determination, the various grounds for

182 *Trade Unions and Technological Change*

differences in pay come into play in varying strengths. Figure 4 gives several examples of this.

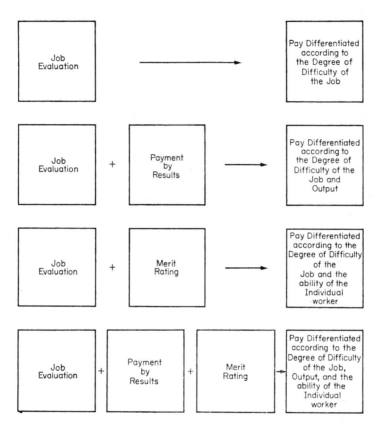

FIG. 4. Different Methods of Differentiating Pay

WAGE SYSTEMS AND TECHNOLOGICAL CHANGE

Wage systems cannot function in isolation from their technological, economic and social settings. Changes in such environmental factors frequently call for modifications in the wage system. The need to adapt wage systems to such changes must be constantly studied and re-assessed. This is not to imply that the basic values that underly the existing system of wage deter-

Systems of Wage Payment

mination or goals of wages policy must be changed. It is merely to suggest that new methods must occasionally be experimented with in order to achieve old objectives.

Many studies have been made of the impact of technological change on systems of wage payment. In the literature and discussion a variety of hypotheses has been suggested and views put forward about the nature of this relationship.[1] There is some consensus that the piecework percentage tends to increase at the technological level at which much of Swedish industry presently finds itself (i.e. 'low' and 'middle' levels of mechanization according to our terminology). The reason for this is that the pace and method of work at this level of technology are not entirely controlled by the production process. Employees are still able to exert a fair degree of influence over the flow of output. At the same time, improved work study techniques have created new opportunities to analyse and measure job requirements as well as the work performance of individuals and groups. Payment-by-results systems are increasingly being based on a work study foundation. One can, moreover, anticipate that systematic job evaluation will increasingly force out the more antiquated job classifications and create new wage classes or categories. In the event, wage incentive systems will themselves change in kind. In view of the nature and content of technological and administrative innovations, it appears likely that individual and pure piecework will be increasingly supplanted by mixed and premium piecework systems, including group incentive schemes.

In so far as technology has progressed to the highest 'level of mechanization', i.e. automation, the bulk of authoritative opinion expects a rather different mix of systems of payment to emerge. The piecework percentage is expected to decrease as work tasks such as monitoring increase. Among wage incentive systems, premium and bonus schemes are expected to become more prevalent. But the most significant difference, it is thought, will be the increases in the percentage of pure hourly rates systems, with or without job evaluation and merit rating schemes.

It is exceedingly difficult to ascertain whether changing technology in the past decade has resulted in such a shift in the mix

---

[1] See, for example, Dahlström, E. (Ed.), *Teknisk förändring och arbetsanpassning*, Chapter 3, Stockholm 1966.

of systems of payment. In practice, the selection of a wage system is a complex process. Technology is only one of a number of relevant factors. The available data on the existing wage systems and their habitats, moreover, contain many conspicuous omissions. Consequently, the following discussion will be based to some extent on speculation.

Table 22 below gives us some idea of the change through time of the distribution of payment by results systems in Swedish industry. For the selected years 1956, 1960 and 1964, there was a slight but steady increase in the piecework percentage for industry as a whole. The increase is somewhat larger for women than for men. In building and construction, the increase in the use of piecework was greater than in mining and manufacturing. The data thus do not refute the hypotheses of a shift from piecework to time work with advancing technology, but at the same time there is no indication that technological change has had any dramatic impact on the mix of systems of payment during the period of observation. The statistics for the individual industries contain more interesting findings. The largest increase in the piecework percentage occurred in the food, beverage and tobacco industries. Even if significant technological changes have taken place in these sectors it seems unlikely that the increase in the use of piecework was attributable to this

TABLE 22

Percentage of Hours Worked on Piecework Systems in Different Swedish Industries During Selected Years

Industry	1956 Piecework Percentage		1960 Piecework Percentage		1964 Piecework Percentage	
	Men	*Women*	*Men*	*Women*	*Men*	*Women*
1. Mining	65·6	41·4	58·3	36·8	56·3	8·9
2. Metal and Engineering Trades	69·2	70·7	68·6	70·7	67·3	71·9
3. Non-metallic Mining, Quarrying	64·1	57·2	66·3	57·7	68·0	56·4
4. Wood Manufacture	58·2	55·1	59·8	55·2	61·6	55·2
5. Paper and Pulp	89·6	62·4	85·1	66·5	84·9	74·3
6. Printing and Allied Industries excluding Newspaper Printing	13·0	31·0	19·0	38·0	30·9	41·9
7. Food Manufacture	18·1	33·0	31·7	44·5	47·8	56·5
8. Beverages and Tobacco	16·1	39·6	29·4	48·3	36·8	50·1
9. Textiles and Clothing	58·4	65·3	56·9	67·0	51·7	63·8
10. Leather, Hair and Rubber	68·2	64·7	68·4	70·7	68·6	68·2
11. Chemicals and Chemical Products	60·6	66·1	53·0	66·7	49·2	59·9
12. All Industries, excluding Newspaper Printing	62·6	59·8	63·7	63·0	64·8	64·0
13. Building and Construction	59·9		63·5		66·6	

Source: Löner, Social Welfare Board.

factor. For the attitudes and policies of the trade unions and employers with respect to payment systems and organizational innovations have been demonstrably influential in these sectors. In the chemicals and chemical products and mining industries, there has been a noticeable reduction in the volume of piecework. The advance of technology in these sectors has been rapid in recent years and 'automated' systems have made considerable headway particularly in the chemical industry. Here we may have some indication that changes in technology and work organization have had an observable impact on the mix of payment systems. According to the data, the proportion of piecework systems in the mining industry has been largely replaced by hourly rates, while the remaining piecework is largely based on work study. The change in the actual percentage of incentive wage systems may therefore be less than the data indicate. The piecework percentage has also decreased markedly in the textile and ready-made clothing industry. But here the average age among the workforce has probably been a contributing factor. Older workers are often changed over to hourly rates even though they continue to work as operatives.

The proportion of piecework has also declined in the paper and pulp industry as a whole though its use there has increased among women workers. Yet given the predictions of the above hypotheses and the extent to which production processes throughout much of these industries have been automated, the piecework percentage is surprisingly high. The piecework systems operated here are probably group incentive and bonus systems rather than pure piecework schemes or others that are commonly found in many other industries. The question that remains to be answered is whether conditions other than technology have ensured the continuance of a high percentage of piecework.

The most radical shifts in the mix of different wage systems have occurred outside the industrial sector. Table 23 offers a good illustration of this. The percentage of piecework has increased in trade even though the number of hours worked had risen. The increase has been more rapid for drivers and chauffeurs than warehouse workers. Plainly, changing technology has contributed to this development. However, changes in work arrangements and the increased use of work study techniques

TABLE 23

The Proportion of Piecework in the Commercial Sector.
The Number of Hours Worked on Piecework as a %
of the Total Number of Hours Worked by
Adult Men and Women

	Swedish Union of Shop, Distributive and Allied Workers		National Co-operative Society	
	1963	1965	1963	1965
Warehouse Staff	18·1	20·5	52·2	57·5
Drivers	18·3	25·9	33·4	60·2

Source: Combined wage statistics of the Swedish Union of Shop, Distributive and Allied Workers and the National Co-operative Society.

appear to be more significant factors. The most important determinant, however, has probably been the demand of trade union organizations in the sector for the increased use of piecework systems.

The available data are insufficiently differentiated to allow a breakdown by type of piecework system and it is therefore not possible rigorously to examine shifts in the mix of wage incentive systems. It seems likely, however, that shifts in the distribution of various types of piecework systems have been more extensive than changes in the overall piecework percentage. Thus, national and regional fixed-price-list systems appear to have broken down under the pressure of the transformation of workshop production engineering procedures. It appears reasonable to assume too that mixed and group incentive systems have become relatively more prevalent in firms which have reached a comparatively higher position on the automation scale. However, group incentive and bonus schemes also operate to a great extent in sectors which are not highly mechanized, notably the commercial sector. The decisive factor governing the use of such systems appears to be the difficulty of measuring the relationship between the output of the individual and total output. The earlier-mentioned study by the Swedish Employers Confederation indicated, moreover, that mixed piecework systems were more extensively operated in larger-sized industrial firms than smaller-sized ones. One explanation for this could be differences in the technological and organizational structures of these production units.

The operation of elemental time data systems such as Methods-time Measurement has long been confined mainly to the larger Swedish firms, though at that rarefied level their use is fairly common. According to a report of LO's work study committee, MTM systems were used as an aid to wage determination in thirteen national union jurisdictions in 1965. Altogether, 158 domestic MTM collective agreements had been signed covering more than 17,000 members. Of these, 120 agreements covering 12,000 workers were concluded in workshops within the metal-working and engineering union sector. Judging from lively growth trend of MTM systems in Sweden in recent years, such systems will probably become quite prevalent throughout most of the LO sector, particularly as an aid to piecework systems.

Systematic job evaluation also appears to be gaining ground in Sweden. In the public discussion, the view has occasionally been aired that the more rapidly changing technology and its new job requirements may unduly complicate or prevent the application of traditional job evaluation systems. This does not appear to be borne out by the Swedish experience. Continuous technological change, however, does point to the need for periodic re-assessment and revision of the systems being applied.

By way of summary it can be noted that technological and organizational innovations have opened up new opportunities for the use of certain systems of payment, while simultaneously setting logical limits for the diffusion of others. Yet such changes are not accurate guides to changes in the pattern of use of particular systems of payment. For the application of wage systems is essentially a matter for collective negotiation, and the type of system selected as well as its manner of installation and operation are largely dependent on the values and attitudes of the parties on both sides of the bargaining table. Consequently, it is not surprising to find no close unlagged association between changing technology and the growth of different wage systems. Occasionally, some systems of payment have spread more rapidly throughout the labour market than would appear to have been warranted by the pace of technological progress. In other cases, wages systems have been retained long after the time that technological change would appear to have rendered them obsolete. However, trade unions and employers should not entirely disregard organizational and technological requirements when selecting a system of payment. For where a wage system deviates too markedly from its social, technological and administrative setting it can create tension and conflict in the workshop and thus decrease labour productivity, lessen the effectiveness of the wage system and adversely affect the occupational adjustment of individual workers.

SYSTEMS OF PAYMENT AND WORKER ADJUSTMENT

In itself, the type of wage system used in a workshop probably has little effect on the level of wage earnings. However, it can have a significant impact on wage differentials. Different systems offer an individual employee or groups of employees varying scope to influence the size of their pay packets. Methods of wage payment vary in their degree of flexibility, adaptability to the labour market situation and to a changing technical environment. On the whole, however, the individual employee tends to regard the method of wage payment as the factor determining his wage earnings. Where it is a general practice for hourly pay to remain below piecework earnings, individual workers tend to accept that this is an inherent feature of such methods of wage payment rather than a reflection of traditional employer policies. This acceptance in turn colours the employee's views of the effort and achievements that are required of him during the course of his performance of the job. Different guiding principles for payment engender different expectations. Not only the pay packet but also the methods and systems used in its determination can therefore be important factors in the occupational adjustment of the individual worker.

The precise rôle of wage earnings in the process of worker adjustment, however, is still a matter of some dispute. Some studies suggest that wages can be a primary factor in job dissatisfaction and in decisions to quit but are less instrumental in improving morale. In one Swedish study of construction workers, however, wages were stated to be the main element in their decision to remain at the job.

Studies in other countries indicate that high wages do not necessarily lead to good worker adjustment. This applies to cases where the work organization is such that employees view the job as uninteresting and not particularly meaningful. However, where the work task itself allows some degree of job satisfaction, wage improvements can noticeably reinforce occupational adjustment.

The level of expectations of the individual worker is obviously an important factor in the effect of wage earnings. If the gap between expectations and actual pay is too wide, workers will look for a new job with higher pay. Where such an alternative is not available—for whatever reason—the result will often be low morale, dissatisfaction and dislike of the job.

Systematic job evaluation is thought to be able to measure differences in the 'degree of difficulty' of various jobs. These differences can then be reflected in the differential rates of pay negotiated by the trade union and employer organization for different classes of workers. In so far as a wage structure based on systematic job evaluation is regarded by all workers concerned as reasonably equitable, such a scheme can promote occupational adjustment. But this is not invariably the case.

What are the implications of systematic job evaluation for manpower adjustment to technological change? Plainly, if technological progress comprehensively transforms job operations and upsets the content and weighting of evaluation point systems, these systems must be revised and re-assessed in order to arrive at an acceptable system of setting wages. In the discussion of this problem in other countries, employers have suggested that in firms using systematic job evaluation schemes, rationalization measures are oriented mainly towards the job requirements that are more heavily weighted under the point system in the attempt to drive down the total wage bill. This practice creates much concern at the workplace and arouses suspicion of the system as such. The mode of installation and operation of a job evaluation scheme and its effect on worker adjustment depend in part on the strength and activity of trade union organizations.

Wage incentive systems are thought to increase productivity by stimulating the worker to greater efforts and higher output. Piecework systems, however, can give rise to conflict and create an unsettled atmosphere in the workshop. Even if the practice of establishing maximum rates of output by informal agreement among a group of operators concerned with a given piece rate system is less common today than before, it nevertheless continues to exist in many workshops. Tradition and experience determine the maximum in the particular firm. New employees with little experience of industrial work occasionally exceed the maximum rate, creating conflict with employees with lengthier terms of service. Conflict can similarly arise between older and younger workers. Moreover, workers who are psychologically unstable can find it difficult to adjust to work that is paid by results.

Most workers generally accept the 'going' system of payment. This is suggested by the results of the LO Membership Survey in which only about 16 per cent of the members surveyed stated that they would prefer a different type of system. Another 14 per cent were not satisfied with the system under which they worked but could not decide upon an acceptable alternative. Among those workers who had fixed monthly and weekly pay there was a relatively small fraction who wished to change to another system. The corresponding proportion was higher among workers on hourly rates or individual piecework rates but highest of all among workers on group or gang incentive systems.

Among pieceworkers who desired a different system of payment, about 55 per cent wanted to have some form of fixed wages. Most of those hourly-paid workers who wanted a different system wanted fixed weekly or monthly pay. Of the members surveyed who wanted to change to a different system of payment, about 36 per cent wanted some type of payment-by-results system.

Those workers who wished to change their system of payment indicated more often than the others that the psychological pressures of their job were excessive. The relationship between the desire to change and excessive physical strain was not as pronounced. The responses to the LO survey also suggest that pieceworkers want to change their wage system to a greater extent than members with a fixed rate of pay and that the pressures associated with incentive systems are often an important factor in their desire to change over to a different system of payment.

On the other hand, payment-by-results systems were thought to have certain virtues. Pieceworkers were generally subject to less supervision and fewer personal constraints than time workers. This relatively greater degree of independence and the discretion within certain limits to choose an acceptable pace of work can result in great job satisfaction for workers on incentive systems. The exact degree of satisfaction, however, probably varies with the nature of the work arrangement. Mechanically controlled work can occasionally be paid under a system which is labelled piecework but offers none of the freedom of other types of work organization.

The responses to the LO survey point to the existence of other problems. Most of the pieceworkers who wanted to change to another system were working under a group or team incentive system. Since many stated that they preferred individual piecework, their views of wage incentive systems as such were not the only factor determining the distribution of their responses.

One likely explanation for worker distaste for group incentive systems is the extent of the demand made on the individual by such systems. With group output and thereby individual earnings dependent on the efforts of all group members, older workers and those with impaired abilities can find occupational adjustment difficult.

In the above discussion we have deliberately refrained from assuming a position for or against the various existing systems of wage payment. For our major purpose was to indicate that the effect of such systems on worker adjustment is multidimensional and does not consist solely of the size of the pay packet. Our information about and understanding of the relationship between systems of payment, the efforts and performance of the worker and his overall occupational adjustment are, however, still extremely limited. There is a great need for a programme of intensified research in this area. For one thing, a more detailed examination of the grounds for and use of different methods of work measurement from the psychological as well as the physiological standpoints would be extremely useful.

Systems of payment and the instruments used in their operation can never be entirely scientific in content or form. The views of the trade union and employer organization of the rôle of wage earnings as a motivating force in human action and their different preconceptions about what is desirable or possible will always be reflected in their selection of a method of wage payment. Such preconceptions will also affect the selection of the factors used as a basis for differentiating payment where a job evaluation scheme is in operation, the elements the system should be based on and the weights to be attached to each element. It is important that the trade union movement clarify its objectives in this area and study in greater depth the consequences of different wage payment systems for these objectives.

In the past ten years, systematic job evaluation has gradually gained ground in the LO sector as a basis for wage differences. The existence of several different systems and the attempts by management and unions to adapt job evaluation schemes locally to existing conditions and practices have, however, not resulted in new methods of comparison of different occupations and jobs capable of application over a wide front. Given the objectives of the trade union wages policy of solidarity, it is clear that the trade union movement would derive much benefit from a general occupational classification system even if this would inevitably be based on rather crude job descriptions. We have earlier sought to show that there is no unique relationship between a given production technology and a system of wage payment. Viewed in a wider perspective the labour market appears to be divided between employees with fixed monthly salaries—a long-established practice in large parts of the white-collar sector—and wage earners whose pay is based on hourly rates or some form of piecework system. Variations in the length of working hours plainly affect the earnings of the latter group but not the former. The difference is further accentuated by the fact that such fringe benefits as sick pay, pensions and income guarantees against displacement due to changing technology and the breaking-in period for new jobs have long been integral to the monthly salary system but not to the systems of payment commonly operational amongst manual workers. These differences have given rise not only to economic inequities but also to unfortunate social prejudices.

Even if we look at differences in systems of payment by industry, as measured by the data for different national unions for manual workers alone, it is difficult to detect any clear-cut association between the level of technology and the system of payment. Tradition and the attitudes of employers and employees appear to be supervening factors. While initially there was some trade union reluctance to go along with employer attempts to introduce piecework systems based on work study, the positions have now almost completely been reversed. Employers are now anxious to have greater control over wage drift, while the trade unions frequently regard a relatively flexible payment-by-results system as a source of special wage advantage. The long period of sustained scarcity of labour has been a key factor in this change of position.

In certain quarters of the trade union movement the view has been expressed that in principle a uniform wage system for a large part of the workforce, such as a guaranteed monthly wage, would be preferable to the traditional array of systems of payment. It appears clear to us that a guaranteed monthly wage would facilitate the solution of a great many problems, prominent among which is that of income security in the face of changing work methods and work organization. We have, however, consciously refrained from taking a position on the desirability of such a reform, because it must be assessed from a number of other viewpoints many of which lie outside the scope of this report. Suffice it to say that technological change at least presents no obstacles to such a reform, if it is found to be otherwise desirable.

CHAPTER 12

Income Security and Technological Change

In Chapter 8, we examined the magnitude and composition of labour mobility and attempted to estimate the amount of labour turnover caused by technological change. We also indicated that displacement and redundancy resulted in readily measurable costs to the individual worker in terms of a reduction in income. In Chapter 9, we treated the subject of vocational adjustment and suggested that there were many other less easily measurable but none the less significant disadvantages in terms of adjustment associated with job displacement.

In the present chapter we shall take up the question of how workers can be cushioned from the adverse effects of displacement, i.e. the problem of job security, though we shall limit the discussion to the somewhat narrower question of income security. We shall examine the extent to which and the way in which current statutory and contractual rules and existing industrial relations practices are designed to provide economic guarantees for employees who are displaced by technological change.

INCOME GUARANTEES AND INTERNAL TRANSFERS

In Sweden, the bulk of industrial jobs are paid by results. Changes in work assignments therefore almost inevitably entail a re-negotiation of piecework prices. In these negotiations, which are commonly at the workshop level between the employer and the union branch or 'factory club', the guides in the national agreements (usually expressed in öre per hour) provide certain guaranteed minimums for 'domestic' piecework pricing. In order to operate as effective floors, however, these piecework targets, whether set in national or local agreements, must be

Income Security and Technological Change 195

set at sufficiently realistic levels to preclude an abnormally large gap from opening between the guide (the money factor) and actual levels of wage earnings. Another form of income guarantee for displaced employees is provided by certain collective agreements which stipulate that the pay in a given workshop cannot be reduced during the term of the contract.

In some Swedish collective agreements, moreover, there are special supplemental payments for training and installation periods which help to offset loss of income for new employees who transfer from one job to another, or whose work assignment is modified owing to a change in methods. Where works study techniques are used as the basis of piecework pricing, it is becoming increasingly more common to give supplementary training and installation payments for newly established piecework rates. Some collective agreements contain regulations providing for supplementary payments during periods of training. These can be paid out for periods of varying length and in varying amounts in accordance with the circumstances of the case. Within the ready-made clothing industry, for example, there is a regulation that a pieceworker who is temporarily transferred to another job is entitled in certain cases to receive a compensatory payment in the new job for a week amounting to the difference between his actual earnings and the 'normal' earnings of an average experienced workman.

For hourly-paid work, the collective agreement provision of a basic or minimum time rate offers some measure of income security. Hourly wage earnings generally consist of an individual minimum hourly rate plus *piecework compensation* which is an hourly compensation payment equal to a given percentage of the hourly rate. In general, the rates set out in the collective agreement lie significantly below the actual level of wage earnings. In practice, hourly rates have been supplemented by cash or percentage payments for skill, age and length of service and difficult job requirements. Since these are largely domestically determined the actual level of wage earnings is generally fixed by negotiations at the local or workshop level.

The system of wage determination for workers in the private industrial sector is highly flexible. Typically, after the central and national agreements have been signed, the level of wage earnings is set by an added tier of negotiations at the local level, which take into account local practices and the local labour market situation. The trends in recent years suggest that a new element has entered the picture. Increasingly, collective agreements are containing provisions that wage rates or piecework targets should be related to the type and requirements of particular jobs. These can lead to cost-saving methods reorganizations.

The public sector offers the best example of rules and practices designed specifically to protect staff from loss of income due to technological change. It is generally true, for example, throughout the entire public sector that individuals holding permanent or 'established' positions are protected against reduction in income owing to transfer or displacement.

The rationalization programme of Swedish Railways has resulted in a contraction of personnel requirements and extensive internal transfers of the existing workforce. Those that hold 'established' positions with the corporation come under the general rule for employees of the State and need fear no loss of income as a consequence of staff changes. In addition all Swedish Railway employees who are compelled to transfer to a new service area, and are unable immediately to obtain new housing in the area, are paid a re-stationing allowance of 27 Sw.Kr. (about £1 17s. 6d.) per day for the lower salary grades for a maximum of twelve months. Another form of assistance to displaced employees is provided by the corporation's internal retraining programme and by housing loans in the new assignment area.

Protective measures have also been taken to lessen the impact of the reorganization on career opportunities. In a special agreement between Swedish Railways and the Swedish National Union of Railway Workers an attempt is made to compensate employees for loss of promotion opportunities owing to the present contraction of the workforce. The regulation provides that all staff who have been employed by the corporation for a period of twenty-three years without obtaining a second promotion are entitled to a personal compensatory payment corresponding to the difference between their current salary and that of the immediately superior salary class. The same provision applies to those employees of seventeen years' service who have been forced to transfer without being promoted.

Another example of economic guarantees in the public sector

Income Security and Technological Change 197

is offered by the Swedish defence system. Within defence establishments regulations drawn up in 1960 provide for payments to employees displaced by reorganizations, plant shutdowns, or internal transfers. These payments take three forms: redundancy payments for workers ceasing employment; payments to salaried employees who transfer to positions at lower salary grades; and retraining payments to employees covered by collective agreements.

The redundancy payments may be disbursed either in the form of a series of fixed annual payments or in one lump-sum payment. The fixed annual payments are essentially pre-retirement pensions but are discontinued after three years if the individual has obtained another non-temporary position. Employees qualify for redundancy payments either if they have worked fifteen years in public service or are at least 50 years of age. In certain cases, both qualifications are prerequisites. The fixed annual payments vary in accordance with the worker's pension entitlement at the time of redundancy. The lump-sum settlement consists of a payment to employees with at least three years of employment of one, two or three months' salary depending on the employee's length of service. Employees must be at least 25 years of age to be eligible for such payments, unless they are married or have dependent children.

Even salaried employees in 'non-established' positions who satisfy the conditions of length of service and age are entitled to continue to receive a salary at the same level upon transfer to a lower position. Employees who do not satisfy the conditions, but have been in public service for at least three years, enjoy a partial guarantee of salary level in the event of transfer to a lower position.

For those employees covered by collective agreements who obtain another position in the government's employ there is a retraining payment for a maximum of six months. The payment is designed to guarantee to the individual employee that his level of income in the new position will not fall below the normal level for the average experienced employee during the period of training and transition. The maximum payment, however, consists of the difference between the individual's level of earnings at the new and the old positions.

In the LO Membership Survey about 18 per cent of the member

responses indicated that they had been transferred to significantly different jobs without changing employers during the past three years. Their response to the question of how their level of earnings had been affected by the change of jobs is shown in Table 24.

From the top half of Table 24, it appears that there is a marked difference between the earnings experience of the sexes in the event of displacement. Technological change appears to hold forth the prospect of financial improvement to men to a relatively greater extent than to women employees.

For almost half of the male employees job transfer meant an increase in income, while for a similar fraction of women displacement resulted in no significant change in income. There is a more even distribution in the numbers of men and women experiencing a reduction in income. Roughly, one-seventh of both groups experienced a reduction of wage earnings as a result of displacement.

The lower half of Table 24 shows clearly that workers in the lower age groups more often experience an increase in income when transferred than those in the middle and higher age groups. For the highest age group, displacement more often

TABLE 24

Change in Level of Earnings for LO Membership as a Consequence of Internal Transfer

	Higher Earnings	Percentage Unchanged Earnings	Lower Earnings	Total
Sex				
Men	46	38	16	100
Women	35	50	15	100
Both	44	40	16	100
Age Group				
−25	55	36	9	100
25–39	50	52	9	100
40–59	40	40	20	100
60–	11	38	51	100

Source: LO Membership Survey, Appendix 1, *Trade Unions and Technological Change.*

means a drop in income. There is a tendency for the incidence of displacement to decrease with increasing age.

However, while proportionately fewer of the elderly workers are displaced, more than half of the highest age group of displaced workers experience a reduction in earnings after transfer.

INCOME AND AGE

The existence of relatively large differences in incomes between different age groups of trade unionists is often disregarded in discussions of income distribution. Figure 5 shows how the LO membership is distributed by age and income groups.

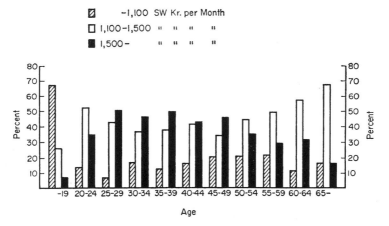

FIG. 5. The Distribution of LO Members in Different Income Classes and Age Groups

The diagram indicates that the percentage of members in the two lowest income groups (i.e. 0–1,000 Sw.Kr. and 1,100–1,500 Sw.Kr. per month) tends to increase with increasing age, and the fraction of members in the highest income group (i.e. 1,500 Sw.Kr. and above per month) tends to decrease with increasing age. The maximum percentage in the highest income group is that enjoyed by the 25–39 age group. A rather sharp decline occurs at the fifty-year level. The reasons for this distribution are several-fold.

For a start, existing differences in pay among different industries appear to account for a significant part of the distribution of age and income groups. The textile industry, for example, is a low-wage industry with a high proportion of middle-aged and elderly workers. Another such sector is agriculture and forestry.

In Chapter 9, we discussed the problems created for certain groups of workers, particularly the older workers, by the increasing level of mechanization and rationalization of work arrangements. The prevalence of piecework systems also affects the relationship between age and income. The forestry sector is a case in point. In one study it was found that the average daily earnings of a 63-year-old pieceworker amount to 75 per cent of those of pieceworkers in the 35–40 age group. In the metal-working and engineering sector too there are differences in average earnings among different age groups, though the differences in this sector were generally on the order of about 10 per cent.

Another factor bearing on the distribution of income among different age groups are existing differences in the level of earnings of time workers and pieceworkers. In 1964, for example, the average hourly earnings of adult male industrial workers on piecework was 16 per cent higher than the corresponding earnings of time-workers. This difference significantly affects the age-income relationship because there are a greater proportion of elderly workers in hourly-paid positions.

EXAMPLES FROM OTHER COUNTRIES

In certain other countries, the collective agreement has been a favoured instrument to 'manage' the introduction of new techniques with the labour contract containing specific measures to protect the displaced worker from loss of income.

In the USA, for example, collective bargaining has produced a number of measures to cushion workers from the adverse economic effects of technological change. Broadly, these range from limits on the rate of displacement, and work sharing, to guarantees to workers of either a job or minimum earnings for a given period of time.[1] One type of limitation on displacement is

[1] See, for example, Shultz, G. P., and Weber, A. R., *Strategies for the Displaced Worker*, New York 1966.

based on the 'attrition' approach and attempts to limit the rate of displacement imposed by management to the natural attrition of employees owing to quits, deaths and retirement. Where the natural wastage rate is too low in relation to intended displacements such schemes are frequently reinforced by incentives to accelerate attrition, notably early retirement benefits. Some agreements incorporate procedures for worksharing in some cases involving complicated schemes for inter-plant transfer. A third type of measure consists of programmes of outright job or economic guarantees.

The agreement between the Kaiser Steel Corporation and the United Steel Workers, for example, contains a guarantee that no worker will be laid off owing to improvements in work methods. Workers who lose their jobs as a result of technological change are placed in a 'pool' of employees and guaranteed their weekly income for a period of fifty-two weeks, even should they be transferred to a lower-paid job.[1]

Similarly, the 1960 agreement between the West Coast Maritime Employers Association and the West Coast Longshoremen's Union contains protection against lay-offs resulting from new methods of handling cargo, i.e. containerization, and a guaranteed minimum weekly wage in case the working week drops below thirty-five hours for all 'Class A' or fully registered longshoremen.[2] Other collective agreements provide severance pay, usually in the form of lump-sum payments where employment is terminated, supplementary unemployment benefits for seasonal and cyclical lay-offs and continued rights to fringe benefits for stipulated periods after redundancy.

Finally, some collective agreements in the USA provide for placement training and retraining programmes for displaced workers. In many cases, these measures to cushion the economic impact of technological change have been incorporated into and financed by 'automation funds' jointly administered by the employer and the trade union.

In Germany as well attempts have been made to limit the adverse income effects of technical change by inserting certain

[1] Reynolds, R., *The Kaiser Steel—United Steelworkers' Long Range Sharing Plan;* Blood. J. V. (Ed.), *The Personnel Job in a Changing World.* American Management Association, 1964.
[2] Kennedy, T., *Automation Funds and Displaced Workers*, Boston 1962.

income guarantees in the collective agreement. Here as in the USA there are contractual provisions for early retirement, severance pay, retraining allowances and other measures designed to cushion the impact for workers who are displaced within the firm.[1]

In Germany, there are several cases of collective agreements providing economic protection for workers with diminished work capacity due to age, illness or disability. One agreement, for example, gives an income guarantee for workers in four instances: disability due to accident; occupational illness after one year of employment; illness (not necessarily 'occupational' as defined in the agreement but caused by the job) after ten years of employment; and diminished working ability due to ageing for workers over 50 years of age with more than fifteen years of service. More typical, however, are labour agreements laying down a minimum period of service of between fifteen and twenty-five years and a minimum age of 55 years.

In the collective agreement between IG Metall and Volkswagenwerk,[2] displaced workers are partially protected against loss of income. Every worker employed by Volkswagen for more than a period of six months and later displaced is guaranteed a minimum wage equal to that received in the previous job—regardless of whether he or she was time or piecework—for a maximum period of three months. The time period can be varied to allow the worker to reach a certain level of competence in the new job.

INCOME SECURITY AND REDUNDANCY

In Sweden, redundancy is largely associated with the shutdown of an undertaking. Only rarely are employees laid off from viable enterprises. This practice gives rise to some degree of real if not formal job security. However, a sizeable segment of those workers who change jobs voluntarily do so because technological change has adversely affected their occupational adjustment. (*Cf.* Chapter 8 on voluntary job changing.) The majority of all job changes caused by changing technology take the form of dis-

[1] *Automation und Technischer Fortschritt in Deutschland und den USA*, p. 321, Frankfurt am Main 1963.
[2] Ibid, p. 375.

placement within the enterprise. Thus, in the LO Membership Survey, about 10 per cent of the responses indicated that they had been made redundant by a contraction in personnel during the preceding three-year period, likewise during the same period 18 per cent stated that they had been subjected to internal transfer. These figures, however, do not indicate the full magnitude of job changes caused by changing technology, for nothing became known of the reasons why employees voluntarily ceased employment.

While employees of the State holding permanent or 'established' positions are not subject to lay-off in the event of technical or organizational changes, there are no unconditional guarantees of job security in the private sector in Sweden. The Basic and Works Council Agreement between LO and SAF contains provisions regulating redundancy and lay-offs. The employer is required to give fourteen days' notice before the lay-offs are announced, before the period of lay-off begins. The period of notice is intended to be used for discussions about the reasons for the announced steps and the selection of workers to be made redundant. This early-warning system offers a measure of job security but its effectiveness is greatly limited by a clause in the collective agreement stating that the employers' need of suitable labour or key employees shall be given priority in the selection of the list of employees to be retained. There is a strong feeling throughout the Swedish trade union movement that such a system of job security is inadequate. Under existing regulations, it is felt, workers' representatives are confronted by a *fait accompli*; all too frequently the decision has already been taken by the employer and cannot be influenced. Another limitation is that the worker dismissed by the employer without reasonable cause is only entitled to damages and has no right to reinstatement.

Most redundant workers are able to obtain a new position. For many, however, the job change involves a drop in earnings. In one Swedish study, it was found that 33 per cent of the laid-off employees experienced a reduction in income of more than 5 per cent and that women were affected more adversely than men.[1] In the LO Membership Survey, 13 per cent of those members changing jobs during the three preceding years had a

[1] *Näringsliv i omvandling*, SNS, Stockholm 1964.

drop in income after the change. The data also indicate that the percentage of redundant workers experiencing a drop in earnings in their new job rises with increasing age. As is evident from Table 25, the fortunes of workers above and below the 40-year mark are markedly different.

TABLE 25

The Number of LO Members who have Experienced a Reduction in Earnings after Changing Jobs as a Proportion of all those who Changed Jobs, by Age Groups

Age Group	Number of LO Members in %
–24	9
25–39	10
40–59	20
60–66	19

Source: LO Membership Survey.

It is also worth recalling in this context, the relatively large segment—about 20 per cent of the total number of redundant workers (*cf.* Chapter 8)—who were not able to obtain new employment. Their income subsequent to lay-off was limited to either unemployment insurance payments or public assistance. Redundant married women who do not succeed in obtaining new positions are often excluded from public assistance by the means test. The figures show thus that redundancy can have serious adverse effects for particular groups of workers. Let us examine the kind of protection and assistance the Swedish government and trade union and employer organizations have provided for the redundant Swedish worker.

During the central negotiations of 1964 LO and SAF agreed to set up a fund for redundancy payments for workers who have become 'unemployed as a result of plant shutdowns or significant production cut-backs in an enterprise where such workers are of advanced age (more than 50 years) and have been employed by the firm for a long period (at least ten years)'. The size of the payment is graduated according to the age of the worker at the time of redundancy from a minimum figure of 2,500 Sw.Kr. (about £170) to a maximum of 7,500 Sw.Kr. (about £510). In the 1966 negotiations, the redundancy payments scheme was expanded and elaborated in certain respects. Thus, the minimum age and length of service required for eligibility have been expressly incorporated in the agreement. And a 'combination rule' has been agreed upon whereby workers who do not fulfil the minimum age condition can still be eligible to receive the payment if their age at the time of lay-off together with their period of service amounts to at least sixty-five years. Also, there are now two types of redundancy payments. There is a basic payment which varies in accordance with the worker's period of service; for every complete year of employment the worker is entitled to a payment of 100 Sw.Kr. (about £7). And there is a supplementary payment, the size of which varies with the age of the worker from a minimum of 1,500 Sw.Kr. (about £100) to 6,000 Sw.Kr. (about £400) and in each case is set 'taking into account the extent of the difficulties experienced by the worker in connection with unemployment owing to redundancy'. Those workers who receive a supplementary payment that is less than the maximum and experience redundancy a second time are entitled to request the maximum supplementary payment at a later application any time during a period of five years after redundancy.

Unemployment insurance is the second form of short-term protection provided to redundant workers. The Swedish unemployment insurance system was improved in 1964 and gives an earnings-related payment of between 27 Sw.Kr. (about £1 17s. 0d) and 40 Sw.Kr. (£2 14s. 0d.) per day for five days a week. The payment can be claimed for a maximum period of thirty weeks during any one year.

In order for a worker to be eligible for unemployment insurance benefits he must register as a job-seeker at the public employment exchange and not without good reason refuse a position that is offered to him. Where a worker refuses the offer of a suitable job, he can be precluded from receiving unemployment benefits for a period of four weeks. The four-week rule is also applicable to those workers who terminate employment voluntarily, such as workers who voluntarily withdraw from a difficult situation.

The services provided for job applicants by the employment exchanges raise important questions. Apparently, the public employment exchanges act as an intermediary only in a relatively small fraction of all job changes, at least if one can judge from the employees' own statements about how they obtained their jobs. In the LO Membership Survey, only 15 per cent of the responses mentioned that they had received assistance from the labour exchanges. And an even smaller percentage of those that stated that they desired to change jobs had attempted to contact their local exchange. Unfortunately, the available data do not lend themselves to an analysis of the reasons for the low 'participation rate' of the employment exchanges in labour turnover.

The kind of services provided by the labour exchanges are determined largely by the circumstances of the individual case: they depend in part on the wishes of the job-seeker as well as his degree of knowledge. But they also depend on the labour exchange official's competence, interest in and interpretation of his job. The foundation of labour exchange work is the so-called golden rule, that the employer shall obtain the best possible job applicant and the job applicant the job for which he is best suited. This rule obviously allows room for interpretation in the individual case. It also contains two occasionally incompatible alternatives.

The services provided by the exchanges are often of crucial importance because their job reference can exclude the job-seeker from other vocational alternatives. It is important to ensure thus that the information preceding a job reference is sufficiently comprehensive. The service of the labour exchange consists of referring a worker to a job vacancy; the actual question of employment is decided after free deliberation between the employers' representative and the job applicant. While the latter individual can return to the labour exchange after commencing a job, he is often disadvantaged by such a step. This is particularly true in the case of unemployment insurance.

The job-seeker's alternative to accepting a job offer from the local exchange is to look for employment in another area or to enroll in a training course for another occupation. In the first case, the unemployed worker is eligible for a grant to cover the costs of removal only if he cannot find employment in his own area. This constitutes a serious constraint on the effective operation of existing measures as stimuli of labour mobility. They

Income Security and Technological Change

are largely limited to job-seekers in contracting labour markets.

A relatively rich variety of vocational training courses have proliferated in recent years. The national retraining programme covers about 40,000 persons annually (about 1⅓ per cent of the occupied population) and is rapidly expanding. The courses are differentiated in purpose, content, length and level. Within building and construction and agriculture and forestry, *further training* courses are arranged to assist workers to adapt their abilities to changing technology. *Retraining courses* are orientated primarily to meet the demand for labour on the part of the metal working and construction industries. There are also special *beginner courses* for industrial workers designed to facilitate vocational guidance. The State grant can also be used for theoretical education to the extent that this is a requisite of vocational training.

Training allowances are disbursable to all workers who participate in the vocational training programme for adults. They are designed to cover living costs during the training period, and include a basic allowance of 450 Sw.Kr. (about £30) per month plus family and housing supplements. The allowances are based on a means test, which to a certain extent results in the disqualification of women. It is stipulated, however, that the qualifying test shall be administered with consideration given to the fact that the allowance is meant to stimulate vocational training.

Our survey of the problems raised by income and employment security is linked to the findings in Chapter 9 that certain groups are particularly disadvantaged by displacement and redundancy. The tendency of the income of displaced workers to decrease with increasing age is one which is to some extent caused by technical and organizational conditions in working life. These contribute, too, to the difficulties of maintaining income experienced by middle-aged and elderly workers or others with diminished working ability.

In a preceding section we described briefly how trade union movements in other countries have created various forms of income and job guarantees for their members through provisions in collective agreements. We have also pointed to examples of income guarantees in the Swedish public sector. The largest worker groups in Sweden, however, still lack formal job and income guarantees, though the favourable labour market situation during the post-war period has ensured a high degree of real job and income security for the great majority of wage earners.

Admittedly, there are certain risks associated with wide individual job and income guarantees, notably the possible limits these can set on desirable mobility of labour. For job and income security measures can come into conflict with the requirements of a high level of industrial efficiency as well as our desire for a large degree of freedom for individual workers in terms of job choice. However, one must also include the productivity gains that flow from an increased degree of job and income security, because of greater employee receptivity to technological change. We do not feel therefore that every form of income and job guarantee must necessarily conflict with the requirement of increased efficiency. The question is essentially how the gains from rationalization are to be distributed, not only between workers on the one hand and employers on the other but also among different groups of workers.

Redundancy creates serious problems for the individual worker. We have earlier indicated that the unemployment and under-employment problems are so grave that larger national labour market policy measures are called for. Even if these measures are expanded, however, situations can arise where cash payments are the only way to provide effective protection to redundant workers.

CHAPTER 13

The Distribution of Income and Wealth

As was mentioned in Chapter 2, the Swedish trade union movement accepts the need for rapid economic and technological progress as the key to a higher overall standard of living and increased welfare. An accompanying objective, as we stated in the same chapter, is that of a more even distribution of income and wealth.

The former goal, rapid economic growth, requires a generous capital formation. In recent years, however, Sweden, like many other countries, has experienced a shortage of capital in the sense that desirable and urgent investments have been waiting and delayed. One problem that arises from the attempt to further the two above objectives is to ensure that the essential increase in capital formation does not occur at the expense of an increase in the concentration of property among the owners of capital.

The potential incompatibility between the dual objectives of economic growth and income equalization has been noted and discussed by trade unionists in many Western European countries, notably West Germany, the Netherlands and Denmark. There the problem has been subjected to lively debate and several concrete resolutions have emerged from the discussion. In Sweden, however, such a debate has been conspicuously absent, possibly owing to the fact that it is generally accepted that wage, tax and social welfare policy measures are sufficiently effective tools of income distribution policy. The value of existing policy instruments should not of course be minimized. At the same time, however, it is important to recognize the limitations of such measures as they are presently formed.

It is therefore appropriate to take a closer look at the important question of how the desired increase in capital formation—on this there is almost unanimous acceptance in Sweden—can be secured without adversely affecting the overall distribution of income and wealth.

CONSTANCY OF THE WAGE AND SALARY SHARE AND GROWING INEQUITIES IN THE DISTRIBUTION OF INCOME AND WEALTH

Changes in the share of wages and salaries in the national income can be taken as an approximate reflection of changes in the distribution of income between wage and salary earners as a group and other income groups. According to the figures calculated by K. Jungenfelt,[1] the wage-salary share displayed a pattern of 'anti-cyclical' fluctuation over the period 1870–1950; that is, the share of wages and salaries in the national income rose during recessions and declined during periods of economic recovery. Various mechanisms in the product and labour markets contribute to this pattern. One example is the so-called 'ratchet effect', whereby money wage rates strongly resist downward pressure. When national income declines quickly, the wages and salary share may rise. However, when national income recovers, there is a compensating fall in the wage and salary share. This movement in the wage and salary share has little or no long-term distributive significance.

The secular trend of the wage share rose continuously from a floor in 1913 to 1933. There was little marked change after 1933 and by 1940 the share of wages had stabilized itself at a level of roughly 5–6 per cent below that of 1933. Since 1940, the wage share has remained fairly constant, rising markedly only during the 1962–3 period. Jungenfelt associates the overall stability or inertia in the wage and salary share—the share of wages in the national income today is not markedly different from that in the late 1800s—with the stabilization of the trade cycle. 'Even if both factors of production gain under full employment, the larger return goes to capital.'

However, given the changes in the employment shares of wage earners and self-employed persons and the marked shifts between manual workers and salaried employees within the wage

[1] Jungenfelt, K., *Löneandelen och den ekonomiska utvecklingen*, Stockholm 1966.

The Distribution of Income and Wealth 211

and salary sector, it is questionable whether the wage and salary share is a sufficiently comprehensive measure of changes in the income structure. In any event, it seems plausible, as Jungenfelt stated, that the trend in the wage-salary share suggests that shareholders—the owners of capital—enjoy the greatest return.

Tax statistics indicate that there has been little progress made towards a more even income distribution during the post-war period. Indeed, there is evidence that there has been a greater than average increase in existing concentrations of wealth. Thus, the Swedish Royal Commission on Taxation,[1] has stated that 'there has been no marked change in the nominal income distribution among married persons as a group since 1948' and that the same has been true for single persons. During the period of observation, moreover, the fraction of persons with a low income (defined as having no more than 40 per cent of the mean income) considerably increased, while at the same time the group with a 'normal income' has decreased and the proportion of higher-income earners has increased. There is thus a demonstrable trend towards a less even distribution of income.

Equally evident has been the growing concentration of Swedish wealth. The data presented by Royal Commission on Taxation indicated that, for the period 1957–61, there was an increase in the total number of fortunes by 26 per cent. Moreover, the number of fortunes in the size group 1–2 million Sw. Kr. rose by 35 per cent and the highest wealth category (over 2 million Sw. Kr.) grew by not less than 48 per cent.

THE DILEMMA BETWEEN INCREASED CAPITAL FORMATION AND A MORE EVEN DISTRIBUTION OF INCOME AND WEALTH

The presentation of the existing data concerning the share of wages in the national income and the distribution of income and wealth has, admittedly, been very summary. However, it does serve to indicate that the post-war period with its relatively swift rate of economic growth, accelerating rate of technological advance, significant increase in overall living standards and continuously high level of employment has not resulted in much success for the wage and salary group as a whole in increasing

[1] *Nytt skattesystem*, SOU 1964:25.

their distributive share. We are utterly convinced that the opportunities to create a more equitable wealth and income structure through more effective wage, tax and social policy measures have not been fully exhausted. The problems of increasing the effectiveness of these policies should be given a high order of priority by the trade union movement. However, since such measures can be applied with varying strength independently of the rate of technological change, they fall somewhat outside the ambit of this report.

In this chapter we are interested in examining more closely the dilemma between the need for increased capital formation on the one hand and on the other the desire for more even distributive share of income and wealth.

There are several different methods of financing the growth of the supply of capital; all with differing distribution effects. One approach would be to increase *company savings*. This would result in a higher self-financing capacity of industry. An alternative method is to increase *personal savings*. A third approach is to secure a higher investment ratio by increased *public savings*. This could be accomplished by tax or welfare fund measures, such as the National Pension Fund scheme. To this list should be added the opportunities offered by the process of collective bargaining, though these represent less an independent alternative than a complementary method to at least one of the other three.

INCREASED COMPANY SAVINGS
(A HIGHER SELF-FINANCING CAPACITY)

Widely divergent views have been expressed on the effect of self-financing capacity on the propensity of companies to invest. Industry has often pointed out that self-financing is necessary particularly for research and development projects of a long-term and risky character. A high self-financing capacity, it has been argued, is necessary to secure that segment of investment which is most productive and most indispensable for competition in the long term. This is an important consideration but it must be weighed against another, namely, that a high self-financing capacity results in—or can result in—a 'sectorization' of the capital market which in turn could create obstacles to

The Distribution of Income and Wealth 213

a dynamic adjustment of production and innovations. A flexible capital market (as well as a mobile labour market) constitutes an important precondition to the successful adjustment of industry to continuously shifting technical and market conditions. Moreover, it should be remembered that investment in research and development comprises only a small fraction of overall industrial investment outlays.

The question of a higher or lower self-financing capacity, however, is not merely an issue of the most appropriate way of utilizing scarce capital resources. Even if it were true that a high self-financing capacity would help to ensure an increase in productivity over the long term, the method would be objectionable because of its adverse effects on the distribution of wealth. A high self-financing capacity tends to increase the concentration of wealth among the owners of capital. And, since the ownership of capital is already strongly concentrated among a small fraction of individuals in the higher income groups—the proportion probably being something in the order of 5 per cent—the increase in the wealth of holders of share capital will produce an even less equitable wealth structure. A high self-financing capacity, moreover, implies a measure of compulsory savings on the part of consumers either through higher prices or lower company taxation (assuming that dividend levels remain constant).

Given these considerations, there are few grounds for complaint that there has been a decline in self-financing capacity in Sweden in the past decade. This is the more true because the growth of the National Pension Fund has amply compensated for the drop in business savings (see Table 26 below). If the self-

TABLE 26

Savings in the Business Sector as a Percentage of Investment, 1955–70

1955–59	91%
1960–64	68%
1964	67%
1970*	64%

* At an unchanged saving ratio.
Source: Kragh, B. Appendix to 1965 Report of the Long-term Planning Commission.

financing capacity of Swedish companies continues to drop to the point where there is a risk that essential investment expenditure might be curbed, appropriate measures should be taken. Nothing in the present buoyant investment situation, however, suggests that we are anywhere near this limit. This view is reinforced by international comparisons which show that in certain countries (notably West Germany and Japan) a low self-financing capacity is compatible with a high investment ratio.

MEASURES TO STIMULATE PERSONAL SAVINGS

The adverse effects of company savings on the structure of wealth can be avoided to the extent that capital formation is based on increased personal savings. Statistically, the picture is clouded somewhat because private unincorporated firms and partnerships in industry, trade and agriculture are calculated as 'households' in the national income figures. The order of magnitude involved here can be illustrated by the observation that the wage and salary bill as a percentage of national income in recent years has been about 65 per cent, while the income share of all 'households' has been about 76–7 per cent. Total personal savings as a proportion of gross national product has remained rather stable for the past decade—at about 7–8 per cent. (The percentage was lower only during the recession years of 1958–9.[1]) The introduction of the National Pension Fund has not had any appreciable impact on the propensity of individuals to save; the slight increase registered in recent years is more directly attributable to the increased rate of increase of earnings. The findings of the earlier-mentioned study by the Swedish Institute of Economic Research, of the savings schedules of a few thousand households, support other observations that the savings ratio increases rapidly with rising income.

The observed constancy of savings habits and the rather fixed relationship between income and the propensity to save limit the scope for and effective operation of measures to timulate saving.

Long experience with such measures in Sweden and other countries with similar economic and social structures demon-

[1] *Hushållens sparande år* 1958. Meddelande från Konjunkturinstitutet B:33' Stockholm 1966.

The Distribution of Income and Wealth 215

strates clearly that their effect is very limited. Unless tax allowances, for example, are limited to a small amount, wealth can be transferred to tax 'havens' in the saving sector. Such subsidies, moreover, only result in rewarding a significant proportion of savings which would in any case have been made. Further, experience shows that when the subsidies are discontinued or when the fixed term of saving is ended, a large part of savings is diverted to consumption.

Wider participation in share ownership is both practicable and desirable. However, it is not an effective means of evening out the distribution of wealth or promoting greater industrial democracy. Moreover, a wider diffusion of share ownership can only be expected to lead to a marginal amount of new savings. Its likely effect will be largely one of changing the form of existing savings; members of the public who turn to savings in the form of shareholding will tend to transfer their savings from traditional forms.

The difficulties of securing a real increase in voluntary savings have repeatedly provoked proposals for various forms of compulsory savings. Apart from situations of economic crisis, which can require exceptional measures, all forms of compulsory savings should be regarded with extreme caution. For in the long term compulsory savings tend to undermine the very foundation of the desire to save. Moreover, such methods are doubtful means of creating a more durable basis of capital formation, since the funds which have been compulsorily saved must one day be released for consumption.

In sum, there appears to be little likelihood that personal savings can be stimulated to an extent sufficient to provide the necessary increase in capital formation. The only remaining course is increased savings by the community.

MEASURES TO INCREASE COLLECTIVE SAVINGS

Taxes and certain types of welfare funds—though rarely viewed as such—are forms of collective savings. From a purely technical viewpoint the most simple method of securing the basis for capital formation would be to adjust taxes so that the savings of the community remain continuously in line with the need for capital. This, however, would entail that a large segment of total capital formation would be subject to government supervision and that the citizen would be required to contribute in accordance with the norms of the tax system. Thus, while tax policy offers a conceivable method of reconciling increased capital formation with the goal of an even distribution of income and wealth, the restrictiveness with which such a fiscal policy would have to be pursued makes it an unrealistic alternative.

A more practicable approach is offered by the creation of community funds such as the National Pension Funds. The difference between taxation and funding is largely a technical one; the State is responsible for capital formation by taxation, while the responsible body of the National Pension Fund is more diffuse. Though the trade unions and employer organizations are represented on the governing boards of the Funds the latter are independent of the labour market organizations and of the State, which has created the legal framework within which the pension system operates but has no authority over the funds deposited. In the present context, the legal status of the fund is of less moment. The crucial point is that the National Pension Funds provide a form of collective savings which already accounts for at least one-third of total net savings and is rapidly growing. This phenomenon is not unique to Sweden. In the Netherlands, for example, collective savings already account for half of the total net savings.

In recent years, the rules regulating the investment of the resources of the National Pension Fund have been criticized from two standpoints. Firstly, there has been concern that the funds are depreciating in real value owing to rising prices. Secondly, there have been pleas for a more active placement policy which would expand investments from debentures and local authority bonds to participation in new industrial projects. The first criticism is directed to the general problem of inflation which lies outside the scope of this report. The second criticism is not unlike the Swedish trade union view put forward in 'Economic Expansion and Structural Change'.

The present division of the capital market into two sectors, with the National Pensions Funds being directed entirely to the bond market with its emphasis on central and local government borrowings and private credit institutions financing the capital

The Distribution of Income and Wealth

requirements of industry, would still be unsatisfactory even were the return on National Pension Funds investments to be tied to a cost of living index to a greater extent than the present restrictions allow. For if the funds were to continue to be placed in housing, local authority construction, etc., though in the form of an index-tied bond, the criticism would remain that the administration of the fund would not have a sufficient degree of influence in determining the overall direction of investment expenditure.

While we sympathize with these views, we do not have any reason to go into this essentially political aspect of capital formation and the use of the resources of the National Pension Fund. The main point for us is that capital formation is currently financed to a significant extent by collective savings. The question of which sectors should be financed by the National Pension Funds or other types of funds is an ancillary one, though it is obviously important in other contexts.

CAPITAL FORMATION THROUGH COLLECTIVE BARGAINING

The objection to self-financing because of its unfavourable income distribution effects, the almost insuperable difficulties involved in significantly stimulating personal savings, and the existing political tendency to favour collective savings as a solution has awakened interest in the idea of incorporating an element of savings or capital formation in the collective agreement. A great many proposals to this effect have been aired in various countries. The discussion has been particularly lively in Western Germany for most of the past decade.[1] The suggestions that have emerged from discussions in different countries can be outlined in the following way:

A. *Collective Agreements at the Company Level*
   1. A Profit-sharing System.
   2. A Negotiated Company Savings Scheme.

B. *Collective Agreements at the Industry-wide Level*
   3. Investment Levy on Wages.
   4. The formation of a 'Socialfund' (The Gleitze Plan).

[1] von Laesch, A., *Die Grenzen einer breiteren Vermögensbildung.* Frankfurt 1965.

5. Deposits to a 'Nationalstiftung' (The SPD Plan).
6. Deposits to 'National Investments Fund' (The CISL Plan).

1. A Profit-sharing System at the Company Level
This alternative has been regularly rejected by the Swedish Confederation of Trade Unions. Its greatest weakness in our view is its incompatibility with our wages policy of solidarity. The system also has the undesirable consequence of binding employees to particular firms. Moreover, there are certain technical difficulties. The current methods of company accounting of profits make it difficult to transfer to employees a real share of the increase in the capital worth of the enterprise.

2. A Negotiated Company Savings Scheme
According to the West German law on the 'promotion of wealth formation among wage earners', certain amount of wage income can be exempted (Aussertarifliche Sonderleistungen) from income tax and social insurance withholding tax. The maximum permitted is DM312 annually and this amount must be placed with a building society, savings bank, in shares in the employees' own firm or given as a secured loan to the firm for a period of at least five years. The arrangement has been applied only rarely, but is of interest principally as an example of a system of bonuses for wage savings. In 1965, the law was changed to cover a certain proportion of the wage determined according to the collective agreement between employer and employees. It is plain that the law even in its expanded form will not involve much more than an incentive to saving through a tax allowance.

3. An Investment Levy on Wages
Under this system, a certain percentage of the wage is paid out not in the form of cash but to an investment trust which issues certificates redeemable after being held for about five years. A variation of this system is one in which the 'investment wage ratio' is fixed by legislation. Both versions, however, are unsatisfactory because they are based on compulsory savings. That such a system is integrated in the process of collective bargaining does not obviate the objections to such a form of savings raised earlier in this discussion.

The Leber Plan[1] (named after the General Secretary of the

[1] Leber, G., *Vermögensbildung in Arbeitnehmerhand.* Frankfurt am Main 1964.

West German Construction Workers Union) proposes that employers deposit 1·5 per cent of the annual wage earnings of employees to a special fund. The employer is then entitled to borrow the funds for his own firm, and pay his contributions to the fund in shares or cash. The fund is administered according to the principles of a unit trust, as far as the employee-beneficiaries are concerned, and can also lend money to construction firms or provide credit facilities for building workers who wish to purchase their own homes. The certificates obtained by members throughout the years can be redeemed when they reach the age of retirement.

Profit-sharing at the Industry-wide or Central Level
All of the following arrangements have one thing in common: they attempt to re-distribute wealth to the wage-earner from company profits. The Gleitze Plan, published in 1957, suggests that the larger companies should transfer a part of their capital to a fund (Sozialkapital) which would issue certificates to employees. According to one SPD plan, a proportion of company taxes should be transferred to a national fund which would issue 'national shares'. One of the 1964 proposals of the Italian Confederation of Trade Unions (CISL) suggests that wage negotiation should determine that a certain proportion of the wage increase be paid out in saving certificates. The scheme would be voluntary in the sense that individual workers could contract out. The funds would be allocated to a National Investment Fund which would be administered by a board on which the trade unions would have a majority of representatives.

From these proposals, it appears that the various groups of measures—to stimulate *savings*, to increase *collective capital formation* through taxation or funding, and *arrangements built into collective agreements* for wage earners to obtain a share of company profits or only for a form of compulsory savings—do not exclude but rather complement one another. In the Swedish situation, the second group appears to be central and the first and third group of measures largely complementary devices. This is not merely because of their limited effect. The decisive point is the strong element of support for company self-financing that characterizes the majority of the above arrangements. A general tax or welfare fund policy would limit the opportunity for self-financing and maintain a more effectively functioning capital market.

Industry Funds
These considerations lead us to reject all forms of company-bound wage savings plans even if they contain a means of fashioning a more reasonable distribution of wealth. The alternative that we recommend is the creation of industry funds along the lines of our proposals in Economic Expansion and Structural Change. In the rather weak debate that greeted this proposal in the 1961 LO Congress, and in subsequent discussion, no serious objections have been raised to such funds. Indeed, we now have the prototype of a fund constructed through free bargaining between employer association and trade union, i.e. the AGB Fund, which is devoted, moreover, to promoting the mobility of labour. The beginnings of organized co-ordination at the industry-wide level have also evolved in the engineering and textile industries. Both industries have discussed at some length the problems of manpower adjustment (particularly those of elderly manpower).

The industrial fund would be established through collective bargaining between LO member unions and their counterpart employer organizations. The method of allocation to branch funds should also be an object for negotiation and the amount need not vary in accordance with the size of firm's wage bill, as in the case with many non-Swedish schemes. The objective of the funds would be to facilitate the adjustment of the enterprise and the workforce to changed technical conditions. Depending on their size, their resources could be allocated to research, market analysis, consultation activity, training and re-training programmes, redundancy payments and pre-retirement benefits for elderly redundant workers. As the funds grow in size, they could be used for more extensive economic operations such as the financing of the winding-up of unprofitable enterprises.

When a similar proposal was presented five years ago, there was some concern lest an uneconomic distribution of the funds among a number of different branches lead to an inefficient use of scarce capital resources.

This concern appears to be undue at least as long as the

amounts in the funds remain reasonably small. A continuous expansion of funds, however, would give added strength to the question of whether the members are bound too tightly to their sectors. A conceivable way out would be to transfer a certain proportion of the funds to a central fund which would not be limited to a particular sector.

The funds should be administered jointly by the negotiating parties and could be regarded as 'foundations without ownership'. As opposed to the majority of proposals in other countries, there would be no issuance of certificates to individual workers. Nor could a contributing firm have claim by right to borrow from the fund. The general economic orientation of the funds could be emphasized by the trade union and employer association agreeing to appoint an independent person as chairman.

As has already been stated, this model for capital formation which could more directly favour wage earners can only play the rôle of a complement to other more central measures for a more even distribution of wealth and income. These would include an intensified incomes policy of solidarity, a tax policy which neither in principle nor in practice favoured certain types of income, a reduced and not unduly large capacity for self-financing in industry which limits a rapid concentration of wealth in the hands of a relatively few owners of capital, and an expanded social policy that ensures to the inevitably large groups of economically disadvantaged—the sick, the aged, the large families and the unemployed—a reasonable share in our general increase in the standard of living.

CHAPTER 14

Technological Change and Labour-Management Co-operation in the Plant

The approach of the Swedish trade union movement to changing technology has been twofold: it has attempted to obtain for its members the largest possible share of the benefits brought about through such change, i.e. higher wages and better working conditions; and it has endeavoured to ensure that particular groups of workers or individuals have not been compelled to bear a disproportionate share of the economic costs of such change, notably unemployment, a reduction in income and less favourable working conditions, etc.

The means with which the trade union movement has sought to achieve these objectives have similarly been twofold: through the process of collective negotiations with employers over wages and conditions of employment; and through political activity. The former avenue has been used largely to acquire a share of the increased output resulting from improved techniques, in the form of higher wage earnings and 'fringe benefits'. Political action has brought us closer to the goals of full employment policy and an active labour market policy, as well as providing a system of social security through legislation on working hours, pensions and sickness insurance.

Despite these gains, Swedish trade unions have not won a direct share in the 'management' of technological change, determination of working conditions or the administration of work organization in many respects. Collective agreements over wages and working conditions in the LO-SAF sector still contain the old management prerogatives provision according to which the employer has the right to manage, to allocate the workforce in accordance with production needs, and freely hire

Labour Management Co-operation

and dismiss employees. True, agreements and common practice over the years have greatly modified the importance of this clause in practice, but the principle is nevertheless still embodied in the formal agreement.

As a rule, national collective agreements in Sweden contain no provisions giving workers a right to participate in decision-making and the management of changes in work methods and organization in the plant or guarantees against loss of income owing to changing technology. The means of achieving these measures of employment security in Sweden have largely been the procedures of joint consultation and labour-management co-operation at the workplace.

LO-SAF AGREEMENTS

The Basic Agreement in 1938 between LO and SAF marked a new epoch in employer-trade union relations in Sweden. It was soon followed by a spate of agreements relating to many aspects of industrial life involving labour-management co-operation not only at the industrial level but also at the place of work. These agreements have generally sought to create the conditions for greater productive efficiency and improved conditions of service. In 1942, the two central confederations signed an agreement on workplace safety arrangements, which was followed by the 1944 agreement on industrial training, the 1946 agreement on works council and the 1948 agreement on work study.

At a less formal level, the LO-SAF Labour Market Committee has approved a 1951 report on women in the labour force, and in 1954 established certain principles for company health schemes.

The LO-SAF agreements that are particularly relevant to questions of production and technological change in the firm are the works council agreement and the work study agreement.

Works councils are intended to provide an instrument to improve productive efficiency in the firm and to give employees some insight into the economics and technical conditions of operation. As well, their functions are to provide a measure of job security, improve working conditions and encourage vocational training within the plant. The rationale underlying the agreement on work study is that an increase in productive efficiency is a necessary condition to a continuous increase in living standards and welfare. Work study, it is stipulated, must take into account psychological as well as physiological factors and requirements for adequate worker protection.

These agreements have created new spheres of activity that require new skills and expertise on the part of employee representatives. In the event trade unions have found it necessary to acquire staffs of specialists such as economists, lawyers, work study engineers and doctors. Moreover, trade union officials have increasingly begun to specialize in various aspects of trade union activity. The wider functions of the trade union organization have necessitated increasingly larger numbers of full-time personnel. To obtain the required financial support for the needed expansion of full-time officials, it has been necessary to increase the average size of the member organizations. This in turn has required amalgamation of separate units at the plant level, i.e. factory clubs, into local union organizational units, or branches.

At the local level, as well, trade union representatives have had to acquire new expertise. For their functions, too, have noticeably expanded. From their original task of bargaining mainly on wage issues, trade union representatives now must negotiate with management on practically all problems that arise between supervision and employees. To effectively discharge these functions today, the local trade union representative must be well versed in production techniques, work study techniques and factory safety measures, ergonomics and bio-technology, occupational physiology, industrial hygiene, business economics and business administration including features of personnel management such as recruitment, selection and training. Since open conflict is a rare occurrence in the Swedish workshop, shop stewards and local union officials must have sufficient expertise in these spheres to represent employees in the give and take of negotiation.

The workshop representatives and local union officials often stand in a middle position between management and the workforce. In many cases, their job includes the task of clarifying management measures to employees.

Developments in the work study field are a case in point. When the bulk of piece rates were set by supervisors, the individual employee as well as the workshop representatives enjoyed a rough equality of expertise in negotiations over work measurement. As more systematic methods of work study have been introduced, the opportunities for the individual worker to control the measurement of effort and the system of payment have greatly declined. The workshop representative has therefore had to acquire a thorough grounding in the various existing systems of work study. For lack of knowledge on the part of employees only arouses suspicion towards the new methods, thereby creating a potential source of conflict.

THE INDIVIDUAL WORKER AND THE PROCESS OF TECHNOLOGICAL CHANGE

New methods, the installation of new labour-saving machinery and changes in organizational arrangements mean to the the individual worker a change from familiar behaviour to a new and unknown situation. In so far as such changes are perceived by workers as threats to their interests, they give rise to anxiety and resistance.

The reaction of the individual worker to any given change, i.e. his attitude and behaviour, is determined largely by how he perceives the change in relation to his own psychological and physical needs. Change, as a rule, has positive as well as negative facets and each individual has different criteria for weighing the advantages and disadvantages. This balancing process is highly personal and its outcome will depend on the individual's overall comparison of all the factors that he deems relevant.

Resistance to planned changes in a firm can be expected if the displacement of personnel is perceived as a threat to job security, living standards, social status, skill or freedom of movement. Conversely, in so far as the change holds forth the promise of improvements in such factors it will be well received by employees.

The foregoing discussion implies that there is an important distinction between the *objective* and the *subjective* consequences of a change. The latter concept refers to the individual's personal interpretation of the nature of a particular change. A necessary condition to employee receptivity to change is that the new situation as a whole does not objectively hold forth the prospect of less favourable conditions. But this by itself is not always a sufficient condition. Psychological resistance to change can also arise where the individual experiences uncertainty about what the change holds in store for him. How can such uncertainties be minimized? Three factors appear to be particularly relevant here:

1. The extent to which the individual has been informed of the change.

2. The individual's opportunity to influence the decision initiating the change, i.e. his degree of participation in its planning and execution.

3. The individual's confidence in management.

To the extent that the individual is insufficiently informed of the planned innovation, he is liable to form an inaccurate picture of its nature and contents.

For the less factual information an individual receives, the more likely he is to read his own preconceptions, values, doubts and fears into the situation. And the steps he takes—which will appear rational to him—will be based on information heavily coloured by subjective factors. Management, in turn, having incomplete insight into employee perceptions and interpretations, view their behaviour with a certain degree of subjectivity, i.e. importing their own attitudes and preconceptions into the situation. This sets the stage for a vicious circle. Where the flow of information is incomplete, misunderstandings arise and consequent suspicion towards the views of the other side inhibits further contact and communication between the two parties.

Adequate information by itself, however, is not enough. There must also be provision for consultation and a measure of active participation by employee representatives in decision-making and management. Experiments have shown that the more consultation that can be established directly with the individuals affected by a change, the more likely they will be to accept the change. Employee confidence in management's responsibility and honesty can be an important factor here. Where confidence is at a low ebb, there is a tendency for employees to give a negative interpretation to all ambiguous management proposals. Under such circumstances, moreover, the basis for establishing a viable system of employee-management co-operation is extremely precarious. For a relationship of mutual confidence between management and labour cannot be developed in a short while.

LABOUR-MANAGEMENT CO-OPERATION IN MANAGING CHANGE AT THE WORKPLACE

Labour-management co-operation at the plant level can take either one of two basic forms:

1. Through organized co-operation, i.e. joint consultation, between management and representatives from trade union organizations.

2. By giving the individual worker a greater *direct* measure of influence in decisions which affect his job and work situation.

These two forms are essentially complementary and must be used in conjunction to obtain the optimum results. The former method consists of formal machinery usually governed by rules set out in collective agreements. Direct employee participation is a less formal process. It relates to intangibles such as attitudes, ways of life, and manners of dealing with other people. In this context, management selection and training in human relation skills, etc., are of particular consequence.

Experience from *inter alia* the activity of works councils has shown that formal consultative machinery, even when fed with extensive information, does not always function satisfactorily as an organ of contact and communication. Employers who imagined that information about the firm's problems could be communicated to employees entirely through representatives in the works councils have been rather sadly disillusioned. But this is largely because they misunderstood the nature and intended rôle of the works council. The traditional chain of command of the managerial hierarchy must be the major channel through which information flows in the firm. It is a vast over-estimation of the potentialities of organized co-operation to believe that all employees will be more productive and feel more closely identified with the firm simply because they have the right to select representatives to a works council. In order for labour-management co-operation to approach the limits of its potential, it must be expanded.

An expansion of direct worker participation through increased daily co-operation between employees and front-line supervisors would supplement rather than supplant a well-developed formal system of trade union-employer co-operation. For employees must have a measure of influence at all levels of the firm. Since technological change occurs over a wide front, the system of labour-management co-operation must extend to all levels of the business organization as well as reach directly to the individual employee. The co-existence of these two systems of communication, i.e. the formal consultative machinery and the direct co-operation between employee and supervisor, suggests that certain problems of demarcation might arise. Is certain information more appropriately conveyed by one of the systems? Do certain forms of co-operation lend themselves more to one of the two arrangements? In general, however, both routes will have to be used to obtain satisfactory results.

The processes of providing information and consulting on problems of production, company finance and personnel management must be used continuously. For employees and their representatives cannot make a constructive contribution in critical situations unless they are well grounded in the general problems of the firm. And only continuous exchange can build up the mutual confidence that can allow both sides to work successfully in a crisis.

It is too late to attempt to create a system of labour-management co-operation at the stage when the firm is about to reduce its workforce. For only by daily and continuous collaboration over a lengthy period can a reserve of good will be accumulated to be drawn on in a difficult situation.

Experience with works councils in Sweden indicates that information and consultation relating to changes in the firm are often provided at too late a stage. Investigations performed by LO's works council division, based on questionnaires to workers' representatives sitting in the councils, suggest that only 25 per cent of the councils obtain information of the more important changes in production and working conditions at a point in time when it is possible to exert any influence over the company's decision through consultation procedures.

DIFFERENT DISPLACEMENT SITUATIONS

It is difficult to generalize about the nature and intensity of the information and consultation between labour and management in the case of various types of changes in the firm. The existing tone of industrial relations at the workplace, previous custom and practice, and the nature of the change itself vary greatly from case to case. The following discussion is an attempt to look at the problem from the vantage point of three different types of changes:

1. Everyday rationalization.
2. Larger changes in production involving production reorganizations, expansions, etc., without any actual dismissals or lay-offs.
3. The close-down or movement of a place of work or other reorganization accompanied by dismissals and lay-offs.

The first case would include the continuous installation of new technical methods. This process is conspicuous externally but it is a significant component of productivity gains. For the workforce, such change often results in displacement, changes in work methods and variations in income.

Generally, no new or special informative consultative bodies are organized to deal with this form of change. The initiative and planning lie with management (though rather low in the hierarchy). As a rule the individuals concerned are directly informed of such changes. The extent to which there is real consultation between employees and supervisors is almost impossible to estimate. Formal consultative machinery, such as works councils, only exceptionally enter the picture. The exceptions are found primarily where the councils have been decentralized into departmental committees or consultative councils in particular workshops with the firm. The trade union officials can be brought in where the individual employee is dissatisfied with the change. The dialogue between union official and supervisor generally covers wage issues, the selection of persons to be transferred and the nature and content of the new work assignments.

In the second type of case, too, the initiative and responsibility for planning lie with management. The difference is that the decision is generally taken at a higher level in the managerial hierarchy. Where firms consist of a number of geographically separated plants, the actual planning and decision-taking processes may be separated from the management of the plant in which the changes are to be made. This of course tends to lengthen the period of time required for planning and execution, though developments will vary from case to case. In general, however, it seems to be true that while management is careful from the start to take great pains in preparing the technical and economic aspects of their decision, they appear to be less concerned about personnel aspects until a relatively advanced stage of the decision-making process.

According to Section 8 of the 1966 agreement on works councils, the employer is required to inform employees in advance of all planned reorganizations within the firm and of the intended installation of new manufacturing, production or work methods or other technical arrangements. Such information is to be passed on through formal channels (works councils, supervisors, staff newspapers, etc.) before the changes are actually initiated. Early warning is frequently given but only at a stage when the basic decision has already been taken by management. It is not unusual for special consultative bodies to be established specifically to function during the period of reorganization.

The third type of case—a change involving dismissals and lay-offs—is the most drastic from the viewpoint of the workforce. As a rule, the taking of such a decision is preceded by careful planning and study. This should occur without exception in the case of the winding up of individual operations in a large multi-operation concern. However, there are far too many examples of business operations being carried on to the point when resources are almost totally depleted, and shutdown procedures carried out under conditions of crisis, with insufficient notice and at too rapid a pace to allow the impact on the workforce to be cushioned in various ways. Such a situation, it is plain, leaves little scope for information and consultation between employers and employee representatives.

Apart from this type of case, however, it is probably true to say that in general plant shutdowns in Sweden are marked by fairly comprehensive information and planning activity. Under the LO-SAF central agreements there are explicit provisions regulating the timing of the early-warning system. Moreover, as in the preceding case, it is common to form special channels of information and consultative groups to administer the reorganization. Generally, the labour market administrative authorities are brought into this activity. Representatives from the local employment exchanges often sit on the consultative committees administering the staff problems arising from the reorganization.

In cases when dismissals and lay-offs are limited to only part of the workforce, there is usually a rather lively exchange between union and management on the number and the persons to be declared redundant. According to the information received by LO's works council division, the trade union branches feel that in general these arrangements have worked out satisfactorily. In some cases it has proved possible to reduce the number of redundancies, and in other cases the branches have been able to voice their views on the principles governing the selection of redundant employees. The final decision, however, has always been taken by the employer.

In many cases, consultation slides over into pure negotiation. It is not infrequent for the central trade union confederation and national unions to be drawn into the deliberations, particularly in questions involving redundancy payments.

TECHNICAL CHANGE AND LABOUR-MANAGEMENT RELATIONS IN THE PLANT

The pace with which new changes are introduced in the firm, as well as the nature of the innovations, can significantly affect the atmosphere and spirit of industrial relations at the workplace. As changes increase in frequency and occur over a wider front, more firms and individuals will be subjected to the requirements of rapid and radical adjustment. Such a process tends to generate strong pressures on labour-management relations. There are greater possibilities for misunderstanding and conflict which can undermine the goodwill and confidence upon which constructive co-operation must be based.

On the other hand, comprehensive reorganizations tend to lead to a greater awareness of the need for effective communication and correct information. The volume and intensity of information fed into the consultative machinery tends to increase in firms which are involved in a dynamic period of expansion, though this will often depend on the quality of industrial relations before the reorganization as well as management's 'organizational ideology'. Nevertheless, there is a general trend among Swedish employees to recognize the need to inform their employees. The premise that the employer has the responsibility and duty not only to shareholders but also other 'interest groups' related to the firm, appears to be gaining wider acceptance. An accelerated pace of change does not inevitably lead to a deterioration of labour-management relations at the plant level.

Of greater moment than the pace of change is its nature and direction. A change viewed by the employees as a threat to their job security, material standard, social status, occupational skills or freedom of movement will generally be met with strong resistance. If such views of the threat are allowed to spread and intensify they can lead to organized counter-measures on the part of employees which can intensify into open conflict. In extreme cases this can spread from the workplace to higher organizational levels. Strikes in the United States in recent years appear to contain an element of 'escalated' resistance to change. To date, industrial relations in Sweden have been free of this pattern of conflict.

The trend here appears to be towards increased information and expanded co-operation and consultation within the plant. The prospects that this trend shall continue appear to be good. Employers' associations and employers have displayed an increasing interest in joint consultation in different contexts and the same is true of the trade union organizations. This is exemplified by the new central agreement on works councils, though it is too soon to be certain about the practical effects of this agreement. Much depends on the quality of industrial relations at the individual place of work.

THE RIGHTS OF EMPLOYEES TO PARTICIPATE IN MANAGEMENT DECISION-MAKING

One question remaining is how change affects the possibilities of employees to participate in and influence developments in the firm. Technical innovations and administrative reorganizations are highly significant but not the sole agents of change. It is not surprising therefore that a wide diversity of views and shifting assumptions about the nature of future labour-management relations have found their way into the discussion.

According to one view, the employees' opportunities to exercise influence over events in the plant will tend to decline. This, it is felt, will be an inevitable accompaniment of the growing trend towards centralization and co-ordination of decision processes in modern business organizations. The new planning instruments and techniques and production engineering methods demand an ever-increasing staff of specialists. Even personnel management is becoming a highly specialized field, administered by specially trained individuals.

These developments it is thought suggest that the importance of worker representatives who lack the wide and varied expertise necessary to participate in planning and influence the contents of changes will diminish. Moreover, to the extent that changes in methods result in increased fragmentation and 'routinization' of job operations, employee interest in the overall problems of the firm will probably decline. And as the pressure 'from below' on workshop representatives to involve themselves in these wider issues decreases there will be a corresponding decrease in the efforts of individual workers and their representatives to influence and direct the course of change.

In our opinion, hypotheses of this sort are not terribly relevant to developments presently confronting us, at least not if we limit our time horizon to the next decade. For a start, changes in technology and administrative systems are not as uniform as is presupposed by the above views. 'Systems analysis' and the efforts to integrate different major operations and processes in production and administrative systems are still relatively rare and show no likelihood in the forseeable future of being adopted by large numbers of firms or installed in many workshops. Moreover, to suggest, as some have, that trade union representatives will not be able to assert their views against management specialists, is to misunderstand the nature of the rôle of the workshop representatives or trade union organization in a co-operative system of industrial relations. It is not the task of workers' representatives to solve the technical and administrative problems of the firm. Their responsibility is to safeguard that reasonable consideration is given to the employees' position and the manpower adjustment problems created by an innovation. In other words, their rôle is to present demands which management experts must take into account when devising solutions. The opportunities to voice such demands appear to be related more to the overall economic and labour market situation and the bargaining power of trade unions than to the technical expertise of employee representatives. Workshop representatives must of course have sufficient technical knowledge to exchange views with management specialists, understand their case and even form an opinion of the consequences of the proposals. The discharge of these function, however, does not appear to present insuperable obstacles.

Further, there are a number of trends in society as a whole which bear significantly on industrial relations at the workplace. For example, the current 'revolution' in Swedish education will entail that members of the workforce in the future will have a totally different educational background than current employees. The individual employee will have increased knowledge of fields which are important in understanding technical, economic and environmental problems. Given the 'deepening' of their education that is in the offing, wage earners will not readily remain on the sidelines of events in their firms. Moreover, the the rising standard of living with its increasing freedom of choice and the growing 'democratization' of consumption patterns will have an effect on labour-management relations. Employees will become more strident in their demands to be treated in their work situation in a manner commensurate with the treatment they receive as consumers and citizens. A high level of economic activity and full employment with its attendant scarcities of labour also enlarges the individual worker's freedom of choice as far as place of employment and type of job are concerned. This can be relied on to make management more sensitive to employee demands with respect to the shaping of the work environment and the administration of innovations.

Last but not least significant in this context is the general attitude of employers and trade unions towards the importance of information and consultation in the overall process of adjustment. In general, there are always opportunities to choose between various alternatives and combinations of organizational structures for any given set of technical or administrative needs. If there is an interest on both sides in co-operation, the preconditions are promising for devising an organizational solution and the manner of its installation which also facilitates and improves worker adjustment. Recognition of this principle appears to be spreading among management and labour in Sweden.

THE ORIENTATION OF INFORMATION AND CONSULTATION

On the whole the trade unions have been fairly successful in upholding the interests of their membership so far as the purely material consequences of technological change and security of employment are concerned. The possibilities of continuing so to do in the future appear to hinge on the level of activity in the economy as a whole as well as conditions in the labour market and the bargaining power of the trade unions rather than changing technology as such. There seems to be no indication that the foundations of trade union negotiating activity in this respect shall be undermined in the next decade. It also seems fair to assume that the trade union officials shall continue to make good use of these foundations.

It is important, however, that we within the trade union movement devote greater attention to the problems of income and employment security that can arise for certain individual workers and groups of workers in conjunction with economic and technical changes. The continuous introduction of new systems of payment and methods of job evaluation can have adverse income consequences for particular groups of workers. Not only might they suffer by comparison with the income in previous positions; their earnings position relative to other groups might deteriorate. New methods are often so complicated that the individual worker can find it difficult to obtain an overview of their construction and practical operation. In the event, it is essential that trade union representatives become familiar not only with the technical aspects of the system but also their income consequences in the long as well as the short term. Moreover, the fact that different systems of payment have differing effects on worker adjustment quite apart from their income consequences must be given careful consideration by trade union officials.

We have thus reached the point where we can make some attempt to evaluate the significance of technological change in terms of worker adjustment as we described this concept in an earlier chapter. Various aspects of the workplace environment and job content emerge as important factors here, notably lighting, noise, dust, health risks and inadequate safety measures. Technical change can also entail less obvious forms of human depreciation. It is important that the trade union representative ensures that the findings of bio-technology and ergonomic research are applied to a greater extent before planned changes are introduced in the place of work.

Since the shaping of the workplace environment and the design of job operations can be crucial for the worker's physical health and job satisfaction, it is important that worker representatives carefully scrutinize the way in which work tasks are constructed. The modern techniques of work study afford an opportunity for systematic analysis of the smallest elements of different job operations. Hitherto, these have been used largely to break down operations into a number of minute and simple repetitive tasks, susceptible to close direction of the pace and method of work. However, the same techniques make it possible to 'enlarge' tasks into operations encompassing a number of different tasks which challenge the skill of the worker to some extent, and allow him some discretion over the pace of work, and avoid much of the tedium and fatigue associated with repetitive work movements. In consultation with management workshop representatives should work to ensure that all such opportunities are realized.

In order for employee views to have an effect in the planning process, they must be put forward at a fairly early stage; when the new machinery is installed or new work routines established it is generally too late to introduce objections.

The higher the level in the managerial hierarchy the decision is taken and the more extensive and time-consuming the planning project, the higher the level and the earlier the point in time must be the trade union's contribution to the consultative process. Management has stated that it is impossible in many instances to give out information at an earlier stage than is now customary.

They have also asserted that it is difficult to integrate additional persons in an already complicated and time-consuming planning and decision-making system. However, management must recognize that the changes they make can have a crucial impact on the jobs and living of individual employees. It is therefore only reasonable that workers be entitled to participate in the planning of such changes. It should be possible in most cases to satisfy this demand without ignoring the secrecy requirements of the firm.

Against this background, it appears necessary at all large workplaces to free one or more trade union representatives from other duties to be able to devote himself full time to discharging responsibility as a trade union representative. Such representatives should be given complete freedom of movement within the workshop. In this way, they will be able to maintain the necessary contact with their constituents—the organized workers—and at the same time have sufficient time to take part in the planning work in connection with changes in methods.

Clearly, the trade union representative must be compensated for these activities. There are several possible ways of dealing with this problem. The decision should be left to negotiation between the parties concerned.

An expanded trade union activity at the workshop and plant requires of necessity increased training of local trade union officials and workshop representatives. For a long while, the trade union movement has provided an extensive training programme which obviously must be continued and expanded. In our opinion, however, the trade union movement neither can nor should assume full responsibility for satisfying the rapidly increasing demand for training facilities for workshop representation. A large part of the training activity must be undertaken by the firm. The training of workshop representatives and other employees in work study, methods study and systems of payment, as well as production engineering and economic questions in general must be viewed as a cost of production and borne by the firm. This implies that the activity shall generally be carried out during normal working hours and that the participants are to be given full economic compensation for their efforts. Certain firms have already gone a long way to meet these requirements. In the great majority of cases, however, the situation is still far from satisfactory.

CHAPTER 15

Conclusions and Recommendations

THE ISSUES

The Swedish trade union movement has long taken a positive approach to technological change, economic expansion and the structural transformation of industry. Its willingness to adjust to events and its capacity for innovation in the past twenty years have been well documented. Previous trade union efforts have been directed along two lines: suggesting a blueprint for a structural policy designed to secure an increase in the growth of the Swedish economy; and formulating the basic security requirements for the individual in a changing society.

In the present study we have attempted to take both ideas a step further and if possible synthesize them into an acceptable overall method of approach as well as to extract from them the guidelines for a trade union programme of action. Our task as we saw it was to investigate how changing technology affects employment and working conditions and to explore the ways in which the search for increased efficiency could be combined with satisfactory work adjustment, i.e. in general how the individual could be cushioned from the adverse consequences of change in the modern industrial society. The focus has not been limited solely to technological changes but has been enlarged to encompass the overall process of change, including changes in technology, organization, structure of industry, composition of demand, import competition or other circumstances.

It seems plain that the objectives of increased economic efficiency and those of adequate job security, job satisfaction and work adjustment for the individual worker can occasionally conflict with one another. A high level of aggregate employment can disguise considerable variations in the employment experience of different sectors, just as changing technology while not greatly affecting the general employment level can have quite dramatic consequences for workers in particular firms, industries or regions. The general, macro-economic measures of economic policy which have the task of securing a high level of overall employment must therefore be complemented by more selective measures in the form of an active labour market policy, a policy for industrial relocation and an industrial training policy.

Clearly the process of transformation creates significant inconvenience and can result in cases of personal suffering. If these consequences cannot be prevented or at least substantially mitigated by public measures, workers will tend to resist change. This in turn can result in a slower rate of growth. It is therefore a matter of great urgency that society allocates resources to neutralize the adverse consequences of change for workers. In the last resort, the capacity of our national labour market policy should operate as a constraint on the pace with which structural rationalization is carried out in Sweden. This is not to pre-judge the issue of just how rapid this pace ought to be. Certain circumstances that have been presented in this report indicate that currently the magnitude of resources assigned to the administration of labour market policy are inadequate in relation to the needs outlined above.

EXPANDED LABOUR MARKET AND LABOUR FORCE RESEARCH

One of the primary obstacles to an improvement in the effectiveness of selective measures in the labour market is our lack of knowledge of its structure and how it functions. Swedish labour market statistics are inadequate in many fundamental respects. Too little is known of such basic phenomena as the composition and direction of labour mobility, how workers look for and obtain jobs and the economic costs and benefits of various labour market measures. It was only as late as 1960 that a systematic occupational classification was introduced in the population census. Consequently we do not know with any degree of precision how the occupational structure has changed in Sweden over the long term. There are, moreover, rather important defects in the system of classification, at least in the cases of employment exchange services and wider occupational comparisons.

In Sweden thus there is much to be done in the way of research on labour market problems. In recent years the government and researchers have displayed a resurgence of interest in this field. In November 1966, the Institute of Labour Market Research, linked to University of Stockholm, was established. Under the auspices of the Central Bank, the Riksbank, funds have been made available to finance research efforts in *inter alia* the labour market field.

One obvious shortcoming of present research efforts is that the National Labour Market Board, which has the major responsibility for practical policy in this sphere, does not have the opportunity to function as an initiating and to some extent co-ordinating agent in research projects on labour market problems. To remedy this we suggest that finances be appropriated to the budget of the National Labour Market Board, in the form of 1 per cent of the Board's total budget, to be granted for research work. The Board would be able to plan, project and carry out research under their own direction or through independent institutes.

THE FOLLOW-THROUGH ON MEASURES TAKEN

Labour market policy measures must often be applied on extremely short notice and in situations which are shifting and diverse. A high degree of flexibility and improvisation are often indispensable. However, given the considerable variation of available measures and the many different possible combinations of these measures, labour market administrative activities are rather difficult to measure and evaluate. It is essential that systematic follow-up studies and new methods of reporting the results of measures that are implemented be integrated into the operations of labour market administration. There has already been some activity of this sort introduced. Among other things, there have been certain follow-up studies of retraining programmes and the impact of the different mobility-stimulating measures. These accounts have, however, rarely provided definitive answers. Indeed, in many cases they have given rise to new types of problems. The measurement and evaluation of labour market

Conclusions and Recommendations

policy measures must be improved qualitatively as well as quantitatively.

In cases of plant shutdowns or large-scale redundancies it is important to make a special report for each case on the measures that have been taken and their results. Preferably, a follow-up study should be done in each case some time after the event. Systematic efforts should be made to establish not only the extent to which laid-off workers could be redeployed but also the nature of the positions to which redundant workers had been referred through the exchanges. The idea would be to clarify how redundancy affected workers in terms of changes in income, job content and other relevant factors. The few studies of redundancy that have been carried out in Sweden show that a disturbingly high proportion of redundant workers are unable to obtain new employment. If the average segment found in these samples—i.e. about 15 per cent to 20 per cent—should prove to be a representative figure, it is essential that this be made widely known and that we direct our energies to the task of reducing the number. It is plain that the number of registered unemployed by itself is an unsatisfactory indicator of the gross labour displacement that occurs. In general, the labour market administrative authorities, firms and trade union organizations should neither be surprised nor taken aback whenever a firm is forced to lay-off large numbers of workers or close down entirely and hastily improvise measures in a psychologically unfavourable atmosphere. We must accustom ourselves to the idea that such situations will soon become a regular feature of our economic life. It is precisely because of this that we need to assign significantly greater resources to the administration of labour market policy measures, expand our long-term and basic forecasting and planning activities and create a more comprehensive information-gathering service.

FORECASTING MEASURES

For the planning of labour market policy measures in general and the training programme in particular, access to reliable forecasts is a basic prerequisite. Currently, our administrative authorities have to operate with forecasts which do not comprehensively cover all occupations in the labour market. They also lack the type of forecasts which are necessary to provide a basis for short-term as well as long-term training plans. The absence of a suitably and sufficiently comprehensive occupational classification system and occupational forecasts operates as a severe constraint on labour market policy and must be removed. Moreover, short-term labour force studies are currently based on relatively small samples which do not allow analyses which are sufficiently refined. The size of the samples for these studies must be widened.

Forecasts of technological developments in different sectors and of different types of techniques should be made to attempt to obtain a clearer picture of the places at which changing technology is likely to create employment or adjustment difficulties for workers.

It is also crucially important, too, to have adequate advance warning of the nature and location of large-scale redundancies and plant shutdowns. To this end, special studies should be carried out seeking to improve our ability to anticipate fluctuations in the production schedules of firms. One problem here is to determine whether certain types of plant shutdowns can be anticipated and whether it is possible to forecast the occupations and qualifications of personnel with a high likelihood of redundancy.

Related to these problems is the need for the National Labour Market Board, trade unions and employers' organizations to take measures to improve the existing system of early warning of plant shutdowns and redundancies. The current statistics on reported lay-offs and notice are extremely unsatisfactory in form. For example, they do not make it possible to distinguish between notifications which have led to actual dismissals and lay-offs and those where redundancy has been avoided. Nor do the figures include data on the establishment of new plants, the relocation of enterprises or cases where firms add on large groups of workers.

THE EMPLOYMENT EXCHANGES

The backbone of modern labour market policy is its system of employment service offices. It is therefore unfortunate that the national labour service acts as agent in such a small fraction of all job changes. Admittedly, the figures are favourable by comparison

Conclusions and Recommendations 243

with those of other countries. Nevertheless, we think it essential that the national labour exchange services be expanded to the point where they function as the central job information service for the entire labour market, and employers as well as job seekers consult the exchanges as a matter of course for information and services.

To achieve this, both the quality of exchange services and their quantitative coverage must be increased. The labour exchanges must not only allow but also encourage persons who are not employed but are none the less interested in a new occupation to register as job applicants. In this way it should be possible to increase the range and quality of labour the exchanges can offer employers and thereby increase the latter's interest in using the exchange services. Management should be encouraged and actively reminded (through questionnaires, etc.) to notify the exchanges of all planned manpower needs. Currently, the State and local authorities, public corporations and administrative agencies do not use the exchanges to the extent that they could.

Information about the manpower needs of employers, the wages and conditions of service of jobs, and the qualifications, income and wishes of the job applicants must be greatly enlarged. In order to increase the efficiency of the job information service and labour exchange activity, continuous development and experimental work should be integrated into the regular activities of the employment service. The modern information and data techniques appear to offer promising avenues in this respect. In California, for example, the public employment services now operate with the assistance of a computer unit. With modern data processing machinery, employment service personnel can be relieved of much routine work and their energies redirected to more complicated and special job placement duties.

Improved and more extensive labour market information and placement services can by themselves lead to increased and more systematic mobility of labour. In many cases, however, information will have to be bolstered by more positive measures to encourage labour mobility. There are already a number of instruments at the disposal of the National Labour Market Board in the form of economic incentives to stimulate mobility.

In this context we wish merely to point out that the financial allowances must be adjusted to take into account the continuous rise in the cost of living and living standards. In order to overcome the resistance of individuals to geographic movement, the various financial allowances must be made much more generous. Moreover, since social and psychological factors as well as economic considerations are important elements in the individual's propensity to move, they should be given greater consideration in a policy designed to stimulate labour mobility. Comprehensive and correct information are the primary requirements for any case of geographic movement. To this can be added the importance of introductions not only to the new work environment but also to the community outside of the place of work. Such activities must be followed up by various types of counselling services.

Presently in Sweden it appears to be a generally accepted practice among employers to avoid dismissals and lay-offs wherever possible during the course of reorganizations and rationalization. Management tends to rely on the natural attrition of their workforces together with internal transfers of existing personnel. We accept this approach in principle but wish to point to some problems that are associated with it. Thus, while the attrition approach has the virtue of avoiding redundancies it exacts retribution in the form of a reduced or halted flow of recruitment. This in turn can have serious consequences for the labour market situation outside the firm—particularly in those areas with a relatively undifferentiated industrial structure. We feel that it is therefore equally important for firms carrying out comprehensive reorganizations and rationalizations to notify the labour market administrative authorities in advance of any intended reduction in their personnel needs as well as intended dismissals and lay-offs. Management should, moreover, help to ensure that the best possible information about labour market conditions is given to the employees to facilitate eventual job changes.

DISPLACEMENT WITHIN THE FIRM

Even at larger places of work, the number of jobs and environments are limited and the employees also have fixed margins as far as their physical and psychological make-up, training and experience are concerned Consequently, the problem of obtaining the 'right man' for the job strictly through internal transfers, even after large-scale technical reorganizations, can often create almost insuperable difficulties. In such a situation there appears to be certain manifest advantages to be derived from co-operation between management, local union officials, the employees affected and the labour market administrative authorities. To start with, firms, prior to any large-scale reorganization, should inform employment exchange and trade union officials of all persons thought to be difficult to place after the reorganization. These persons should obviously be given an opportunity to discuss the problem but should also be reassured that they are not to be made redundant. The rôle of the employment office at this stage would be to attempt to find and offer alternative employment to this group of workers. The workers should then be given the choice of either accepting the offer of new employment or remaining with their present employer. In this way it should be possible to increase the individual's degree of choice while simultaneously giving him the chance to learn of and consider different possibilities without being compelled by unemployment to accept the first available offer of employment.

SPECIAL MEASURES FOR DIFFICULT-TO-PLACE WORKERS

Even if management makes great efforts to avoid making employees redundant in conjunction with technological innovations, it is inevitable that the economic and structural transformation will entail that many individuals will lose their jobs. Given our present overall labour market situation in Sweden, it seems fairly likely that unemployment will be a relatively short-term experience for most individuals. However, for certain workers the opportunities to find new jobs will be quite limited. This will be particularly true for workers with limited physical or psychological capacities or inadequate training and education. This will also be true for women workers. In many cases, the placement difficulties are real problems which can only be solved by special public policies. At present, the government provides emergency works, 'sheltered' employment, and various forms of financial allowances. One cannot ignore, however, that discriminatory practices by employers contribute to the placement difficulties of many workers. An important task for the labour market administrative authorities is to attempt to reduce such practices and remove irrational obstacles to recruitment. Here, State and local authorities should take the lead and set a good example for private employers. The objective should be to arrive at agreements with private employers on placement of individuals who are difficult to place on the open market or have been employed for a long while. Employers should receive a subsidy from the National Labour Market Board for taking on such workers. It should be clear from the outset, however, that such workers are not to be singled out for special treatment but, rather, to be integrated with the regular workforce, receive wages according to the collective agreement and be assigned to normal jobs. To accomplish this, employers will have to institute extra training and vocational guidance measures. The costs for these should be partially borne by the public.

For many unemployed workers, the only suitable measure is a long-term rehabilitation programme designed to give them the opportunity to return to normal work. The rehabilitation programmes that are presently being carried out by the National Labour Market Board are under-sized in relation to the need and should be significantly increased. Given our general value premises, it is extremely important that individuals are provided an opportunity for active and meaningful employment; society should therefore not hesitate to assign more resources for such programmes even should it prove possible to demonstrate that it is more 'economic' simply to pay a financial allowance to difficult-to-place workers than to offer them employment in 'sheltered' workshops or other forms of rehabilitation activity.

It is vital that individuals feel that their jobs are meaningful. Jobs which are obviously 'make work' schemes should not be tolerated. The notion that the individual is eventually to return to normal working life must be continually stressed. There are formidable obstacles here—largely in the form of the negative attitudes of employers. These obstacles must be overcome.

RETRAINING AND THE OCCUPATIONAL STRUCTURE

In Chapter 7, an attempt was made to throw some light on changes in the occupational structure. Given the limitations of the available data, the picture presented was very crude. In Sweden, it appeared that the labour force had proved to be relatively flexible during the post-war period owing largely to the favourable overall employment situation and the rapid and comprehensive expansion of our educational system and training programmes for young people. By the end of the decade, the comprehensive school reform will be fully completed. The various educational 'lines' after the period of compulsory education have also been built up. The grammar schools have been reformed and a new type of school has been set up—the vocational secondary school. Vocational education has been a subject of reform as well. The capacity of post-grammar school educational and training courses has been markedly increased.

The number of trained and educated workers who enter the labour market today is four or five times larger than the number of workers who leave the labour force owing to advanced age. Because of the vast expansion in educational facilities in Sweden in the most recent decades, there will be even greater disparities between young people and middle and elderly workers. We feel therefore that it is imperative that society take strong measures to prevent a further widening of the 'educational gap' between generations. The objective should be to reduce differences between different generations of workers.

A significant expansion of adult education and training is necessary to maintain a balanced labour market over the course of the structural transformation of the Swedish economy. This expansion of adult educational facilities must include general education as well as vocational education. For this is necessary to ensure that the work interests and capacities of all individuals are used to the fullest extent. Basically, however, it is a question of facilitating the adjustment of individuals to a changing society. An educational system should be created that gives individuals practical opportunities to educate themselves and, moreover, encourages whatever interest that manifests itself. The need for adult education—by which we mean the resumption of education by individuals whatever their age after a certain period of time in working life—will grow with the expansion of the basic educational system. It is important to ensure that standards of education are adjusted and levelled out in this process. We regard an expanded system of adult education, moreover, as an instrument to achieve greater social equality. The necessary reforms would include *inter alia* a radical expansion of the system of studies, a wider diffusion of educational centres and a forward-looking leadership of adult education.

Certain comments on the nature and content of vocational education are warranted. The requirement that only unemployed workers are entitled to subsidized retraining must be discontinued. In this way we could obtain a preventive as well as a curative labour market policy. The retraining courses must be differentiated and made more flexible in respect of length. Retraining, both for the unemployed workers and for persons with employment, entails an important step in the individual's vocational development. The choice should be carefully weighed and supported by extensive vocational guidance and advice. One basic difficulty at present is that it is not always possible to offer a comprehensive training programme in every locality. The provision of the widest possible programme of courses should be given high priority; where a widely varied programme is not practicable, economic support should be given to allow individuals to enrol in training courses in another district. The scope of the programme offered in the immediate locality has hitherto constituted a constraint on the choice of training of many individuals. This is particularly true for persons undergoing retraining courses. One explanation for this is that retrainees as opposed to beginners generally have dependants to support. Even if the retraining programme corresponds fairly well to the future occupational structure, measures can be ineffective if individual desires are not met.

The nature of structural change suggests that adult education must be highly varied and designed to increase the abilities of individuals to be transferred and redeployed to new jobs. The proposals for the future basic vocational education programme that have been recently put forward in Sweden will also help towards this end. What is needed in most cases is a course in general theoretical and practical subjects which can provide a basis for later specialization. The retraining programme to a greater extent than other training activities must be designed with the idea that it shall provide individuals with extremely varied educational background, age and desires. Retraining can facilitate the adjustment of the labour force in the long term while simultaneously providing a measure to cope with acute short-term needs. Courses which aim to further the general theoretical knowledge of individuals should normally be included in the retraining programme. The contents of the courses should be planned on the basis of observations and forecasts of the occupational structure. At present, however, the information and statistics in this field are extremely limited. Measures should be devised to improve the planning of training courses. We suggest that the trade unions be given a greater measure of influence in the design of and the preparation of the contents of training courses run by private firms. Trade union participation could occur in the form of an advisory service, the costs of which should be subsidized by the State.

WAGES POLICY AND SYSTEMS OF PAYMENT

The wages policy of solidarity—the foundation of trade union wages policy—can if successful promote industrial efficiency by compelling low-wage firms either to rationalize or if they are not able to compete for labour at the going rate, to release their manpower to expanding firms. A more rapid pace of technological change, however, will entail greater differences in the ability of different firms to pay and thereby generate strong pressures against an egalitarian wage policy. It is therefore urgent that wages policy instruments be designed to allow it to carry out its important functions.

Were we to obtain more data on wages and other labour market phenomena and more effective analytical tools, the level of the wage policy debate could be considerably raised. What we require here is first a systematic classification of different occupations according to function and work load from the individual's point of view. At the moment, we lack a system of classifying jobs which allows us to compare wage levels over a wide front. True, detailed systems of occupational classification can be found within certain industries, but what we need is a system that allows comparisons to be made over the entire LO sector and ultimately the entire labour market. With the aid of such broadly based wage statistics, the contents of different systems of payment can be better evaluated over the long term.

We start from the premise that trade unions seek a further specification of the purposes of systems of payment and the dependence of these on different types of production technology as well as technological change. In some cases there may be a shift towards increased piecework, in other cases the shift may be to fixed hourly wages. In all circumstances, the trade union rank and file factory clubs and local union branches should be informed of the basic factors involved.

We wish to underline the importance of courses, study groups and other types of systematic information about work study methods and job analysis in the widest sense. The object of the exercise should be, however, not only to understand a particular system of payment techniques and procedures but also to provide a foundation for evaluating whether the methods and forms of organization are rational, to provide guidance to job analysis methods in general, and to cover the ways of measuring physical and psychological stress and strain from the viewpoint of the individual worker.

The basis for and consequences of the methods which are used today in the work study field are not clearly understood in all respects. There is a great need for multi-disciplinary investigations encompassing the technical, physiological, medical and sociological aspects of work.

In these investigations, the problems of on-the-job training and breaking-in periods should be treated, since these workshop problems are becoming increasingly important, particularly in questions of wage setting.

INCOME AND JOB SECURITY

Unquestionably, rationalization leads to a higher real wage level in the long run. However, those workers who are displaced—i.e. compelled to change jobs or place of work—often experience a reduction in income. Furthermore, such changes, in conjunction with present systems of payment, can cause wages to decline for workers of advanced age. It is neither acceptable nor

Conclusions and Recommendations 251

necessary that particular groups of workers should by themselves bear the risks of a drop in income associated with technological change. Where there are no guarantees against loss of income, innovations will naturally be met with greater suspicion.

It seems only reasonable therefore that changes in methods and internal displacement should be combined with guarantees against reductions in income. The task of creating flexible rules for the purpose appears to be more difficult in the case of incentive systems than in the case of hourly wages systems. Indeed, fixed time rates can be viewed as a method of guaranteeing a reasonable income in the long term, independent of small changes in job content. Even under piecework systems, however, it is possible to construct guarantees which cushion workers against the adverse income effects of displacement, production stoppages and changes in methods. As we have shown, several different approaches have been tried.

In all likelihood, a well-developed occupational nomenclature will facilitate the assessment of changes in income owing to displacement. With such an instrument, local union officials whose job it is to safeguard the interests of the members in such a situation, can pinpoint employers' attempts to use work reorganizations to reduce wages. When entirely new jobs are introduced, inter-firm and inter-industry comparisons can be helpful in questions of wage and job descriptions.

The present Swedish redundancy payments system provides some guarantees against the economic consequences of cutbacks in production and plant shutdowns. The system offers an example of income guarantees which are necessary to protect the individual worker from loss of income. Owing to the limitations of its total sum, and its age and length of continuous service requirements, such insurance is altogether too narrow in scope and coverage. It seems evident from an examination of the system that redundancy payments should be developed and expanded in many respects.

We have marshalled much evidence of the need for an expansion of existing labour market policy measures. Even when such an expansion is complete, there will probably be difficulties experienced by redundant elderly workers in finding new employment. Of course, these individuals will have the opportunity to accept early retirement pensions. For those who have not reached 66 years of age, however, such a step would entail a considerable decrease in the size of annual pension payments. For not only will the annual payment be reduced owing to normal actuarial practices, but the number of years of service that constitute the basis for calculating the overall pension entitlement will be reduced. Early retirement pensions appear therefore to be a disadvantageous approach in comparison to that of continuing to work until the normal retirement age or obtaining a pre-retirement pension on the grounds of lost working ability due to illness. The difficulties created by the present system for redundant elderly workers should be eased. This can be done in several ways. For example, the present SAF-LO system can be improved. As well, another method of calculating the size of retirement pensions could be devised. A third possibility is that of resorting to industry funds along the lines we discussed in Chapter 13.

We want to emphasize that there is great social injustice in management's willingness to provide extensive guarantees of job security and compensation for loss of income to those groups that occupy the higher positions on the income scale while giving the large number of manual workers only meagre protection. It is a highly unsatisfactory state of affairs that the individuals who have hitherto been least affected by technological change should enjoy the best forms of protection, while the wage earners who run the primary risk of suffering from changing technology have the poorest guarantees. The trade union movement will assign high priority to the task of gaining improved security of employment and income for all employees.

The somewhat special problem of the income security of elderly workers is of wide consequence but at the same time has no direct connection with technological change. In so far as there is a shift to systems with fixed hourly wages, the scope of the problem will automatically be reduced. But even in such a case complementary measures—such as supplementary age wage payments—will be called for. Special studies of how wage levels vary with age would be required to provide guidelines for such a policy.

OCCUPATIONAL ADJUSTMENT

The consequences of technological change from the viewpoint of occupational adjustment depend on many factors, notably personnel administrative efforts in conjunction with the installation of innovations, the climate of industrial relations in the firm, etc. The concept of adjustment is multi-dimensional and the individual has many different needs that can be affected in different ways by technological changes. The extent to which these needs can be satisfied depends on the design of the job as well as a number of factors in the work environment.

Against this background, there is a manifest need for increased knowledge of the situation of individuals in their work environment. An increased programme of research in this field is warranted and desirable. Labour and management should initiate studies in conjunction with the government and scientific institutions.

The development council established under the 1966 agreement on works councils would be the appropriate initiator and co-ordinator for such research activity.

Research should largely be experimental in nature; it should attempt to test the practicability of different alternatives and arrangements in the firm (feasibility studies). This requires active involvement on the part of management and interest on the part of employee organizations. It seems only reasonable that the State-owned corporations should set an example in this respect.

In view of the complicated nature of occupational adjustment, we feel that it is not possible to give hard and fast recommendations about concrete measures. Instead we will try to point out some of the key problem areas which deserve the close and continuous attention of the trade union movement. This is not to suggest that in all cases it is the trade union's job to assume full responsibility for various practical measures. For the rôle of the trade union is to make demands of and suggest initiations to other centres of authority, notably the government and management.

The discussion in Chapter 9 indicates that the importance of taking into account the medical and job hygiene aspects in industrial planning and job design must be conveyed more widely to the management and technicians responsible for these tasks.

Within the field of worker protection there are stated rules which must be followed in the workshops. There is a public inspection agency whose job it is to ensure that these rules are observed. The rules, however, are often too general in nature and too vaguely formed, and the inspection agency lacks the necessary resources to make adequate checks and carry out development work. This has adverse side effects on trade union activity in this sphere; the trade union factory safety agents do not receive the support they need.

Science has given us increased knowledge of man's make-up and abilities as well as how the job design and machinery can be adjusted to these. We also have greater possibilities at our disposal today to identify and measure different risk elements in the work environment such as dust, noise and toxic objects. It is imperative that all such risk elements be removed from the workshop and that the worker safety agent be continuously on his guard for new risks. In the case of the installation of new machinery, the alteration of work methods and the design of new jobs, bio-technical aspects must be taken into account at the pre-planning stage. This would be in the interest of employers as well as employees; worker safety pays! Efforts to increase labour-management co-operation in this sphere should be redoubled.

The extent to which bio-technical and health aspects are taken into account as changes in technology are introduced depend largely on the resources available in the firm for medical care. Adequate medical care is provided today only by the larger firms. The facilities in the smaller firms must be greatly expanded. By organized co-operation among several firms in a locality, even smaller places of work can be covered by such services.

Firms should be encouraged to study new job tasks from a physiological viewpoint. At the same time, the attributes and capacities of the labour force should be studied and clarified. In this way it should prove easier to place every individual in a suitable job. In the event, even persons with limited working capacity will be able to make a complete contribution. Overly uniform work methods and work tasks limit the opportunities for placement. Greater scope must be given for individual variations.

Conclusions and Recommendations 255

A number of other conditions affect opportunities to satisfy psychological needs at work. Let us point out a few of these.

The *design and content of the job*. Jobs which are broken down into simple and repetitive tasks, and which are mechanically controlled, can entail great psychological stress, particularly if they require continuous attention. The job can easily be perceived by the worker as meaningless. Morale can be low and the possibilities of involvement small; in the more extreme cases, the outcome can be a deterioration of psychological health.

Modern work study techniques present new opportunities to analyse and measure job operations. This speciality has hitherto been used largely to divide job operations into simple, uniform work tasks. Yet the same techniques can be used to *enlarge* jobs by combining a number of tasks in one logical sequence. In recent years, this aspect of job design has begun to be studied in the USA. It is urgent that similar research and experimentation be started in Sweden. An important task for workshop representatives should be to ensure that jobs are designed which not only take into account the physical needs of the worker but also his psychological needs.

The *overall work organization*, i.e. conditions such as the distribution of authority, the decision and control systems, the communication system and the shape of personnel management policy in the firm. Several empirical studies have shown that an authoritarian and highly centralized order and control system can have a negative influence on morale and job satisfaction, while a more 'democratic' organization can have a positive effect. The nature of the system of control is a crucial factor in the employee's feelings of freedom and his possibilities for contact and social exchange. The worker's degree of knowledge of the firm and its situation as well as different conditions in the workshop are also significant factors. Similarly, the nature of personnel policies and job methods are of consequence. Management's manner of discharging its functions has a direct and strong bearing on the employee morale and job involvement.

The traditional authoritarian work organization is still extant among Swedish firms even if the most extreme examples have disappeared. The fundamental dogma that this is based on, however, has been questioned from various quarters. New types of organizations have been experimented with in various contexts—for example, in large research organizations. As well, experiments have been carried out with self-directing groups. The trade unions should attempt to increase development work in this field.

The form and orientation of personnel services in the firm can be extremely important for the individual's occupational adjustment. Consequently, it is only reasonable that employees should have some influence over its content. These views have been satisfied in part by the 1966 agreement on works councils, which in section 9 states that the councils shall be informed of and be the forum for consultation about the general guidelines of the firm's personnel policies.

The individual worker must be encouraged to interest himself and participate in the design of his job and the layout of his work environment. This is particularly true in the case of the selection and design of new methods. Here of course the manner with which supervisors and foremen carry out their functions is of major importance. Increasingly, however, methods selection and planning operations are being centralized. In the event, the opportunities of individual workers to participate in decisions about innovations are reduced. To the extent that such a step is economically necessary it must be the responsibility of senior workshop representatives or local trade union officials to function as connecting links between the individual employee and the central planning authority of the firm.

HOURS OF WORK, PART-TIME WORK, SHIFT-WORK

Changing technology has made possible a reduction in working hours together with a significant rise in the standard of living. The reduction in hours of work in Sweden has not been part of a concerted effort to create employment for unemployed workers. Full employment, it is felt, should be secured through a high level of effective demand and not through the sharing of a given number of jobs among a greater number of workers. On the other hand, a reduced work week is a way of providing jobs for groups who are able to offer their services only for a limited number of hours per week. Such workers should be given part-time work.

Conclusions and Recommendations

It is important for the trade unions carefully to follow the trends in the disposition of hours of work. At the local level, officials should continuously watch out for individual adjustment problems, physical as well as others, that may arise from shift work.

A MORE EVEN DISTRIBUTION OF INCOME

It is imperative that the capital formation essential to increased industrial efficiency is secured by methods that will not adversely affect the overall redistribution of income and wealth. From the distribution viewpoint, the most appropriate methods for capital formation are those that build on increased collective savings, such as taxes or deposits to public funds. A conceivable complement to this could be methods of increasing private savings through collective agreements. This latter type of method would have the additional virtue of giving wage earners some degree of economic influence. In this context we have chosen to put forward once again our suggestion for 'industry funds' to be formed by collective bargaining, with the objective of furthering and facilitating the adjustment of capital as well as labour to changing technology by financing research projects, training and retraining programmes, redundancy payments, and pre-retirement pensions to redundant elderly workers, etc.

THE 'MANAGEMENT' OF CHANGE

The way innovations are installed is of decisive importance for the way in which employees will react to such changes and also to their adjustment in the long.

It seems only reasonable to assume that changes will be planned carefully with questions of personnel adjustment entering the picture from the start. In order to satisfy this requirement, trade union officials should be called in to participate in the planning of the larger technical and organizational changes.

A careful strategy must also be drawn up for the introduction and initial operation of proposed innovations. It is precisely at this stage that the information and consultation organs must play a key rôle. The recent revision of the agreement on works councils means that there are increased opportunities for consultation during changes. We hope that these opportunities will be taken advantage of in the future. Any consultation can scarcely be held on an equal footing, however, as long as the clause in the basic agreement giving management the exclusive right to manage, allocate labour and freely hire and dismiss workers remains in the collective agreement.

The issues of the individual's adjustment to changing technology must be solved through co-operation between the local union branch and the management of the works. This activity must, however, be supported by the central trade union and employer confederations. The development council which was established under the 1966 agreement on works councils and the recommendation for increased co-operation at the works level, which is included in the agreement, are important steps in that direction.